Thomas Watkins

Travels Through Swisserland, Italy, Sicily, the Greek Islands, to

Constantinople

Through part of Greece, Ragusa, and the Dalmatian Isles, Vol. I

Thomas Watkins

Travels Through Swisserland, Italy, Sicily, the Greek Islands, to Constantinople
Through part of Greece, Ragusa, and the Dalmatian Isles, Vol. I

ISBN/EAN: 9783743418622

Manufactured in Europe, USA, Canada, Australia, Japa

Cover: Foto ©Andreas Hilbeck / pixelio.de

Manufactured and distributed by brebook publishing software (www.brebook.com)

Thomas Watkins

Travels Through Swisserland, Italy, Sicily, the Greek Islands, to Constantinople

TO THE RIGHT HONOURABLE

The Countefs POULETT.

YOU in a manner confented that I fhould dedicate the firft volume of my Travels to you, on condition that I did no more than merely *infcribe* it to your Ladyfhip. The requeft was embarraffing—I wifhed to comply; but the recollection of your good qualities has prevented me.

Had your rank, Lady Poulett, been the motive of this addrefs, I probably had infcribed it to you; it were eafy to follow that mode of dedication: authors have introduced it, who thought it neceffary to compliment thofe whom they could not praife. For me it is not *neceffary* to dedicate to any one, but I feel it *honourable* to do so to you; because, after much reflection, I can scarce among a numerous acquaintance find a Lady who is your *equal* in merit, it were in vain to look for your *superior*.

I have the Honour to be

With the greatest Respect and Esteem,

Your Ladyship's most obedient Servant,

THOMAS WATKINS.

London, Nov. 5, 1792.

THE following Letters are the same as were written by the author to his father. The first part of his travels in France and Spain he has suppressed, from the desire of limiting his publication as much as possible. The favourable reception they have met from a few friends to whose inspection they were submitted in his absence, has induced him to lay them before the public; but as the judgment of the former has probably been influenced by partiality, he waits, *and indeed with no little apprehension*, for the decision of the latter. These Letters would have been published soon after his return, had not his intention been prevented by illness and family concerns. He thinks it incumbent upon him

him to apologize for the numerous *errata*, false pointing &c. of his first volume. They must be attributed to an ignorant amanuensis, and in some measure to the hurry of the printer, as the author's residence at a considerable distance from town being necessary, he was obliged to leave the correction of the press to him.

CONTENTS.

CONTENTS

OF TH

FIRST VOLUME.

LETTER I.

ARRIVAL at Geneva. Its situation. Resort of the English. Villas of the Lake. View of Mont-blanc at sunset. Outline of the history of Geneva. Its Government. Civil quarrels. Triumph of the Aristocracy. Old form of Government. Its commerce. Revenue. Public Buildings. Inhabitants. Their number.

LETTER II.

We quit Geneva. Enter Savoy. Salenche. Waterfall of Cheyde. Mountain d'Enterne. Cerve. Vale of Chamounie. Its rude and sublime scenery. Mont-blanc. Mêr de Glace. Les Aiguilles. Grotto of the Arveron. The Vaillais. Martignie. Pisse Vache. Sion. Much disappointed with the Vallais. Rousseau's

false

falſe account of it. Brieg. Ober Gheſtenen. The Goitres Government and population of the Vallais

LETTER III.

Source of the Rhone. Mount Furca. Canton of Uri. Urſerren. Its grotto. The Devil's Bridge over the Rheuſs. Deſcent to Altdorf. Embark on the lake of Lucerne. Its many beauties. Our boatmen converſe with us in Latin. Tell's intended priſon: Land at Brunnen. Schwertz. Lower part of the lake. Lucerne. General Phiffer's model. Hiſtorical ſketch of the Foreſt Cantons. Government of Schweitz and Underwalden. Alſo of Lucerne. Its military force. The patriot Winhelreid. A facetious innkeeper.

LETTER IV.

Zug. Its fertility. Government. Anecdote of the Lucernois. Good inn. Landlord's daughter. Mount Albis. Zurich. Its ſituation. View from the hotel. Principal buildings. The reformation. When begun. Zurich firſt in rank of the Helvetic corps. View of its hiſtory. John Gaſpar Lavater. Phyſiognomy. Abbey of Einſidlen.

LETTER V.

Wooden bridge over the lake of Zurich. Rapperſchweil. Utznach. Heriſeau. Canton of Appenzel.

Agri-

Agriculture. Manufactures. Climate. Government. Simplicity of the inhabitants. St. Gall. Its commerce. Subject to the Abbot. People Protestants. Its government. Turgow. Lake of Constance. Rorshach. Constance. Its council in 1414. *Stein. The Rhine. Schaffhausen. Its bridge of one arch. Government. Population. Fall of the Rhine. Anecdote of an innkeeper.*

LETTER VI.

Dogguerne. Conrad Ebner. Dress of the country. Hercynian forest. Basil or Bâsle. Situation. Buildings. Holben's paintings. Government. Population. Clergy. Mechel's gallery of prints. Bienne. Isle of San Pierre. Rousseau's Asylum. Neuville. Neufchatel. Situation. Buildings. Constitution. Revenue. Commerce. Population. Extent. Anecdote of an English traveller.

LETTER VII.

Journey to Berne. Swiss agriculture. Berne. Its public edifices. History. Government. Education and discipline of the clergy. Military establishment. Freyburg. Its buildings. Historical sketch of the Canton. Anecdote of Thuring de Halwyl. Government. Population. Hermitage of John de Prè. Yverdun. Outline of its history. Society for the prevention of begging,

and

and the encouragement of labour. Anecdote of a maître d'hotel.

LETTER VIII.

Lausanne. Lake of Geneva. Miellierie. Nouvelle Heloise. Vevay. Privilege of a certain street in Lausanne. Mr. Gibbon. Morges. Rolle. Copet. Pays de Vaud. Union and alliance of the Cantons. Military establishment, &c. &c. Character of the Swiss in the democratic Cantons.

LETTER IX.

Geneva. English gentlemen imprisoned for a riot. Fernay. We pursue our tour to Italy. Remellie. Chamberry. Grenoble. Survey of its history. Carthusian monastery. The garrison of Grenoble ill affected to the Court.

LETTER X.

Journey to the foot of Mount Cenis. Anecdote of a French traveller. Ascend Mount Cenis. Excellent trout on the summit. Arrive in Italy. Passage of Hannibal over the Alps. Turin. Its public buildings. Presented to the King and royal family at Montcallier. A view near Turin.

LETTER XI.

General account of Savoy and Piedmont. Agriculture. Commerce. Revenue. Government. Military establishment. Compendious history of these countries.

LETTER XII.

The Apennines. The Bochetta. Genoa. Its public buildings. Short character of the Genoese. Their commerce. Bank of St. George. Anecdote of two Venetians.

LETTER XIII.

Republic of Genoa. Its soil and produce. Its government and history. Conspiracy of Fiesco. Arrogance of Louis XIV. Corsican revolt.

LETTER XIV.

Pavia. Milan. Its edifices. Manufactures. History. Government. Military force. Novi. Parmasan cheese. Piacenza. Banks of the Trebia. Parma. Modena. Bologna. Its population. an ill built city. School of the Caracci. Collection of paintings. Bologna subject to the Pope. Punishment of the Corda. A curious concert. Mode of reckoning time.

LETTER XV.

La Pietra Mala. Florence. Public buildings. Celebrated gallery. The Tribune. Venus di Medici.
                                                                    Short

CONTENTS.

Short account of Tuscany. Family of Medici. The reigning Duke. Account of the produce &c. of Tuscany.

LITTER XVI.

Pisa. Reduced by the Florentines. Its present condition. Its buildings. Leaning tower. The galley slaves. Story of Rossiter. Leghorn. Its great commerce and population. Anecdote of an English Consul.

LETTER XVII.

Sienna. Its pure dialect. Radicofani. Lago di Bolsèna. Viterbo. Journey to Rome. Modern Rome. Il Corso. Public fountains. St. Peter's. St. John di Lateran. Santa Maria Maggiore. The Vatican. Its inestimable contents.

LETTTER XVIII.

Monte Cavallo. Other palaces. Villas Borghese and Albani. Anecdote of Prince Borghese. Castle of St. Angelo. Bourbon's Armour. Dagger of Beatrice Cenci. Her unhappy fate. Campus Martius. Trajans column. Antonine's pillar. The Pantheon.

LETTER XIX.

The Capitol. Tarpeian rock. Tower of the Senatorial Palace. Via sacra. Arches of Septimius Severus,

verus, and *Titus*. *Temples of Antoninus Pius and of Peace. Flavian amphitheatre. Mount Palatine, Golden palace of Nero. Forum Romanum. Cloaca maxima. Circus maximus. Baths of Caracalla and Diocletian. Catacombs. Fountain of Egeria. Campus sceleratus. Cura Pompeii. The Tyber. Proposals for scowering its channel. Frascati. Tivoli. Campagna di Roma.*

LETTER XX.

Papal territories. I. Paludi Pontini. The Pope occupied in draining them. Who are eligible to the Papacy. The electors. Negative voices. Mode of election. Cardinal de Bernis. Princess Santa Croce. Operas. Anecdote of an English gentleman. The Pretender. Disgraceful custom of the Mancia. Vindictive character of the commonalty. A poor assassin. Bank of Monte di Pietà.

LETTER XXI.

Road to Naples. Naples. Its situation. Number of inhabitants. San Carlo. Royal palace. Capo di Monte. Grotto of Pausilipo. Virgil's tomb. Puzzuoli. Zolfatàra. Lake Agnano. Cumæ and its environs. Herculaneum and Pompeii. Museum of Portici. Ascent to the crater of Vesuvius. Caserta. Furcæ Caudinæ. Society at Naples. Our Minister

and

xvi   CONTENTS:

and the French Ambassador. Introduced at Court. Carnival at Naples. Académie. Musick. Lazaroni. Anecdote of an English boatswain. Frequency of assassination. Anecdote of an aged murderer. Acqua Toffana.

LETTER XXII

Our departure for Sicily. Pæstum. Agropoli. Cape Palinuro. Capo di Infreschi. Beat on the shores of Scalèa. Hospitality of the Monks. Soil and produce of Calabria. An English hermit. Stromboli. First view of Sicily. Gioja. Ravages of the earthquake in 1783. Utter desolation of Oppido. Faro of Messina. Land in Sicily.

TRAVELS.

LETTER I.

Geneva, July 22, 1787.

AT length, my dear Sir, we are arrived at Geneva. I thought that my friend and companion Mr. Pocock could not be more known to me than he was at college, but have difcovered fince our departure from England many noble qualities, that had before efcaped my obfervation. To an excellent underftanding and an extreme fweetnefs of temper, he joins the trueft fenfe of honor and propriety; but I was at firft convinced of his merit from his attention to his father, the moft amiable and refpectable of men. This city is fituate upon the fummit, summit, the sides and at the bottom of a hill, where the Rhone issues out of the lake, in a smooth, deep, and rapid stream, the blue transparency of which resembles that of the ocean. Behind it the Alps of Savoy bend into a magnificent theatre. At some distance on the frontiers of France, are the mountains of Jura; and up the lake on its northern bank, is the rich Pays de Vaud, fronted by the rugged hills of Chablais. As it was built at a time when its thrifty citizens had probably no taste in architecture, I cannot speak favourably of it in that respect. However, it has some good edifices, and the upper part of it on the Savoy side, being entirely new, and composed of large houses, presents a very noble appearance. The language of the place is French, though much German is spoken by the Swifs mechanics who are settled here. Provisions and house-rent are moderate; in a word, Geneva is admirably calculated for a place of abode, as indeed is evident from the many English gentlemen who do, and have resided here during the summer months.

The

The little villas on the lake are now entirely occupied, the gardens of which are moſt convenient for bathing, or for parties on the water. Here too the proſpect is much finer than from the city, as the objects of ſight are enlarged and multiplied. Among theſe the moſt wonderful is Mont Blanc, that giant of the Alps, which is ſo much higher than the lofty mountains that ſurround it, as to have the ſun's light upon its ſides full twenty minutes longer than it can be ſeen on their ſummits. This is more particularly noticed, from that rich ſhade of deep crimſon, which the ſnow of the mountain reflected on by the ſetting ſun aſſumes. But I have diſcovered this vaſt land-mark with the circumſtance above-mentioned, from Mount Afric behind Dijon, at a diſtance that, taken in a direct line, cannot be leſs than an hundred Engliſh miles. The ground on which the city ſtands was probably, from the advantage of its ſituation, inhabited at as early a period as any of theſe parts of Europe. After it had been taken from the Allobroges by Julius Cæſar,

Cæsar, he fortified and made it extremely ferviceable to him in the reduction of the Helvetii, or ancient Swifs. It was then called Geneva, which the middle ages corrupted into Gebenna. At the general partage of the empire, it fell to the Burgundians, and they were fucceeded by the Franks. Charlemagne, who might be faid to imitate the example of Cæsar in healing the wounds of conqueft by civilizing the people he had fubdued, beftowed on it confiderable immunities, when he affembled his army here for his famous expedition againft Didier king of the Lombards. After his death it made part of the new kingdom of Burgundy; was again united to the German empire under Conrad the fecond; and then governed jointly by its own bifhops and counts, who, taking advantage of the diftractions in the empire, and their diftance from the feat of government, threw off all dependance on their liege fovereign. The jealoufy and oppofite intereft of thefe rulers proved favourable to the citizens, who wifely made the conceffion of new privileges,

LETTER I.

privileges, the price of their support, to either the one or the other party; but a third power, much more dangerous to their liberties, arose in the Counts of Savoy, who claimed the exclusive sovereignty of Geneva and its district; but the people, aware of the despotism that these new pretenders exercised over their own subjects, rejected their demand, and acknowledged their prelate as their only ruler.

To enter into the particulars of their history is by no means my intention. I shall therefore pass over in silence their various quarrels with their bishops: their civil troubles: their alliance with the cantons of Berne and Freyburg: with the various pretensions of the dukes of Savoy, and the consequent wars. Their sovereigns had been won over to the interest of these princes, and had therefore so far excited their contempt, as to produce in them a resolution of renouncing their authority, as the bishops had done that of the emperor. When inclination and power are united, a pretence for rebellion is seldom wanted, but

in the inftance before us, the beft that could
be for a people who were defirous of depofing an ecclefiaftical ruler, prefented itfelf
in the new doctrine of reformers. This was
firft introduced by William Farel, in concert with one Froment, a young Frenchman,
to whom were affociated Lambert and Bouf-
quet, two monks; but it required a more
daring fpirit, and greater abilities, to effectuate a work of this magnitude, and they
were foon found in the celebrated John
Calvin, who happened to arrive here in
1536. The fame of this man, whofe moral
virtues are deeply fhaded by extreme pride
and intolerance, had reached Geneva before
him. He was recommended by Farel as
the moft proper perfon to complete what
they had begun, and being intreated by the
citizens, undertook to form a body of ecclefiaftical fervice and difcipline; but in the
mean time, thofe who adhered to the church
of Rome, and others that were offended
with the feverity of his precepts, created a
party, and procured his banifhment. However, the new fectaries, finding it impoffible

LETTER I.

sible to overcome the many difficulties that surrounded them, without the aid of his abilities, recalled, and not only employed him in the reform of religion, but consulted him on the manner of establishing a system of civil government at Geneva, where his opinions on all subjects were ever afterwards adopted as the standard of orthodoxy. In little more than half a century from the introduction of the reformation, their religion and liberties were in the most imminent danger of being crushed by an attempt on the city, which from the manner of making it, was called *L'Escalade.* In the winter of 1602, Charles Emanuel, son of Philibert duke of Savoy, though at peace with the republic, assembled a body of troops in the neighbourhood, and determined at midnight on attempting the city by surprize, as there was no suspicion of so base an action (but what species of treachery has not been used by princes to increase their power?) they approached the walls unperceived, and having silently planted their ladders, about an hundred of them mounted

mounted one of the baftions, and were on the point of entering the city, when they were fortunately difcovered by the inhabitants, a few of whom rufhed out to oppofe them, and, like the followers of Manlius on the Tarpeian rock, foon cleared the rampart of the invaders. The anniverfary of this fortunate efcape has, till the laft revolution, been kept facred at Geneva, and celebrated with every mark of joy; but, fince that time, the magiftrates, fearful of offending fo powerful a neighbour as the king of Sardinia, have difcontinued the feftival. From this epoch may be dated their internal commotions, which ended in the fubverfion of their liberties, and the eftablifhment of the prefent abfolute ariftocracy. The moft remarkable of thefe infurrections were in this century, particularly in the years 7, 30, 37, 62, 70, and 81; fo that the hiftory of the republic, during this period, is little more than a recital of incroachments on the one fide, and of popular difturbances on the other. The legiflative power and election of the chief magiftrates

belonged

LETTER I.

belonged to the general affembly of the burghers; and the executive government to the councils. The former, tenacious of their own authority, and diftruftful of thofe who were the more immediately concerned in the public adminiftration, watched with fufpicion, and examined with prejudice their every action; whilft among them were many, who by nature turbulent and factious, reprefented the whole conduct of the ariftocracy as tending to undermine and to fubvert the conftitution. On the other hand, the magiftrates, impatient of continual oppofition from the burghers, and defirous (if we may conjecture from univerfal example) to render themfelves abfolute, gave juft grounds of fufpicion, by acting with fecrecy, and declaiming againft all popular enquiry as rebellious. Such were the motives of difturbance, or I fhould rather fay, fuch was the direct confequence of a republican government, in which the power of the ftate is equally divided between the patricians and popular affembly. Thefe contefts, which were frequently fo violent, as to require the

intervention

intervention of their Swifs allies, generally ended in favour of the people, till the year 81, which proved fatal to the liberties they had ever been fo jealous of maintaining. Some members of the great council, who were friends of the conftitution as then fettled, finding it was the intention of the chief families to acquire abfolute authority by various incroachments on the rights of the people, boldly oppofed their defign, and would have fucceeded in the caufe of freedom, had not the weaker party, affured of fupport from the French minifter M. de Vergennes, called in the affiftance of France, which marched a large body of troops to befiege the city. This giving alarm to the bordering ftates of Berne and Savoy, they alfo fent their forces to the fame place, fo that Geneva faw itfelf betrayed by its own magiftrates: befieged by three powerful nations: and reduced to accept of their mediation, partial and influenced by the fuperior power of France, which eftablifhed the prefent defpotic government on the ruins of the democracy. The leaders of

the

the oppofition were banifhed for life, and many of the citizens entered into voluntary exile.

After this triumph of the ariftocracy, they found it neceffary to fupport their authority by foreign troops, who rule the inhabitants with a rod of iron, and are, I am fatisfied, more infolent, more rapacious, and more oppreffive than ever were the thirty tyrants of Athens; but from the general tone of converfation, I believe the citizens will again affert their former privileges, whenever a proper opportunity fhall prefent itfelf,—and may fortune crown the patriotic enterprize with fuccefs.

Before this change the government of Geneva was democratic, inafmuch as the fovereign power refided in the general affembly of burghers; in which was vefted the privilege of enacting laws: eftablifhing impofts: ratifying treaties of peace and alliance: together with declarations of war, alienations, or acquifitions of ftate domains: and

and finally of electing the principal magistrates, such as the four syndics, lieutenant, auditors, treasurer, and attorney general. The executive power and public administration were intrusted to three colleges or councils; one of twenty-five, called the senate, another of sixty, and a third or great council of two hundred, with which both the former were incorporated. The senate acted as supreme in all political, œconomical, and criminal matters; every vacancy in this assembly was filled up by the two hundred; and the members could be elected only from that body.

The council of sixty, of which the senate made a part, seldom assembled, as they transacted no other than foreign business.

The two hundred, originally of that number, but afterwards increased to two hundred and twenty five, and again to two hundred and fifty, judged in dernier resort all matters of the inferior police, as well as all civil causes of importance. It had the

power

power of pardoning criminals, or of extenuating the severity of the law pronounced by the twenty-five. The senate filled up annually the places of deceased members in the council of sixty, and half the vacancies of the two hundred when they amounted to fifty, the other half being reserved for the nomination of the burgher. The four syndics at the head of the republic held their office for one year, and could not, according to the constitution, be rechosen before the expiration of three. Their precedency depended on their seniority in the senate; the first presided in all the councils: the second was commandant of the city: the third chairman of the assembly of finance: and the fourth director of the public hospitals, the chambers of justice, police, &c. Every year the councils proposed to the burghers eight senators for their syndics, and the general council had the right of rejecting the whole number, or part of it, by voting for a new election. On this rested the chief power of the democracy. The lieutenant, who ranked after the syndics, was chosen annually from those who had served that office : he presided at a tribunal of the police, and high court of justice in the first instance; was assisted by six auditors taken from the two hundred, who remained in place three years, and with him formed a court for the first examination of all criminal matters.

The treasurer was elected from the body of the senate, and held his office for three years, at the expiration of which he might have been rechosen for the same period.

The important office of attorney general was instituted in 1534. The person who filled it was taken from the council of two hundred. His charge, like that of the treasurer, was for three years, and like it also could be renewed at the end of that time. His business was to prosecute and plead for the state in all criminal proceedings and forfeitures: to watch over the public interest : to guard the constitutional rights of the people: to enforce a general observance of the laws :

laws: and to protect and govern the wards under his charge. In regard to the inferior offices, I shall only observe to you, that what in monarchies are confined to individuals, in republics are generally carried on by councils or chambers of several members.

I must not omit the public magazine of corn, in which, the superintendant officers are obliged to keep a large provision for supplying the city, and preventing monopoly. They dispose of it to the bakers, who are obliged to furnish the inhabitants with bread at a fixed price; but so many abuses have crept into this department, as to render it almost useless;—the citizens finding they are able to procure their wheat in France and Swisserland, on more reasonable terms than from their own government. I am informed these establishments are kept up on a more equitable plan in the Swifs cantons. Might not something of a similar kind be adopted for charitable purposes in the country towns of England?

Before

Before the two laſt diſturbances in the years 70 and 81, the commerce of Geneva was very flouriſhing, particularly in books, plate, jewelry, leather, and watch-making; in the laſt of theſe trades were eight hundred maſters, who employed one third of the inhabitants, for men and women work equally at this buſineſs. But the moſt lucrative profeſſion is that of banking; from the advantageous ſituation of the place, which is, as it were, the center of ſo many different countries. The annual revenue of the republic was then computed at 20,833l. which aroſe from ſtate lands, fee farms, tithes, and alienation fines, taxes on induſtry, cuſtoms, duties, and tolls on whatever merchandiſe paſſed through the territory of Geneva. After the deduction of ſtate expences, little remained for contingencies, or extraordinary calls. The penſions annexed to public places ſwallowed up more than one fourth of the revenue; the annual expence of the garriſon amounted to 4200l. Theſe, and the repair of public buildings; of roads; of fortifications;

LETTER I.

cations; various fums for the police; and many fmaller charges, amounted to the nett product of the whole.

In addition to this might be mentioned the public hofpital, the expence of which is annually between three and four thoufand pounds; but as the revenue allotted to it is inadequate, the deficit is fupplied by annual collections, legacies, private donations, and eleemofynary contributions in churches.

Foreigners are generally fhewn the univerfity, which is well endowed with profefforfhips; and the public library, in which I faw a large collection of books and manufcripts. The former was founded in 1368 by the Emperor Charles the fourth. In looking over the library, I took occafion to enquire for De Lolme's Hiftory of the Britifh Conftitution; but to my aftonifhment was anfwered, they had it not. On hearing it, I could not but obferve to the gentleman who conducted me, that *a prophet was not without honour, save in his own country;* and indeed he seemed to be of the same opinion.

It is a very general and a very just observation, that the inhabitants of Geneva are remarkably well informed, which is in consequence of the care taken of their education, and their frequent intercourse with foreigners. I found many of the second order of citizens, who had been in London, and were intimately acquainted with our customs and constitution. For the purpose of seeing the real genius of the people, I have frequently visited the coffee-houses of the mechanics, and there heard conversations both moral and political, that have surprized and pleased me beyond measure. They seem to pique themselves very much on speaking with propriety, and I could not but observe, that in these conversations they exerted themselves the more when an Englishman was present; to whom they would tacitly appeal on the justice of their argument, by a look that sufficiently indicated their meaning. I know no people on the continent fo ingenious, particularly as draughtfmen; indeed, this is in great meafure the effect of a public drawing-fchool, in which fixty or feventy fcholars are continually inftructed, and rewarded with different medals, according to their degrees of merit. Having faid fo much of the Male inhabitants, you would fuppofe me to have affumed the cowl of St. Francis, if I were not to mention the other fex, particularly when fo interefting as the Females of Geneva. The Bourgeoifes are the prettieft women I know of their condition, and their drefs is peculiarly elegant and fimple. Laft Sunday evening we walked out to admire the fcenery of the lake, but were met by fo many charming faces, that I am fure we faw as little of the profpect, as if we had remained in our apartments at the inn.

They eftimate the population of the city at 22,200 fouls. Adieu.

In a few days we fhall begin our tour of the cantons.

LETTER II.

Prieuré in the Vale of Chamounie,
July 26, 1787.

ON Monday the 23d we left Geneva, with a determined resolution of overcoming all difficulties on the road, and I believe that never were two men better qualified for a Swifs tour. We expected our amiable friend Western to join us, but were disappointed. Having entered the territories of his Sardinian majesty, we soon came to the little town of Bonneville, built at the foot of a mountain called the Mole, which from its height, and fine sloping peak, is an object of great beauty when seen from the lake of Geneva. Our road continued up a deep valley, through which the polluted Arve runs with great rapidity, and empties itself into the Rhone. The exact resemblance of the opposite rocks, on the one side concave, on the other convex; their correspondent qualities, equal height, and little distance between them, convince me,

that

LETTER II.

that this valley was formed by some great convulsion of nature. We stopped a short time on the road to admire two noble waterfalls that rushed over a mountain, and formed two large streams below. They appeared to the greatest advantage from the heavy rains that had lately fallen. Soon after we crossed the Arve, and arrived at Salenche, a place that has given me a most unfavourable idea of the Savoy towns. Our inn, though bad, is the best habitation in it; the other houses present an appearance miserable in the extreme, and the streets are so dirty, that it was impossible to walk out. However, the accommodations were better than we expected, and fortunately for us, as the continued rain which fell the next day, prevented our departure. On leaving Salenche, we continued our rout up the same valley on the banks of the Arve, and under Mount Varens. Having travelled about five miles, we left our horses, and were conducted by our guide to the waterfall of Cheyde, at a little distance from the road; we stood on the side of a deep woody dingle,

dingle, oppofite to a lofty rock overgrown with wild fhrubs, from which, about twenty feet below the brow, rufhes a large body of water, dafhing down a confiderable height in an irregular direction, the fpar of which, produced by the breaking of the current againft the projecting parts of the rock, extends itfelf in a thick mift to the diftance of forty or fifty yards; and we, being fortunately there whilft the fun's rays were ftrongly reflected on it, beheld a moft beautiful rainbow with all its variety and happy mixture of colours. On leaving this charming fpot, we rode along the mountain d'Enterne, which was confiderably higher than it now is. In 1751 clouds of thick fmoke iffued out of it for fix weeks fucceffively, when all the upper part gave way with a moft tremendous crafh, and covered the fides and bottom with its ruins. Under it is the little hamlet of Cerve, in which a company of French miners is eftablifhed near fome copper and lead mines of great value. Thefe gentlemen permitted us to examine different pieces of the ore, which

an-

LETTER II.

answered the description we had heard of it. They also shewed us a very large model of the neigbouring country finely finished. This should be seen by all travellers who visit the Alps of Savoy, as they are more naturally represented than they possibly can be on a chart. The mountains of this country abound in Chamois, a quadruped of the goat species, and very similar to that animal, but rounder in the head, and much lower in the shoulder than the hinder part. We saw two of them at Cerve quite tame. The further we proceeded, the worse we found the road, which had been so broken up by the late rains, as to be almost impassable. However, we entered the vale of Chamounie, and arrived at a comfortable little inn, kept by one Taire, whom I have found to be an honest and an attentive landlord.

Before I say any thing of our present situation, I must intreat you to assist the poverty of my description, by giving your fancy the most ample range. This attention, I think, due to every writer of Travels, from those who read him, as without it the most lively imagery would be flat and uninteresting. Conceive then this little village in a deep valley, fronted by the most vast, most sublime, and most beautiful objects of savage nature. When looking up in an almost perpendicular direction, I beheld a chain of rocks higher than I could possibly have conceived from description, which, as their cragged and spiry sides terminate in acute points, are called Les Aiguilles, or Needles. Amidst, but far above these, is Mont Blanc, the highest mountain of the old world, and covered with eternal ice or frozen snow. Its perpendicular height, as taken from the level of the Mediterranean, measures little short of three miles, that is, 15,663 feet. It was first ascended in 1786 by Monsieur Paccard, a physician of Prieuré, and this year three guides, after much labour and difficulty, effected the same dangerous enterprize. They lay the first night on the ice, where, though prepared with warm covering, it

was

was with extreme difficulty they withstood the cold; proceeding, however, the next morning, they gained the top, after a journey of twenty-one hours. The professors Bourrit and Sauſſeur, of Geneva, are now here waiting for a favourable opportunity to aſcend, and, I think, I never longed ſo much, as to be of their party; but our time will not admit of it.

The morning after our arrival, having hired a guide and mules, we croſſed the vale of Chamounie, and aſcended through groves of immenſe fir trees by a rugged path, a hill, much ſteeper than any of our mountains in Brecknockſhire. I was ſurprized to find the animals we rode ſo ſure footed, as not to make one falſe ſtep. When they had carried us more than half way up the mountain, we alighted, as it was impoſſible for them to proceed any higher; and, after great fatigue, arrived at a little wooden hovel, which the Engliſh travellers, who have viſited theſe icy regions, have dignified with the appellation of Blair's Caſtle;

Castle; probably in honour of the gentleman who built it. I here found the names of many of my friends carved on the castle walls, particularly those of lord Breadalbane, and his brother Mr. Campbell. This hill is named Mont Anvert, and ascended for the purpose of seeing to advantage what is called La Mer de Glace, or Sea of Ice, which is directly below it. From this place I beheld above us, at an immense height, the Aiguille de Charmeaux, which I thought, from its very superior elevation, would command a much fuller prospect of the object of our curiosity than Blair's Castle. I therefore quitted my company, and after an hour and a half's walking, climbing, and creeping along a ridge of sharp rocks, arrived under the second point of this Aiguille de Charmeaux, which, I believe, no mortal ever touched before. Indeed I must acknowledge, now the danger is over, it was extremely young in me to have attempted it. From this pinnacle I looked down on one side over the vale of Chamounie, and on the other over the Sea of Ice, which I
perceived

LETTER II.

perceived communicated with Mont Blanc by two broad channels, and then left it, but not without extreme difficulty. Having rejoined my companions, we defcended and walked half way acrofs this Mer de Glace with the affiftance of our guide, who had provided long poles with fpikes in the end to prevent our falling. It is almoft impoffible to give a perfon, who has never feen this extraordinary production of nature, an adequate idea of it. However, to make the attempt, I muft defire you to fuppofe a deep valley full of ice, little lefs than a mile in breadth, that winds down from Mont Blanc into the vale of Chamounie, the furface of which you may conceive, by fuppofing the feas round the northern pole frozen into a folid mafs, when raifed into immenfe waves by a tempeft. Now I recollect, the following lines in Thompfon's Seafons are very defcriptive of its appearance.

> Ocean itfelf no longer can refift
> The binding fury; but in all its rage
> Of tempeft taken by the boundlefs froft,

Is

Is many a fathom to the bottom chain'd,
And bid to roar no more; a bleak expanfe
Shagg'd o'er with wavy rocks, chearlefs.

We had the curiofity to look down many of thefe vaft chafms, where the ice had opened as deep as forty or fifty feet, but they were inconfiderable when compared to others, as our guide, who is an admirable pilot in thefe frozen tracts, affured us, that in many parts of them they meafured from two to three hundred. It is thought impoffible to form any right conjecture of the caufe of this phænomenon, as its prefent appearance leads but little to an inveftigation of it. One circumftance, however, might perhaps afford a clue, and that is, its being known to increafe and decreafe by the immenfe mounds of earth that are forced up in its fwell. Whenever any of the projecting parts give way, and fall in, the noife is inferior only to that of thunder. We were fo full of admiration at this grand and horrid object, as to continue on it almoft an hour; after which, we were obliged to reclimb the Mont Anvert for the purpofe

of

LETTER II.

of descending to the place where this sea of ice terminates in the valley below. We here found an arch seventy feet high, equally wide, and I should suppose not less than thirty deep, out of which rushes a rapid stream called the Arveron. We got to some rocks in the channel that stand before the center of it, from which we gazed with delight and wonder on this beautiful grotto of clear and solid ice. However, as there was danger from the falling in of its parts, we thought it prudent to quit our situation, and return to Prieuré, where we arrived much tired, but not more tired than pleased with all the wonders of the scene.

Gheſtinen, July 30th.

WE quitted the vale of Chamounie, having ascended, at its southern extremity, the Col de Balme, a steep hill, from the top of which we took leave of Mont Blanc, the Glaciers, and Needles, whose points we had so frequently seen above the clouds. On the other side we enjoyed a most noble prospect.

prospect. The depth and windings of the vale below; the surrounding mountains, and their hanging woods of aged pine, made the view most solemn and majestic. After a long walk up the Col de Balme (for we gave our mules but little trouble) Pocock discovered two boys, who were employed in milking a herd of goats. We immediately approached them, and almost drank a pail full of exquisite milk, with which we were so pleased, that we paid them ten times more than its real value. At the bottom of this deep descent we had to mount another hill, called La Fourcle, from which we gazed with the most favourable anticipation on the Vallais, Rousseau's terrestrial paradise. At the beginning of it is the little town of † Martignie, or Martinac,

† Near this place was the winter station of Sergius Galba, Cæsar's lieutenant; but I could find no remains of his encampment. Cæsar, says "Galba, having fought some "successful battles, many of the enemy's castles being "taken, ambassadors from all parts being sent to him, "hostages given, and peace concluded, determined to "station two cohorts among the Nantuates, whilst he with "the others of his own legion should winter in a village "of

tinac, built of wooden houses on the banks of the Drance, over which hang the mouldering ruins of a castle, the former residence of the bishops of Sion. I climbed the ramparts, and had an extensive view of the country through which we were to travel. We retired early to rest for the purpose of rising with the sun, but were so stung and pestered with venomous gnats, as to put sleep out of the question. The next morning I made an excursion to see the celebrated water-fall of the Pisse Vache, about two leagues from Martignie. Though considerably higher and larger, it did not please me so much as that of Cheyde, on account of its naked situation, and the straight direction in which it falls. The spar of the water extends, without being urged forward

"of the Veragri, called Octodunes, which being situated in
"a narrow valley, is shut in by lofty mountains. As it
"would be divided in two parts by the river Drance, he
"assigned one to the Gauls, and the other (being left by
"them) he appointed for the winter quarters of his cohorts,
"and fortified the place with a rampart and trench." Cæs.
Gall. War, book 3. chap. 1.
 This is the exact situation of Martignie.

by

by any great wind, above five hundred yards. I continued some time at this place, and then returned to Martignie.

Having read such favourable accounts of the Vallais, both in the Nouvelle Heloise of Rousseau, and in the publications of modern travellers, we were impatient for the contemplation of its beauties. The description of Rousseau is the most pleasing picture of rural scenery I ever read. It really induced us to consider this vale as a second Tempè, or even a country to which nature had been singularly bountiful. How surprized will you be when I add, that our impatience was punished by the greatest disappointment imaginable. I think it most unpardonable in Travellers implicitly to adopt the opinions of their predecessors, and retail them on the public. Of this you shall never complain in my Letters; for however singular I may appear, I am determined, on these occasions, to think for myself.

LETTER II.

The Vallais, or, as it is called in German das Walliferland, is an independent republic allied to the Swifs, and fituated between the canton of Berne and the Alps. Its direction is eaft to weft, extending from a mountain called the Fourche or Fork, to the glaciers of Fautignie. It is reputed to be one hundred and nine miles in length, and in its broadeft part forty eight; but I believe this latter diftance confiderably exaggerated. It is watered by the Rhone, which entering at one end, paffes nearly to the other, where it turns off, and empties itfelf into the lake of Geneva. There are two principal paffes that lead out of it into Italy; the firft by the great St. Bernard, and the fecond through Simplon. A few other roads are known, but from the difficulty and danger of attempting them even in the fummer months, they are only travelled by fmugglers, or huntfmen, who purfue among thefe inhofpitable rocks the Marmot, or wild Chamois. The moft frequented of the two paffes is that of St. Bernard, where there is a convent of Auguftin friars

friars built upon the moſt elevated part of the road, which receives the traveller of the Alps, and by affording a comfortable ſhelter from the inclemency of their frozen regions, has preſerved the lives of many. Such a convent is indeed uſeful, and, I believe, would even meet the approbation and patronage of the emperor, if in his dominions.

From Martignie to Sion, the capital and extremity of the Lower Vallais, the country preſented no object deſerving of attention. The land is ſo low, that we ſuppoſed it marſhy from the frequent overflowings of the Rhone, and our ſuppoſition was afterwards confirmed by the declaration of the inhabitants. However, we did not complain, as we expected to be more ſatisfied with that part of the Vallais which lay beyond it. This city (for ſuch it is, being an epiſcopal ſee) is built on the banks of the Rhone, which, inſtead of flowing in the ſame clear ſtream as we had left it at Geneva, is like the Arve polluted by the melt-
ing

ing snow, and the white clay through which it passes. Of all the miserable places I ever had the misfortune to visit, Sion is the most disgusting. The houses are meaner than the poorest suburbs I had ever seen; and so insufferably dirty, that I really am at a loss to find any thing by way of simile or comparison to it. For the purpose of diverting our attention from objects so offensive, we walked up a steep hill to the ruins of an ancient castle, which was of great extent, and considerable strength. When returned, we found our entertainment at the inn perfectly consistent with the appearance of the town; the scanty dinner they served being so dirty, that though pinched with hunger, it was impossible to satisfy it; as to avoid disgust, it was necessary to cut off all the outside of the food; indeed the appearance of the people was sufficient to damp the appetite of a Hottentot. You may be assured we were very happy when the following morning appeared, and delayed our departure no longer than the necessary time for putting on our cloaths, and paying the bill;

bill; but with our journey to Brieg, a wooden town, that for filth and misery is no less remarkable than Sion, we had as little reason to be content as before. The mountains on each side of us, and part of the country through which we travelled, were covered with dark groves of gloomy and ragged fir, unmixed with any trees of a more lively green, that might have relieved the tiresome and melancholy sameness of their appearance. The land, though in many places fertile, had but little sign of cultivation. No inclosures, few herds or flocks, and fewer inhabitants, who were in a condition to labour. From Brieg to the place in which I am now writing (Ober Gheftinen) the Vallais is more elevated, and less desolate, our road lay on the banks of the Rhone, many parts of which were extremely dangerous from its narrow limits, and from the precipices that hang over the river. The nearer we approached to Gheftinen, the more the land appeared cultivated; but far, very far, from the condition that Jean Jaques describes. The appearance

pearance of the houses is singular; they are built of wood, and generally painted red. The upper part is the abode of the family, and the lower converted into stables or hovels. This village is, to our great joy, situate at the extremity of the Vallais. We are lodged in a private house (there being no inn in the place) where I am sorry to find a great scarcity of provisions, bread and cheese excepted. The different climates which authors remark in this country are indeed very perceptible, and consequently, as the land is rich, in summer and autumn many fruits may probably be found in the same day's journey, which in other countries are only to be had in succession, or as the seasons advance. This advantage (if it may be so considered) is in consequence of the different gradations of the sun's heat, and the freer or more confined circulation of air occasioned by the mountains; an advantage which must exist more or less in all hilly countries, in proportion to their southern situations. Such is the real state and appearance of the Vallais, though so differently described in the 23d letter of Rousseau's celebrated novel. But what is still more unaccountable, he speaks of the inhabitants in higher terms of praise than he does of the country, particularly of the women, whom St. Prieux, the hero of the piece, raises by comparison even to his angelic Julia. Instead of these *rare beauties* (for such is his expression) the eye is offended with a stinted race of females, ill formed, and worse featured; whose complexions are of a settled sallow, and whose singular dress would appear to no people but themselves, an embellishment of their persons. But there is another impediment to their beauty which is much more serious, and this is, a loathsome disease called the Goitres, that affects a considerable number of the inhabitants. It is an excrescence in the neck, which though in some no larger than an egg, in others hangs half way down their bodies,—in appearance the most unsightly and disgusting that can be imagined. These Goitres are preceded (as I had frequent opportunities of perceiving in the children)

children) by a yellow and sickly countenance, deformed features, and a languor or heaviness in their eyes. They bring on, for the most part, a total privation of the intellectual faculties, which we considered a happy circumstance for these poor creatures, from its rendering them insensible of their situation; but very different are the sentiments of the Vallaisans with regard to goitrous appearance, for, from ideas as happy in effect, as they are absurd in principle, they consider these people as a blessing in their family, and regard them with affection as the gifts of Providence preserved by the intervention of this malady, from sin and future punishment. They go still further, and marry them together, as they are known even in this state of mental imbecility, to be prone to sensual enjoyments; though without assistance they would remain seated in the same place, until nature sunk under the oppression of hunger.

The causes that are assigned for this evil are physical and moral; that is, its origin is attributed to the former, and its increase to the latter. We perceived, that the greater number of goitrous persons was in the neighbourhood of Sion; and there it is that the water, which the people drink, is more impregnated with *tufo* stone. I was well informed (being very particular in my enquiries) that this was the principal cause of the disease, as in the dissection of these Goitres, several particles of *tufo* had been lately found. As another proof (though a surer I think cannot be adduced than the former) it was told me, that the children of goitrous parents being sent out of the country, or even to the mountains that bound the Vallais, are quite free from the complaint. It is increased by their inattention to cleanliness, and that supine and torpid state in which they live. This, my dear Sir, is the melancholy situation of so many of the Vallaisans, and you will now judge whether I could, with any degree of propriety, join in the panegyric that is bestowed upon it.

LETTER II.

The republic of the Vallais is compofed of feven great commonalties; in French called Dizains, in German Zindhen. Six of thefe have popular governments, and their adminiftration of juftice is committed to twelve magiftrates, over whom prefides a fuperior officer. The names of thefe commonalties are Siders, Leuk, Vifp, Raren, Brieg and Goms. The city of Sion, and its diftrict, make up the feventh Dizain, the government of which is ariftocratic, and the police adminiftered by a council of twenty-four, the prefident of which is ftiled Burgomafter.

Near Sion are three caftles, which belong to the fee; the firft, called Majoria, is inhabited by the bifhop; the fecond, Valeria, by the dean and fome of the canons; and the third, Tourbillon, formerly ferved as a retirement for the bifhops. When a vacancy happens in the fee of Sion, the chief officer of the country calls together, in the caftle of Valeria, the chapter and the deputies of the Dizains; the canons propofe four candidates,

didates, one of whom is elected by the deputies, and confirmed by the general body. This affembly, called Landrath (of which the bifhop is prefident) is generally convoked in May and December by the chief officer of the country, or Landfhauptmann, for the purpofe of deliberating on the general intereft of the Vallais, and determining caufes in the dernier refort. It is by the inftitution of this fupreme council, that the different parts of the republic are united in one political body; they are neverthelefs fo independent of each other, that formerly one or more Dizains contracted feparate alliances, or waged war with the neighbouring ftates. The language of the upper valley is Swifs-German, and of the lower a corrupt French.

The firft treaty of alliance entered into by the bifhop and people of the Vallais, was with Berne in 1250. In 1473 all the Dizains united in a perpetual confederacy with the four foreft Cantons, or Waldftœtt, being alfo at that time allied to Freyburg and

LETTER II.

and Soleure. By thefe different leagues the republic attached itfelf to the Helvetic corps, as an affociate of the general confederacy. Its firft alliance with France was in 1500. The population of the Vallais is eftimated at 90,000 fouls, and the military confifts of 18,000 men.

Since I have written this letter, we have felt a fevere fhock of an earthquake; but I am happy to find it has done no damage in the village.

LETTER

LETTER III.

Altdorf, Aug. 1, 1787.

I BELIEVE that Dr. Johnson, with all his prejudice, never quitted Scotland with greater satisfaction than P—— and I did the republic of the Vallais. On leaving Gheſtinen, we began the winding aſcent of a mountain called the Fourche, or Furca, that preſented the moſt rude and extravagant ſcenes of rocks and precipices. On one ſide we were overſhadowed by lofty woods, and on the other looked down on the rapid torrent of the Rhone, which carried with it trees of immenſe bulk that had fallen into its channel. P—, whoſe glance no object that deſerves attention can eſcape, ſhewed me a diſtant view of the Mont St. Bernard, and of a nearer Alp, whoſe high ſummit ſeemed to reſt upon the clouds. About half way up this aſcent is an opening, where we beheld an extenſive glacier; but as we had ſeen and examined the ſea of ice in the vale of Chamounie, this engaged but

LETTER III.

but little of our time, our attention was more taken up in tracing the Rhone to its source, which is here so narrow, that I stept over it at the place where it empties itself into a foul current that comes down from the glacier. We went about a hundred yards higher to the * fountain head, which we found so clear and sparkling, that we were each of us tempted to lye down and drink of it. Then proceeding, we gained the top of the Fourche, but not without much labour, as we walked all the way. We here entered Swisserland by the canton of Uri, and descended gradually to the town of Urseren. The appearance of this country had been hitherto very naked and uninteresting, but the next day the scenes varied. At a small distance from Urseren, the road is cut through a solid rock. We found the passage about sixty yards in length, narrow and dark. On the other side we

* We were informed, not only by our guide, but by several inhabitants who happened to be upon the spot, that this is the real source of the Rhone, and not as many travellers have naturally supposed from its larger body, the current that issues from the glacier.

crossed

crossed the Reuss by the Devil's Bridge, built of one arch, and so called from its difficult construction over a stream as rapid as any great body of water confined to a narrow rocky channel, and rushing down a long descent that is only not perpendicular, can possibly be. We were much surprized to find a good road cut out along the sides of the steep rocks, and carried over places that would probably have overcome the fortitude and perseverance of the ancient Romans. We were four hours in descending, and frequently crossed the Reuss, in some places continuing on the bank of its channel, where the roar of the torrrent prevented us from hearing each other when we hollowed, though close together: in others so far removed from it, that the lightest murmur of the water only reached us. The sides of the mountains were covered with pine trees of enormous size and height, which nevertheless are frequently torn asunder, and hurled down by great fragments that fall from the rocks above, so that the road is frequently obstructed by the ruin of the woods,

or

LETTER III.

or made impassable by the streams that pour down from the mountains, and swell the current of the Reuss. We were so charmed with these sublime prospects, as to break out continually in expressions of wonder and admiration to each other, frequently stopping to gaze at the various objects in their different points of view. And here let me observe to you, how fortunate I am in having so polished and amiable a friend, who is as passionate a lover of nature as myself, to whom I can communicate my remarks on every thing I behold, and hear his in return. This mutual exchange of sentiment constitutes a principal part of the pleasure that is experienced on a tour; and believe me, I would not for the world possess the disposition of those recluse and selfish animals that think otherwise.

When arrived at the bottom, we entered the vale of Altdorf, and found as great a contrast as can possibly be imagined between it, and the scenes we had just quitted. The one was drest in the gayest liveries of nature,

and

and prefented a moſt happy mixture of mountain, wood, and water, whilſt the appearance of the other was rude, bold, and magnificent. The vale of Altdorf would have ſatisfied the rich fancy of Claude Lorain, and the defcent of Urſeren the romantic genius of Salvator Roſa. If either of theſe great maſters of painting had added any thing, the one would probably have introduced a diſtant view of the ſea with ſhipping; and the other gibbets of banditti on an eminence. Though we had been four hours in going down, we were ſo delighted with this valley, as to paſs on *ſlowly* to Altdorf, a *little* town, but clean, well built, and full of inhabitants.

Schweitz, Auguſt 2.

HAVING amuſed ourſelves with writing during the ſultry hours, we walked from Altdorf to the little village of Fluellen, where we embarked on the lake of Lucerne. It is impoſſible for me to form an idea of any thing more beautiful than this noble piece water, of water, and the furrounding cantons. The woody fcenery of its banks: the depth and tranfparency of the lake: its gloffy furface, and the general filence of the evening, produced an inward calm of happinefs, and fuch mild fenfations of pleafure, as I never before experienced. If the mind then be capable (as I have here found it) of attaining fo great felf-enjoyment, how is it that men are fo mad, fo blind to their intereft, as to ruffle and diftemper it with anger? Why is their reafon fo much weaker than their paffions, when even thefe inanimate objects of nature make fo pleafing an impreffion upon us, and feem, as it were, to perfuade tranquillity of foul, as the moft exquifite pleafure we can enjoy? I was roufed out of this revery by one of the boatmen, who, finding that we did not underftand the German, addreffed us in Latin, fpeaking it with great fluency. You will fuppofe that I was not a little furprized at this, but no; my aftonifhment gave way to the reflection, that it was in confequence of their being born to freedom, and legif- lators

lators of ther country. There is a manly eafe in their converfation and behaviour, that indicates their independence. They look on all other men, however diftinguifhed by fortune, as their equals only, and value them according to their merit. I confider the inhabitants of the Swifs cantons, whofe government is democratic, to be a freer body of people than the yeomanry or mechanics of England; and for this reafon, that as there is a greater equality among them, they have more independence, without which I believe I fhould find no difficulty in perfuading *you* that liberty can be be only partial. Neverthelefs, were I of the loweft order of my countrymen, I would not exchange fituation with a citizen of thefe cantons, as I look upon our trial by jury: our act of habeas corpus: and our liberty of the prefs, to be infinitely above all their privileges.

As we rowed along the rocks of Uri, we came to a fmall chamber cut out in one of them, to which there is no approach but by
water.

LETTER III.

water. This place was intended by Greifler, the Auſtrian governor, for the impriſonment of Tell, the celebrated burgher of Schweitz. It is now converted into a chapel in memory of the man, who, by refuſing to comply with the inſolent injunctions of Greifler, excited his companions to revolt, and to emancipate their country.

When we had been about three hours on the water, we obſerved the ſcenery of the lake ſtill more beautiful from the mellow and ſofter tints of the ſetting ſun. We proceeded on ſlowly, and about eight in the evening landed at the little village of Brunnen, from which we walked to Schweitz, through a country equal, if not ſuperior in appearance, to the vale of Altdorf. This place, the capital of its canton, is built on an eaſy aſcent about three miles from the lake; and like the towns, or rather villages that we have hitherto ſeen in Swiſſerland, is ſimple in its conſtruction; convenience, not ornament, being the principal object of the inhabitants. However, the

houſes

houses are large, and the place supplied with fountains of water at the public expence. Contrary to expectation we are lodged in a good inn, well stocked with provisions. For this, however, we are indebted to a great concourse of people assembled here to day for the purpose of seeing two remarkable malefactors beheaded. These men belonged to a most desperate gang of no less than forty robbers, who had plundered so many people, as to compel the inhabitants of this and the neighbouring cantons to form armed associations, and pursue them. We were happy to hear that the wretches were driven to the frontiers of Germany, where the two who suffered this evening were taken. The continual perpetration of crimes had made them callous to the dreadful preparations for the scaffold, so that the priest, who attended, could neither exhort them to a discovery of their accomplices, or the confession of their guilt. They were therefore delivered over to the executioner without absolution, and underwent the

the punishment which the violated laws of their country had condemned them to suffer.

The population of this canton is estimated at two and twenty thousand souls, and the military consists of four regiments of eight hundred men each.

Lucerne, Aug. 4.

THE morning after our arrival at Schweitz we returned to Brunnen, and reimbarked for Lucerne. The nearer we approached it, the more the prospect improved, till at length it became complete and *faultless*. On passing a narrow strait between the two cantons of Schweitz and Underwalden, we came to that part of the lake where it extends itself in the form of a cross, and looked on each side over a long expanse of water, upon the banks of which were pleasantly seated towns, villages, and hamlets, that added new beauties to the scene; on the left was Mount Pilate, which terminates in a lofty peak 6074 feet from its base.

This mountain, which cannot but attract the admiration of all travellers, is washed by the lake, the surface of which was so smooth and transparent, that the reflection of Mount Pilate appeared almost as strong as the substance. Directly before us was Lucerne, built at the bottom of a steep hill laid out in vineyards and plantations. Can you conceive scenery more beautiful than that of the surrounding objects which I have described? I am sure I cannot, and though I had often heard Swisserland painted in such glowing colours, as to make me believe it the most picturesque and romantic country of Europe, yet my ideas could never do it the justice it merits. Lucerne is much larger than any place we have as yet seen on our Swifs tour. The river that issues out of the lake, and divides the town in two parts, is called the Reufs, from the vulgar notion that it is the same stream which enters by the descent of Urseren, and passes through the lake without mixing its water with it. Whence is it that similar ideas prevail in almost every country where

the

LETTER III.

the fame occafions offer? The bridges here are of fingular conftruction, being built of wood, clofed in on each fide, with windows to admit the light, and covered at the top. In walking about we were obliged to be continually bowing, as the inhabitants take off their hats to every ftranger they meet. Pocock, the fecond time of going out, had fome ideas of walking round the town bare headed, to avoid the very troublefome ceremony of returning the compliment; but on reflection did not, being apprehenfive that the people might confider it as a fatire on their polite cuftom.

Having previoufly fent in our names, we had permiffion to vifit the cabinet of General Phiffer, a veteran Swifs officer in the French fervice, whofe ingenuity as a draughtfman is generally known. We were fhewn a moft curious model which this gentleman had made in wax on a plaftick compofition, reprefenting all the canton of Lucerne, with parts of Uri, Schweitz, Underwalden, Zug, and Berne. This admirable piece of work is is finifhed with fuch precifion, as not only to comprehend the mountains, lakes, and villages; but each particular wood, field, and country feat; all which are painted, and finifhed with fuch art, as when feen through a glafs to affume the appearance of the real objects they imitate. It is in length twenty-three feet, in breadth twelve, and reprefents a country that meafures 225 fquare leagues. It is impoffible for me to fpeak too favourably of the defign ahd execution of this ingenious work. For though I had feen many things of the kind, I never met with any that could be put in competition with the model of General Phiffer. We alfo beheld fome fine plans and drawings, but had not the fatisfaction of feeing their owner, who was then abfent from Lucerne.

Mindful of the injunctions you laid upon me at my departure, to write you fome account of the hiftory and government of the countries I fhould vifit on my tour, I fhall trouble you with a fketch of thofe in which I now am, generally called the four Waldftœtt,

Waldſtœtt, or foreſt cantons. The three firſt of theſe, Uri, Schweitz, and Underwalden, have long been united by the cloſeſt alliance, and known to have enjoyed their liberties in full extent from the earlieſt times of modern hiſtory. In 1115 Uri and Underwalden determined to aſſiſt Schweitz in repelling thoſe enemies who ſhould make war againſt it, at the inſtigation of the monks of Einfidlen, alluding to the dukes of Auſtria; and in 1291 the three cantons entered into a league offenſive and defenſive, which afterwards became a model for the confederacy of the Helvetic body.

By their union and vigilance theſe cantons prevented the eſtabliſhment of an arbitrary government amongſt them, attempted ſoon after, under the falſe pretext of legal authority. Early in the thirteenth century Rodolph, Count of Hapſburg, was raiſed to the ſupreme dignity of the empire. Having ever proved himſelf the friend and protector of the Swiſs, they immediately after the aſſociation of Zurich, and the three Waldſtœtt,

and

and during the long interregnum that succeeded his predeceffor, chofe him as the chief of their union. After his elevation he continued every mark of his good will to them, and confirmed all their immunities. Neverthelefs, defirous of raifing his family, he won over the nobles to his intereft, and prevailed upon them, by honours and emolument, to acknowledge the fovereignty of his houfe. He alfo perfuaded the rich abbeys to put themfelves under his protection, and the leffer communities to do him homage; by this politic management he acquired rights, authority, and jurifdiction in all the northern countries of Swifferland.

His fon Albert, who inherited all the ambition without the policy of his father, having flain his rival Adolph, raifed himfelf by force of arms to the imperial dignity, and purfued the fame project of aggrandizing his family. Stung with the ingenuous refufal of the foreft cantons to fubmit to his abfolute authority, he eluded the confirmation of their privileges, and fent them for

judges

judges men, whom he had particularly selected as fit instruments to crush their high spirit of liberty, or by oppression to force them to revolt, and so furnish him with an opportunity of reducing them to the level of a conquered people. Greisler, one of the imperial bailiffs resident at Kussnach in Schweitz, excited the indignation of Werner de Stauffach, a person of consequence and character, by having reproached him with severity for building a house too noble for the inhabitant of a village. Stauffach had long perceived the insolence and arbitrary sway of these delegated tyrants, and had formed with Walter Furst of Uri, and Arnold de Melchthal of Underwalden, the generous design of vindicating their common liberty. They associated the principal of their countrymen, and swore them to secrecy; but during these transactions the famous Tell, unable to bridle his indignation, had nearly discovered their intention by the untimely sacrifice of Greisler. Fortunately, however, this did not break in upon their plan; for on the first day of the year 1308, they

they seized and banished the imperial officers without striking a blow. Albert, enraged at this violence, but happy in the opportunity of putting his project in effect, had prepared a considerable army against them to execute his vengeance, when he was assassinated near Windisch by his nephew, from whom he had unjustly withholden his patrimony. This was a fortunate circumstance for the associates, as it gave them all necessary time to prepare for their defence, and particularly, as the death of Albert was followed by a contest between two rivals for the imperial throne. The next attack made against them was excited by the monks of Einsidlen, of whose convent I shall probably give you some account in a future letter. Leopold duke of Austria, protector of the monastery, having espoused the cause of the monks, though founded on injustice, assembled a numerous train of his noble vassals, who were all mounted. With this cavalry he imprudently engaged the Swifs in the narrow passage of Morgarten, situated between a small lake called in German Eger-

zée,

zée, and a steep mountain. About 1400 men, but ill supplied with offensive weapons, deliberately waited his approach. Exclusive of these were between fifty and sixty outlaws, who, on account of their crimes not being able to obtain the honour of fighting for liberty in the ranks of their virtuous countrymen, posted themselves on an eminence which commands the Strait, and at the approach of the enemy assaulted them so fiercely with fragments of the rock, as to throw them into general disorder, so that the main body had little more to do than slay the fugitives with their clubs and halberts. This victory was gained with the loss of only fourteen men on the Swiss side; but as many hundred of the other perished in the flight. Was not this another band of Spartans and Thespians at the Straits of Thermopylæ? In 1323 the Emperor Lewis sent John Count of Arberg and Valanjen as governor or imperial judge to the forest cantons. But this commission was principally intended to carry on the league against the house of Austria. Since this epoch, Uri,

Uri, Schweitz, and Underwalden have been governed by magiftrates of their own choice, and their entire independence, as well as that of the other members of the Helvetic corps, has in 1648 been ratified by the principal fovereigns of Europe.

Their form of government is democratical, the fupreme power being vefted in the general affembly of the people called Lanfdgemeind.

Schweitz, according to the limits determined at the firft confederacy, is divided in fix quarters or diftricts, each family being attached to its refpective quarter, in whatever part of the country it fhould be fettled. Every male, born with the right of member or colonift, has at fixteen a vote in the general affembly, which takes place annually the firft Sunday in April, and is held in the open air *. Each man comes girt

* At Ibach, about a mile and a half from Schweitz, there is a field for this purpofe. The prefident of the affembly ftands leaning on his naked fabre, furrounded by the principal officers of the ftate.

with

with his fword, for the purpofe of electing the principal magiftrates, and tranfacting the more important bufinefs of the ftate. The firft men of the government are the Landamman, or chief officer. The Stathalter, or lieutenant, and the Pannerher, or ftandard-bearer, together with fome military officers; all which places are conferred by the people. Government police and juftice are adminiftered by the Landrath, or public council, compofed of fixty members, ten from each diftrict, exclufive of the officers of ftate, and thofe who have ferved. Thefe Landraths are doubled once a year for the purpofe of determining all fifcal matters, and twice a year the council is increafed to three times its number, for giving inftructions to their deputies intended for the general diet of the Swifs cantons: for hearing their accounts of fuch diets, or tranfacting thofe matters which are not according to the conftitution determinable by the public council.

As

As I have told you that Uri and Underwalden are democracies, I shall not enter into a detail of their political administration, as it would be little other than a repetition of that of Schweitz.

But the government of Lucerne is aristocratic, the sovereign power residing in a hundred members chosen out of the body of the burghers. Thirty-six counsellors, selected from the hundred, form the senate or privy council, which is divided in two bodies that govern alternately every six months; on which account they are called the summer and winter divisions. A candidate for admission into these bodies must be a citizen by birth, or have served the republic for a certain number of years. The grand council is the dernier resort of criminal justice, under which are various committees, which take cognizance of the other branches of government.

The first officers of state are the two presidents, who are elected for life, and preside

preside in turn over the two divisions of the senate, and the great council. The elder member of each division is honoured with the title of Stathalter, or lieutenant of the presidents. After these magistrates, the most honourable are the treasurer and the standard-bearer; so high is the dignity of the senate esteemed, that every person admitted into it is ennobled, and the nobility of his family acknowledged by the order of Malta.

The military of Lucerne is divided into five brigades, and each brigade into five battallions of six hundred men. The cavalry consists of three companies, and the artillery of five.

This canton is very fertile in historical fact. It allied itself to the union of Uri, Schweitz, and Underwalden, in 1332; and has, on several occasions, distinguished itself against the house of Austria; particularly in 1386, when near the little town of Sempach in Lucerne, the patriot Winkelried, by the sacrifice of his own life in grasping and turning aside the pikes of the German infantry, opened for his countrymen a way to victory and freedom.

We found every thing agreeable in Lucerne, except our bill at the Golden Eagle (der Goldener Adler); the landlord told us very laconically, on remonstrating with him, that the summer was his only sporting season, and Englishmen his best game.

LETTER

LETTER IV.

Zurich, Aug. 6, 1787.

WE were unanimous in thinking, that if any scenery could be preferable to the road from Lucerne to Zug, it must be that, and that only, from Zug to Lucerne, from the vicinity of the last mentioned city; with which we were so charmed, that with difficulty we could persuade ourselves to ride away from it; nor did we, without frequently looking back on this incomparable country, much doubting our ever being again in a similar situation. Other views might be more grand, and more interesting, but few, I think, can be more pleasing. However, it is not impossible for me to alter this opinion before the conclusion of my travels.

We observed the country between Lucerne and Zug, to be for the most part laid down in meadow, the Swiss farmers being as well acquainted with the advantages which accrue from turning water in the winter and spring over their paſtures, as ours are in England; and therefore the cuſtom is as general. We travelled on the banks of the Aar until we came within ſight of Zug, which is pleaſantly ſituated on the other ſide of its long and narrow lake; we were therefore obliged to make a ſmall circuit previouſly to our arrival. This canton is not above twelve miles long, and as many broad; however, its fertility compenſates for its narrow limits. The produce in wine, corn, cheſnuts, and paſture being ſo abundant, as to exceed the conſumption; an advantage which probably no other part of Swiſſerland can boaſt. The town too is ſmall, but well built, and populous.

The government is ariſtocratic, the eſtabliſhed religion that of Rome, to which, if I may judge from a ſhort converſation I had with ſome of the inhabitants, who ſpoke a little bad French, they are very much attached.

LETTER IV.

People of all countries wish to enter into discourse with foreigners; and this propensity I ever indulge, as it not only pleases them, but frequently *improves*, and always *amuses* me. I here met an open-hearted Swifs, who told me that he thought the English the best people in the world, but lamented their being heretics. Indeed, said he, I believe our neighbours of Lucerne are of the same opinion, though their interest induces them to be the allies of France, for there is not a male from sixteen to sixty in the whole canton, that is not a pensioner of that nation. I thought this rather an extraordinary anecdote, and made further enquiry concerning it, when it was confirmed by a second person; yet it still seems so improbable, that although I do not reject it, I know not well how to give it credit. We found an excellent inn at Zug, and the master attentive, and moderate in his charges. However, we were less pleased with him, than with his beautiful daughter, who was constantly in our company, as the family interpreter in French, which she spoke in a pretty German manner. Pocock was quite in raptures with her; and I am inclined to think that our landlord's daughter at Zug will be our conftant toaft, until her image be obliterated by fome newer beauty, or the recollection of others whom we have left behind us, though not forgotten, in England.

On our departure from this town we afcended to a little folitary inn on Mount Albis, where we lay that night. Though our road paffed through a charming country, we had not many views of it, as the woods often intercepted them; but we were amply compenfated by the various profpect which we enjoyed the following morning at funrife from the fummit of this hill. Exclufive of every thing we had before feen in Swifferland, we looked down with aftonifhment on new cantons, new lakes, new towns; and among the latter Zurich, at which we arrived in a few hours.

Having faid fo much of the fituation of
Geneva,

LETTER IV. 71

Geneva, how can I tell you that I prefer this of Zurich to it? I know you will say that young people are hasty in decision, and indeed with infinite propriety, as I feel and acknowledge myself guilty; but will it not be some little extenuation of the fault, if I ask you, how it is possible to refrain from saying every thing I can, when I behold such a paradise as Swisserland? I believe I am rather an enthusiast in the rural beauties of nature, but it must be little short of apathy to be cold and reserved in expression, when writing on a country like this. From my windows at the Epée, the principal inn of the place, I look up its extensive lake, a distance not less than forty miles, and see the country on each side rich in every object of inland prospect that can engage and please the attention. Zurich is fortified, and not ill built. The principal edifices are the town hall, academy, library, and arsenal, which consist of several detached buildings, and is said to be the best provided with arms and ammunition of any in Swisserland. The streets are clean: the people more in-

F 4   dustrious

duſtrious than their Roman Catholic neighbours, conſequently more opulent. The reformation was begun here in 1524 by Ulricus Zuinglius, who ſurvived its commencement but ſeven years, being ſlain in a ſkirmiſh againſt the enemies of his new doctrine.

This canton is in ſize the ſecond, but in rank the firſt of the Helvetic body, and therefore addreſſed in all letters written by the ſtates of Europe to the Swiſs. The people of Zurich, in imitation of Lucerne, formed themſelves into a canton in the year 1351. The city was always free, and had never conſtituted a part of the Auſtrian dominion. The dukes Albert and Otho of Auſtria, having formed the deſign of beſieging it, the inhabitants united themſelves to the foreſt cantons, took poſſeſſion of that country which is now Glaris, and forced them to give up their intention.

Its government, a mixture of ariſtocracy and democracy, is carried on by bailiffs
divided

LETTER IV.

divided in three classes. The first, which consists of ten members called Administrators, manage the public rents: the second, named the interior body, as those who compose it are always resident at Zurich, is made up of nineteen, who fill offices appointed for the administration of such public business as must necessarily be transacted in the seat of government: and the third class is formed of thirteen members, who dwell in the castles and villages of the canton, being employed in posts of inferior consequence. There are also a great and lesser council, which together amount to 212 members (162 of the one, and 48 of the other) to these are added the two chiefs of the state called burgomasters, who are elected by the counsellors and burghers, and govern alternately every six months. These, with the four Stathalters, or masters of companies, and two treasurers, make up the members that administer the government of Zurich, all of which are elective; each tribe of the burghers furnishing twelve persons

sons for the great, and three for the lesser council.

It is here that the celebrated Lavater resides, a gentleman who has acquired, and I think most deservedly, great reputation by his writings on physiognomy. It has been the lot of this science, and indeed of many others whose advantages are not evident at the first view, to be decried and ridiculed as ideal and erroneous; but surely it must appear in a very different light to those who consider a knowledge of the human mind (of which the countenance is generally the index) as essential to our happiness. Is it not founded on nature, and in a greater or less degree given by nature to every individual whose mental faculties are rational? Our opinions of the temper and disposition of others are considerably influenced by their physiognomy, and indeed *should be*, as a criterion which seldom fails. However, as it sometimes does, we ought to be reserved, and not publish our sentiments to the prejudice of any person. Habit

and

and education might correct our natural dispositions, and lead the physiognomist into error, as we find in the anecdote of the person who pronounced so unfavourably on the character of Socrates; but this by no means derogates from the utility of the science, or affords a handle to ridicule it, as we may infer from the declaration of that great philosopher to his disciples, who had so hastily rejected the opinion of the physiognomist with contempt.

———

Einsidlin, August 8.

WE were so tempted by the beauties of the lake, that we determined on going to Richtiswill, a little town on its western bank, by water; and accordingly, having hired a boat, embarked at Zurich. As we proceeded we lay musing at our ease on the fine scenery that surrounded us, and were both (for I know my friend's mind as well as my own) completely happy. I hope we may continue so to the end of the tour; for happiness,

piness, though often crossed by misfortune, is more frequently destroyed by imprudence, *Nullum numen abest si sit prudentia*. Though our boatmen exerted themselves, it was late before we arrived at Richtiswill; however, when that happened, we were so fortunate as to find a good inn, and some fine fish for supper, among which were *Tench* taken in the lake, but not so large or well tasted as yours in Brecknockshire. The next day we rode through a hilly country to the ancient abbey of Einsidlen; which, I am induced to believe from what I read in Swiss history, has destroyed more bodies than it has saved souls; for before the general confederacy of the Cantons, the monks, who are Benedictines, instead of preaching the word of peace, were eternally fomenting quarrels, and stirring up the ambitious dukes of Austria to oppress their flocks.

The abbey, which is a most extensive pile of building, and endowed with great property real and personal, is called *Our Lady of the Hermits*. We were conducted

over

over the whole by a French monk, who, I believe, had it been in his power, would have asked us to dinner; but the fraternity seems now to have lost the only virtue it was ever supposed to have possessed—hospitality. Their treasury is immensely rich with the gifts of weak enthusiasts, and the church most magnificent. Having entered it by the great door in front, we saw in the aisle a small detached house or chapel, said to have been built many years prior to the abbey by a certain St. Eberard, duke of Franconia, and to have been consecrated by God himself. We descended into it through a door, over which, in a stone covered with a silver plate, are five holes for receiving the four fingers and thumb of the hand. They tell you that God touched the stone, and at the instant this miracle was performed. Under it is a block of wood to accommodate those who are not tall enough to reach up and put in their fingers. You may be sure that both of us took advantage of our situation, though I do not know that either found himself the better for it.

Having

Having descended into the chapel, we beheld through a grate (put up to keep the degenerate pilgrims of the present age from picking and stealing) an image of the Virgin superbly dressed; but by a most unaccountable whim, exhibiting a face of black marble, so that had I not been prepared for this rary show by a knowledge of my situation, I really should have taken her for Prince Memnon's sister, or the Æthiop Queen. At the altar of this *Sanctum Sanctorum*, which, like the presiding deity, is most richly ornamented, and illuminated with a profusion of tapers, we found three pilgrims, two kneeling and praying most fervently, and the third, a female, singing hymns to the image; in doing which, at every other stanza, she altered the tone of her cracked voice, which had the most ridiculous effect; but we were so shocked to see these poor deluded creatures the victims of superstition, that it was impossible to laugh; had we done it, it would have been a satire on the imbecillity of human nature, and we might have said to ourselves; *Quid rides? de te fabula narratur.*

narratur. It was told us, that not less than 80,000 pilgrims come here annually; but even if one half be admitted, the evil is most serious, and cries aloud for redress. Many peasants travel three or four hundred miles on this pilgrimage, and never depart from Einsidlen without leaving some gift to the Virgin, which you may conclude, without my telling you, is applied by these lazy and luxurious monks to their proper use. What is still worse, the journey has no effect whatever in reforming the morals of those that make it. They come not only for a remittance of all *past*, but of all *future* crimes, as we learnt from a Swiss gentleman, who assured us, that the women, both in going and returning, are frequently guilty of the most scandalous debauchery, fully persuaded that they may act with impunity. The French government, from experience of its bad consequences, has wisely enacted a penal law against it; and though not altogether put an end to, has considerable checked the religious emigration of its subjects.

LETTER

LETTER V.

St. Gall, Aug. 10, 1787.

AS Einsidlen contained no other object of attention than the abbey, we left it on the day of our arrival, and descended to the lake of Zurich, which we crossed by a wooden bridge little short of a mile and a half, or 1850 feet in length, to Rapperschweil, a town built on the opposite bank. A bridge similar to this was constructed as far back as the year 1358; since that early period we may conclude from its materials that many have succeeded. It is formed of loose deal rafters, supported on each side by large pieces of timber driven into the ground like piles. However, though simple in construction, even the length must of necessity make a work of this nature attended with great trouble and expence, and not undeserving of regard. Pocock having travelled with hack horses, which he had hired at Einsidlen, dismounted in this place, and walked over the bridge;

but

LETTER V.

but as I had purchafed a mule for the tour (a moft beautiful animal fifteen hands high) I was under the neceffity of getting him over; and being informed by the guide that there was no danger in paffing, undertook the atchievement myfelf. I had not proceeded above a hundred paces before I found the boards fo loofe and rotten, that I moft fincerely repented of the attempt. I would have turned back, had I not perceived it to be more dangerous than to go on; I was therefore under the neceffity of walking forward, full of apprehenfion that every ftep would be my laft; but by good fortune arrived without accident on the other fide.

Rapperfchweil is pleafantly feated on an eminence that rifes from the lake, and commands an advantageous view of it. We there made acquaintance with a gentleman, who gave us all the information we could wifh relative to that part of Swifferland, and politely fent us a bafket of fruit, the produce of his own garden, among which was a lemon of uncommon fize, no fmall rarity for a country so far to the north as this is. In return we asked him to supper, and had the pleasure of his company. The next day, unable to obtain at Rapperschweil as many horses as were wanted, we repassed the lake to the little village of Utznach, whence we travelled through a hilly country, highly cultivated and woody, to an inn on the road side, where the landlord was more obliging (if possible) than our honest friend at Zug; *but he had not so pretty a daughter.* However, our loss in that respect was in some measure made up by the polite attention of the son, an officer of one of the Swiss regiments in the French service. The next morning we continued our tour over hills, and through deep valleys, to Herisseau, in the canton of Appenzel, and from Herisseau to St. Gall. I cannot tell you how much we were charmed with this part of Swisserland. It is laid down in pasture and small inclosures, that seem quite alive with the industry of the inhabitants. The appearance of the towns and villages denotes the success of the manufactures, which consist of of muflins and linen. They are very confiderable in all this country that lies between Zurich and St. Gall, and the correspondence of the different houses most extensive; as the former of these articles is equal, if not superior, to any made in Europe. A traveller might immediately pronounce on the prosperous commerce of Herisęau, from its general appearance. No idlers are to be seen in the streets, nor beggars at the doors, but the whole town wears the happy aspect of industry and opulence.

The climate of this charming canton is, from its superior elevation, much finer than that of the surrounding countries, as the thick vapours, which rise in the winter months from the lake of Constance, never reach and affect it. In the summer it has also the advantage of being free from the intemperate heats which are often felt in the plains below. Then it is that the cool air of its glens and valleys, the excellent quality of its fountains, its milk, its honey, its vegetables and fruits, together with the
rich

rich and extenfive profpects that furround it, attract the inhabitants of other countries lefs favoured by nature, in hopes of participating the health of its happy people, by breathing for fome time the fame air, and imitating the fame temperate and peaceful life.

The government is democratic, but as the religion is mixed, the canton is divided in two parts, diftinguifhed by their refpective names of interior and exterior Rhodes; the former inhabited by Roman Catholics, and the latter by Proteftants. Thefe portions form two little independent ftates, whofe government, police, and finances, are different; but whofe intereft is the fame. In each divifion every male at fixteen has a vote in the general affembly, which is held annually, either in the open air, or in a church, according to the feafon and weather. In thefe affemblies they elect the magiftrates; the principal of which are the Landammann, Stathalter, treafurer, captain general, edile, and ftandard bearer. They have alfo a great

and

and leſſer council for the adminiſtration of juſtice and government. Each diviſion ſends a deputy to the diet, but they have together but one voice; and it is conſequently neceſſary they ſhould be of the ſame opinion to give it effect.

The inhabitants of Appenzel were originally ſubject to the abbey of St. Gall, but impatient of the oppreſſion and rapacity of that monaſtic government, in 1400 they followed the example of the other cantons in aſſerting their liberty, and not only repulſed the forces of the abbey, and their German allies, but carried their arms into Suabia and the Tirol. However, theſe rapid conqueſts were not effected without the loſs of men, and they were too inconſiderable a people to maintain offenſive war againſt enemies ſo much more powerful than themſelves. Having received ſeveral checks, particularly at the ſiege of Brigend, they were at length compelled to retreat within the boundaries of their own country, where they continued in an unſettled ſtate till 1513.

They were then admitted into the general alliance of the cantons, and ranked as the thirteenth. Two circumstances are mentioned in their history, which denote the genuine simplicity of their character. When the bishop of Constance, to whose spiritual directions they had submitted, had on some trifling occasion put them under the bann of the church, they called a general assembly for the purpose of deliberating on this affair, when they unanimously determined, *that they would not be put under the bishop's bann,* and made a decree of their resolution.

The other happened when they had carried their arms into Suabia. Having taken by storm one of the enemy's castles, they abandoned to the flames the plate and rich furniture, being too busily employed in dividing equally among themselves a large quantity of pepper, which they had discovered. The Protestant division can upon an emergency bring 10,000 men into the field, and the Roman Catholic 4000. The population amounts to 51,200,—a surprizing number

LETTER V.

number in proportion to the country's extent, which contains only 180 square miles, great part of which are uninhabitable mountains; but this is the happy effect of their industry and freedom.

The city is, I think, in size and population, inferior to none that I have as yet seen in Swisserland, and in commerce it is much before all, as is evident from the appearance of its bleaching fields, which are covered with linens. Though subject to its abbot, who is a temporal as well as spiritual prince, its inhabitants (who are all Protestants) have the government in their own hands, which is a mixture of aristocracy and democracy. The burghers are divided into six corporations or tribes, exclusive of the noble families. Each of these tribes elect three tribunes or presidents, who assist in rotation. Twelve so chosen compose the minor council, with an addition of three burgomasters, and nine counsellors, chosen from the general body of the citizens; to these twenty-four are added eleven from each tribe to make up

the

the great council of Ninety. The burghers elect their burgomaster, the corporation the tribunes, and the senate choose their members from the council. For the defence of the city the burghers are divided into nine companies of militia, one of artillery men, and two of grenadiers; one of which is a troop of cavalry. Ever since the separation of its inhabitants from the church of Rome, its venerable cathedral is frequented only by the monks, and a few wandering strangers. The greater part of this country is the property of these useless ecclesiastics, who, happily for them, are just out of the emperor's reach, otherwise he would most probably have appropriated their revenues to better purposes than what they do, and would not, I think, by such an act excite the resentment of the citizens, so much as he has that of his bigotted subjects in the Austrian Netherlands.

———

Constance, Aug. 11.

ON leaving the canton of Appenzel and St. Gall, we entered Turgow, and in all
these

LETTER V.

these countries found admirable roads, the consequence of their commerce. From St. Gall our route lay through a country not less fertile or pleasing than the environs of Heriseau. Having rode a few hours, we came suddenly in sight of the lake of Constance, the most noble and extensive in Europe, and then descended to Rorshach, a little town built upon its margin. This lake was called by the Romans Acronius; it now has three names, Bodmerzee, Unterzee, and Bodenzee, or rather its different divisions are so distinguished. Its breadth is sixteen miles taken in the widest part, and its length forty. It abounds in fish, particularly in trout, of the white species, many of them weighing from thirty to forty pounds. Having examined our inn, which was not over excellent, we wandered through the town, and about sun set walked on the borders of the lake, surveying its unruffled surface and the distant shores. Directly opposite to us is the circle of Suabia in Germany: at the eastern extremity immense mountains on the confines of the Tirol,

which

which project over the water; and, at the other end, the city of Conftance and its diftrict. I was pleafed beyond defcription with our fituation, and thankful to the great Author of Nature for the happinefs I enjoyed. As we walked back, we found that the inhabitants of this town were mufical, and liftened for fome time to a concert well executed. The day following we continued our journey along the lake to Conftance, the *ne plus ultra* of our tour from Geneva. This city was the winter ftation of Conftantius Chlorus, the father of the emperor Conftantine, and fuppofed to have been named from him. It was taken from the Romans by Attila king of the Huns, and afterwards became fubject to the monarchs of France, by whom it was confiderably enlarged, and ftrongly fortified. The emperor Charles the fifth annexed it to the Auftrian territories, part of which it ftill is, and enjoys privileges and immunities which are not granted to the other cities of Suabia. Neverthelefs, it is much declined from its ancient grandeur and population;

for

for though well built, there are not inhabitants to occupy its houses. However, the change of government at Geneva in 1771 has added confiderably to the number, and improved its commerce. The emperor has in confequence wifely permitted them the free exercife of their religion, and done every thing that can induce them to continue there.

The council of Conftance took place in 1414. It affembled at the inftigation of the emperor Sigifmund, to make an end of the fcandalous fchifm that then exifted in the church of Rome; when three pretended fucceffors of St. Peter roamed about, venting their curfes and excommunications on one another, and on the adherents of their adverfe parties, while each declared himfelf infallible. Unhappily for their divine authority, the council at the end of four years depofed *both*, and elected in their ftead Martin the fifth. It alfo condemned the doctrines of our Wickliff as damnable and heretical, and in its bigot zeal fentenced to

the

the flames Jerome of Prague, and John Hufs, who were in confequence burnt, although the latter had a pafs, and affurance of fafety given him by the emperor. This celebrated council confifted of four patriarchs, 29 cardinals, 346 prelates, 564 abbots and doctors, attended by not lefs than 8000 fecular princes and noblemen.

Schaffhaufen, Aug. 12.

THE lake of Conftance, like thofe of Lucerne and Geneva, receives its river (the Rhine) at one extremity, and, according to the vulgar error, difcharges it unmixed with its own body at the other. We were recommended by our landlord (whofe good character may be read in his countenance) to go by water to Stein; and accordingly having walked to the village of Stekborn, two miles from Conftance, we hired a boat, and embarked on the inferior lake. Six hours, and two indefatigable boatmen, brought us to the place of our deftination; but the time feemed fhort, as the rich fcenery of the

furround-surrounding country entirely diverted our attention from our watches. The nearer we approached Stein, the more we perceived the force of the current; so that at a small distance from the place it became quite rapid, being contracted in a narrow channel where the lake terminates, and the Rhine begins. Stein being in the circle of Suabia, we lay that night in Germany. It is a little town of no great trade, though so well situated. The chief employment of the inhabitants is in agriculture, which they carry on to advantage from the fertility of the soil. Their herds are tended by one man, who, at dawn of day, walks round the town, and with his bugle horn gives the people notice to drive out their cattle to him; and when he returns in the evening, informs them by the same means of his arrival.

The next day we travelled along the woody banks of the river, which winds down its course in a swift, clear, and deep stream to Schaffhausen, the capital of its canton. The

The town is large, and, upon the whole, not ill built. The inhabitants are fond of painting their houses on the outside, and of covering them with glazed tiles of various colours. In the upper division is a large tower or bulwark, which in early days was the principal fortress of the town, and probably served as a citadel; but is now of little use.

The only object deserving of attention in Schaffhausen is the bridge over the Rhine. The river is so extremely rapid, that several built of stone have been carried away by the force of the current; and the magistrates, after the destruction of the last in 1754, were at a loss how to replace it, when Ulrich Gruebman, a common carpenter of Appenzel (to whom nature, by way of compensation for the most unfavourable appearance, had given an uncommon genius) proposed to throw a wooden bridge of one arch across the stream, which is between three and four hundred feet in breadth. This offer, though it astonished those to whom

it

it was made, was *in part* accepted. They employed him in the undertaking, but diftruftful of his ability to execute what he had propofed, ordered him to make ufe of the center pier of the late ftone bridge as a prop for the new building. This injunction he literally obeyed, though he was determined for his own fame (as ambition is the foul of genius) to effect what he had originally intended. He fo formed the bridge, that no portion of its weight fell upon this pier; and thus it is, though not in appearance, one arch, the angle of which is not lefs than 45 degrees, over a river that meafures between three and four hundred feet. Does not this bring to your recollection the celebrated one-arched bridge of Pont y ty Pridd over the Taaff in Glamorganfhire, and its ingenious builder Edwards?

Hiftory informs us, that Schaffhaufen originated from an abbey of Benedictine monks, founded in 1051 by Eberard Count of Nelemburg. In 1330 it was fold by the Houfe of Bavaria to Frederick Duke of Auftria,

Auſtria, in whoſe family it continued near a century, and performed ſignal military ſervices. In 1424 it leagued with Zurich and St. Gall, and thirty years after joined the confederacy at Zurich, Berne, Lucerne, Schweitz, Uri, and Underwalden. The religion of this canton is Proteſtant, the reformation having been introduced here by Riegius Ritterus, and Hoffmeiſter. The government ſeems originally to have been formed by the Dukes of Auſtria, at a time when the town was ſubject to their authority. Frederic, in 1411, divided the whole body of the burghers in 12 tradeſmens' companies called Abbeys, or Zünfté; each of which was to elect a certain number for the councils. This form ſtill remains, with the exception of a few changes made in 1689. The twelve abbeys ſend each five deputies to compoſe the great council of ſixty, and two for the leſſer of twenty-four or ſenate; ſo that theſe combined aſſemblies, with their burgomaſter or preſident, amount to eighty-five.

The

The law enacts that every vacancy should be filled up within four hours after the death of a member, and on the eighth day after the election the person chosen is admitted by the lesser council, provided there be no legal objection to him. He takes what is called the Oath of Purgation, which is, that he has neither corrupted the electors, nor made use of any intrigue to procure their voices; and what will seem wonderful to you in England, there is no instance of any member having perjured himself on this occasion. The burgomaster, stathalter, and two treasurers are elected by a plurality of voices in the great council, with which the supreme power rests; the different branches of the executive government; such as the police, civil and criminal jurisdiction, public œconomy, military department, &c. being committed to subordinate chambers, where they are transacted in a manner very similar to that of the other aristocracies in Swisserland. They estimate the population of this canton, including the city, at 30,000 souls. But what makes Schaffhausen the resort of so many travellers, is the famous fall of the Rhine, about a mile from the town.

The river, a little below the bridge, is so rapid, as to make it impossible for any boat to attempt the current, so that the fall might be said to begin there.

We were conducted by our guide to the place, where we saw with astonishment the whole body of the Rhine tumbling with a noise of thunder down a declivity of eighty feet, and producing clouds of spar that rose to a considerable height. We took a boat, and crossed the stream to a rock that leans directly over it, where we beheld it in different points of view, from a little winding walk that leads from the summit almost down to the water. The sight and sound of this cataract were tremendous, but what must be the falls of Niagara? We were informed that Loutherburg, who is a native of Swisserland, is now in this country, and means, in a few days, to paint this wonderful scene. Should he do

it

LETTER V.

it juftice, the picture muft, from the fubject it reprefents, be very interefting, and receive great attention in England.

Unfortunately for travellers there is only one inn at Schaffhaufen, and this kept by a man, who, from riding a good horfe, and being enrolled in the town militia, is become fo infufferably proud, as to forget the humble duties of his ftation. The animal may be eafily known by a fmart cocked hat, a fierce pair of jack boots, and a tail that hangs down to his heels.

He confiders himfelf a gentleman, and behaves to thofe, whom neceffity forces to his houfe, with unpardonable infolence; infomuch, that a few years ago he was kicked down ftairs by fome German officers, who fhewed the coxcomb how well they knew to refent the impertinence of a military innkeeper.

LETTER VI.

Basil, Aug. 14, 1787.

HAD we not seen the most beautiful countries imaginable since our departure from Urseren, we probably might have been pleased with our first day's journey from Schaffhausen; but as it was, we were by no means so. On the contrary, it appeared chearless and uninteresting; that is, the remaining part of the canton from Scaffhausen to Waldshut. For with the last stage to Dogguerne, we had every reason to be satisfied, particularly on the banks of the Rhine at Waldshut, where the river winds under the town, and a little on this side washes one of the boldest natural terraces I ever saw, over which the public road passes. At Dogguerne we beheld in our landlord Conrad Ebner a most singular and venerable figure, the genuine representative of the ancient inhabitants of this country. He is a man in years, much above six feet high, large and well proportioned. His hair is

thick,

thick, short and grey, his beard long, and whiter than his head. His dress is that of the country, which has continued many centuries without any alteration, and is as follows. On the head the men put a small straw hat curiously cocked, and tied with ribbons. This hat (if I might so call it) is only meant for ornament, as the crown is not above three inches in diameter, and two in depth. Instead of a coat they wear a jacket, under which they gird themselves with a broad leathern belt. Their breeches are similar to those worn in England in the golden days of queen Bess, or what are still seen among the common people of Holland; that is, preposterously large above, and close at the knees. They fasten their shoes with strings, over which the upper leathers or vamps turn back, and reach to the middle of their feet. The singularity of the womens dress consists in their short petticoats, that fall but very little below the knee: in their shoes, which resemble those of the men; and in their head dress, the fore part of which is closely bound up, whilst the hair behind * hangs down to the small of their backs in thin braided tails. We were very desirous of conversing with our venerable host, but he was quite ignorant of the French, and we of the German language.

The emperor, when he passed through this country, called to see him, and was not only delighted with his dress and figure, but with his conversation and manners. Indeed, the gentleness of his disposition is manifest in his every action. Early the next morning, having taken honest Conrad by the hand, we left Dogguerne, and travelled through woods of noble oak, the remains of the Hercynian, or Black Forest, which is so particularly described by Cæsar in his Gallic war. I had determined on reading this description in the wood, and in con-

* I am informed by an ingenious friend, who is intimately acquainted with the manners and dress of the German people (having long resided among them as a foreign minister) that this manner of wearing the hair is peculiar to unmarried women, and denotes their celibacy. When no longer single, the chignon is turned up, and fastened on the top of the head by a large pin or skewer.

sequence

fequence carried his Commentaries in my pocket. As I think the tranflation will not be impertinent in this place, I fhall take the liberty of inferting it. Cæfar firft obferves, "that this foreft was known to Era-
"tofthenes and other Greeks, and by them
"called Orcynia." In the fubfequent chapter he continues, " The breadth of this
" Hercynian foreft above-mentioned is an
" expeditious journey of nine days, for it
" cannot otherwife be defined, nor have
" they afcertained the meafure of thefe
" journeys. It firft rifes on the borders of
" the Helvetii, the Nemetes, and Rauraci,
" and extends from the right fide of the
" Danube to the frontiers of the Dacians
" and Anartes. Here it bends to the left
" through regions at a diftance from the
" river, and reaches the confines of many
" nations from its great extent; nor is there
" any one in this part of Germany, who
" can fay that he ever arrived at the place
" where the wood begins, although he had
" travelled fixty days, or that has even heard
" where it firft rifes.

"There are many kinds of wild beasts in it, which are not known elsewhere. Among such as differ from all others, and should be transmitted to memory, are these. The first is an ox formed like a stag. From the center of its forehead between the ears rises a high horn, straiter than is generally seen. At the summit of this horn, branches like those of the palm tree, spread out. The male and female are similar to each other, their horns being of the same form and size." Cæsar then proceeds to mention the two others, which I should suppose to be the elk and buffalo. Should you wish to refresh your memory, I beg leave to refer you to the twenty-seventh and twenty-eighth chapters in the sixth book of his Gallic war.

We travelled, as you will suppose, with great pleasure through what remains of this classical wood, which is now called the Schwartzwald, passed Laufenbourg, and the forest towns of Seekingen and Rheinfelden, and

and in the evening arrived at Bafil or Bafie, where we now are.

This city, called by the Romans Bafiléa Rauracorum, is fituated on uneven ground, and divided in two unequal parts by the Rhine, which forms a noble arch as it paffes under the windows of the houfes. The fmaller divifion on the north eaft communicates with the larger by a ftrong bridge of ftone, and the whole town is fortified. It was formerly an epifcopal fee under the metropolitan of Befançon, and its bifhop a prince of the empire. But he being attacked by the Proteftants, fled from Bafil to Perentrú in Alface, and his chapter to Freyburg in Brifgaw. The cathedral, built by one of the German emperors (I believe Henry Auguftus) is a curious Gothic ftructure. Its materials are red ftone of a very deep colour, found near the town. We vifited the arfenal and the palace, where the councils, &c. convene; but what principally engaged our attention were the library, where we faw a curious manufcript of Virgil

and

and the Alcoran, together with the repofitory of Amberbach and Erafmus, which belong to the univerfity. Thefe contain many original drawings, and a dead Chrift by Holbens, who was a native of this city. There is alfo another work by this great artift painted in frefco againft the wall of a church, which has confiderable merit. This is the dance of deaths, a fubject rather fingular. Bafil has the honor of having produced many great men, and of having been fome time the refidence of that elegant Latinift Erafmus, who died and was buried here in 1536. It can alfo boaft of the two Galicions, the inventors of ordinary paper, and of Richel, who firft began the art of printing in 1478; that is, I fuppofe, who fet up a regular office for that bufinefs, as the art was invented and exercifed by Scheffer of Mentz in the year 1450.

In the government of Bafil the citizens alone are eligible to public employments: the fovereign power is lodged in the two councils united; the greater confifting of

216 members chosen from the eighteen tribes of the larger and smaller division of the city, and the minor council composed of sixty, selected from the fifteen tribes of the larger divisions. The two burgomasters, and four chief tribunes, make up 280. The sovereign council, which generally assembles on the first and third Sunday of every month, decides on all the great œconomical and political business of government, exercises the power of legislation, and disposes of the principal employments. The lesser council is composed of two divisions, over each preside a burgomaster, and chief tribune, who succeeds the former in case of death. They govern by turns, each being a year in office, and enter on their charge at Midsummer. They judge in all criminal causes, decide on matters of appeal from the burghers, present to church benefices, and appoint all inferior offices in the police. The other principal tribunals are the council of state called the thirteen, the œconomic chamber, assembly of appeal for the canton, that for the government of churches and colleges, the chamber of commerce, the

consistory

consistory for matrimonial causes, and the court of common law. The military consists of six companies of burghers, and two regiments of the canton, each containing nine companies of fusileers, one of grenadiers, and a troop of dragoons. The population is about 24,000 souls. The clergy, whose head or superior is the chief pastor of the cathedral, form a convocation in the city, and three chapters in the country. They are excluded, not only in Basil, but in all the Protestant cantons of Swisserland, from any share in the public administration, except in trials for adultery and fornication, and in these they only assist the civil magistrates appointed for that purpose. I cannot take leave of Basil without mentioning a large magazine and gallery of prints, which is as well furnished as any in London, Boydell's not excepted. The proprietor, Mr. Mechel, conducted me through a variety of apartments hung with the most rare and excellent, and shewed me his numerous workmen, whom he continually employs in etching and engraving. His correspondence must

LETTER VI.

muſt be very extenſive to make this great branch of buſineſs anſwer; but what ſurprizes me is, that he ſhould have ſettled in a town ſo inconſiderable as Baſil, though the largeſt in Swiſſerland.

Neufchatel, Auguſt 16.

HAD we found between Baſil and Bienne a country abounding in ſuch rich landſkip as we have ſeen on the greater part of our Swiſs tour, we ſhould have been ſurfeited with delicacies; but fortunately we met with ſcenes, which from their variety were calculated to refreſh and ſtrengthen, not cloy our appetites, being ſimilar to thoſe we had left behind us in the deſcent of Urſeren, ſuch as mountains, rocks, precipices, and water-falls. We lay the firſt night at Munſter, a place too ſmall for a town, and too large for a village, and the next morning arrived at Bienne, the capital of its republic, and an ally of the cantons. We found it well built, and well kept, or, in other words,

as clean as any town we had vifited in Swifferland. It is fituated at the foot of Mount Jura, in a fine country, rich in pafture, woods and vines, but the wine is not much efteemed. Of the government of thefe fmaller republics, I fhall not enter into a detail, as I have already put your patience to a fevere trial, in writing thofe of the cantons. Let me only obferve, that this of Bienne is ariftocratic, confifting of a great and leffer council; the latter was for fome time almoft abfolute, and even now indeed enjoys much the greater fhare of the public adminiftration. We walked about a mile and a half from the town to its lake, on which we embarked in the afternoon, and were rowed by three men, and a woman, whom we thought much too pretty for fo laborious an employment; but fhe, though French, was obedient to the commands of her hufband, and pulled luftily at the oar. I think this inferior in point of fcenery to the lake of Lucerne, but preferable to that of Zurich, as it is lefs uniform, and more romantic. We proceeded along its rocks and
filent

silent shores, till we came opposite the little island of St. Pierre, where we directed the boatmen to land us; and oh! with what pleasure did we set foot on this charming spot, which afforded an asylum to so great a genius as Rousseau, when forced to fly from his native city. It is about two miles in circumference, and contains almost every thing within it that can contribute either to its proper ornament, or to the use of the inhabitants. Wood, water, corn land, pasture, and vineyard. On landing we walked up to the summit of the island along a sideland glade, where we found a summer-house built by Rousseau. From this place we descended on the other side to his habitation, in which the farmer with whom he lived is now resident. Having walked up stairs to the room in which he lay, and examined the house as particularly as if we had carried with us a search warrant, you may be sure we were very inquisitive with the honest man, relative to the manner in which Jean Jaques passed his time. He told us that in summer, when the weather would permit,

he

he sauntered in the woods, or was out on the lake; that he would often meet and pass by him unperceived, and that he was generally silent, thoughtful, and melancholy. He was for some time the inhabitant of this island, which belongs to the states of Berne; and they (to their disgrace be it spoken) were prevailed upon by the government of Geneva to drive him from an asylum, in which otherwise he probably would have continued to his death.

We crossed over from this island to the little town of Neuville, where we lay that night, and the next morning travelled through a country of vineyards along the lake, which here takes its name from Neufchatel, where we arrived in a few hours after our departure from Neuville. This town is most pleasantly situated on the side of a steep hill that rises from the water, and is much the best built of any that we have hitherto seen in Swisserland. Its situation, together with the abundance, the excellence, and the moderate price of provisions, make

it

it a place of great resort for foreigners, and consequently its improvement is very progressive. We saw several workmen busily employed in the construction of some handsome dwelling houses, and a public hall; which, though small, being proportioned to the size of the town, displays much taste in architecture.

Neufchatel was originally governed by its own Counts, the descendants of Amo, who lived at the beginning of the eleventh century. After the extinction of this family and its successors, the last of which was Mary of Orleans, duchess of Nemours, who died in 1707, several princes laid claim to the sovereignty, and agreed that their pretensions should be decided by the states of Neufchatel. These accordingly assembled, and having resolved on certain preliminary conditions of government for the maintenance of all their former privileges, rights and immunities, the observation of which was sworn to by the different pretenders before the determination of the states: they decided

decided in favor of the king of Pruſſia, as heir to the Houſe of Challons, the family of ſome of their former Counts; and to him ſwore allegiance, after having adminiſtered the proper oaths. He is repreſented by a governor, who under his direction diſpoſes of the civil and military employments, the principal of which are thoſe of the ſtate counſellors : of the chancellor : of the attorney and ſolicitor general : of the chief commiſſary : of the caſtellans : of the mayors and preſident of the court of juſtice : neither of which can, according to the conſtitution, be offered to any but a burgher or ſubject, originally of Neufchatel. Indeed the only public charge, that can be given to a foreigner, is that of governor.

The conſtitution is compoſed of three eſtates, repreſented by twelve members, four nobles, four high officers called caſtellans, and four counſellors of the town. In them and the governor (whoſe conſent is neceſſary to make valid every law and reſolution) the ſupreme power reſides. The moſt important

LETTER VI.

tant conditions propofed to and accepted by the Houfe of Brandenburg before its fucceffion were, that the rule and authority of the ftate can exift no where but *in* the ftate, confequently that the prince in his abfence can only fpeak to the people by the governor and ftate council: that no fubject can be judged elfewhere than in the principality, and by the conftitutional judges: that the interefts of the people are feparate from thofe of the prince's German dominions: or, in other words, that Neufchatel fhould not enter into any of the king of Pruffia's wars: and finally, that the inhabitants might engage in any foreign fervice. Thus this little ftate being confidered as independent of the Pruffian territories, and the ally of the Swifs cantons, is not expofed to the incurfions of an enemy, when their prince is at war with any power on the confines of Swifferland.

As the political fituation of this principality is fo very fingular, being in great meafure free, though fubject to a prince, whofe whose authority in all his other dominions is absolute, I shall beg leave to dwell a little longer on the subject; and here let me observe, that I neither expect nor merit your praise for what I have written to you on the government of the cantons and their allies, as I, *like all modern travellers*, have done little more than translate from the histories of the country. Do not suppose that in a few weeks any person, however industrious, has time, or even inclination, in such a charming part of the world as this is, to ask many questions on government. Indeed it would in every respect be ill judged. In the first place, as giving much unnecessary trouble by the inquiry; and again, in probably not receiving sufficient information. What foreigner would think of consulting an English gentleman on the History and Constitution of Great Britain, when there are so many excellent books on the subject? But to proceed:—The inhabitants of Neufchatel cannot be tried for any crime without having previous intimation of their judges: all punishments

and

LETTER VI. 117

and fines are determined by law: and in all criminal matters the prince has the power of pardoning the culprit. How similar are those to some of the most essential privileges of our constitution! The property of the inhabitants cannot be subject to any new contribution: the land-tax (which is very moderate) may be paid either in money or kind, and the commerce is possessed of the most extensive immunities, as not being subject to any export or import duty: in consequence of all this, the revenues of the prince are very small, not amounting to more than 100,000 French livres, or 4,166 *l.* 13 *s.* 4 *d.* English. This happy constitution, which is made up of so many advantages for the subject, is naturally productive of general opulence and prosperity. Several branches of trade are carried on with great success, particularly watch-making, lapidary work, and lace manufactures, which the inhabitants export to a very considerable amount.

The population amounts to six and thirty thousand souls—an immense number for a country not more than thirty-six miles in length, and fifteen in its broadest extent, the greater part of which is lofty and barren mountains. If princes knew their real interests, they must be conscious, that the more free, the more flourishing would be their dominions.

As we arrived at the inn when dinner was serving up to the *table d'hote*, and were not only pleased with the dishes, but with the appearance of the company, we added ourselves to the number. During the repast, I happened to notice the excellence of the wine (for this of Neufchatel is famous) when a gentleman, who ingrossed the conversation of the table, asked me whether I was fond of wine; I replied I was, *in moderation*. Then, Sir, said he, I fear we shall not have your company in this town, so long as one of your countrymen (for I presume you are an Englishman) staid in Champagne. "Twenty years " ago," continued he, " I was quartered
" with

LETTER VI.

" with a company of the Swifs regiment
" de Courten at Challons fur Marne, when
" an Englifh gentleman" (or as he termed
him, un Milor Anglois) " drove furioufly
" up to the inn. As he was going through
" in a hurry he ordered his dinner imme-
" diately, and told the landlord to bring
" him fome of his beft wine, which when
" he fat down to table he tafted, and ap-
" proved; but before a bottle was finifhed
" he faw the people harneffing the horfes to
" his carriage. However, this did not in
" the leaft difconcert him, for he bade them
" wait half an hour, and ordered another
" bottle, in which he had not proceeded
" far, before he called in the landlord, and
" afked him what [quantity of this wine he
" had by him? who anfwered, a *room full*.
" Well, faid he, fend the horfes back, and
" put my carriage into the coach-houfe,
" for I fhall not leave your inn, till I have
" finifhed the whole." " And do you know,
" gentlemen," faid the officer (addreffing
himfelf to the company) " that this Milor
" Anglois, with the affiftance of his valet

de

" de chambre, (who served him in the triple
" capacity of footman, interpreter, and
" companion) finished nine dozen in three
" weeks, when he was put dead drunk into
" his carriage to complete his grand
" tour, and improve himself by travelling."
Though I was conscious that the merry
Swiss at my elbow had romanced, yet knowing how general this kind of imputation was against my countrymen, and how many of them deserved it, I was under the necessity, for the better grace, of joining in the general laugh; but another gentleman present, who was an admirer of the English, did not suffer this pleasant fellow to enjoy the triumph of his good story longer than the laugh continued; for addressing himself to him with a very serious countenance, he told him that he had mentioned the circumstance with admirable grace, but unfortunately the great quantity of Champagne, which the English gentleman and his servant had drank in so short a time, made it appear a little suspicious. However, Sir, said he, as you are so intimately
acquainted

LETTER VI.

acquainted with the particulars, it would be unmannerly in me to doubt the reality of them. I will therefore suppose, that *you*, Sir, occasionally, made up the *trio*, that your anecdote may appear less wonderful, and more consonant with truth. You may conceive how the laugh of the table was turned against the wit, insomuch that he was entirely disconcerted, and (I will venture to say) will not in future be so fond of relating his good story.

Adieu.

LETTER VII.

Berne, Aug. 18, 1787.

TO purſue our intended rout, we were obliged to travel back ſome part of the road we had come, and then croſſing the neck of water that forms a communication between the two lakes of Bienne and Neufchatel, paſſed through a part of this canton (Berne) to the town of Arberg. Early the next morning we continued our journey through a country, which convinced us of the induſtry of its inhabitants, and pleaſed us with its beauty, being not only highly cultivated, but finely varied with wood and water. Indeed the attention of the Swiſs huſbandmen to agriculture is become proverbial. In ſome modern publication I have read, that the plough is uſed in places ſeemingly inacceſſible. Nevertheleſs, I muſt in juſtice to my native country obſerve, that I have there ſeen arable fields much ſteeper than any we have noticed ſince our departure from Geneva. Indeed all Swiſ
ſerland

LETTER VII.

ferland cannot boaſt a ſociety for the encouragement of agriculture, ſo laudable in its inſtitution, as that ſet on foot in Brecknockſhire by my worthy old friend Mr. Powell of Caſtlemadock.

On entering Berne, we were much pleaſed with its ſituation, to which I never ſaw any thing ſimilar. It is built on a bold eminence or peninſula, three ſides of which are waſhed by the river Aär, and the fourth or entrance, which I ſhould not ſuppoſe to be above 100 feet in breadth, is defended by ſtrong walls and baſtions. Though it is not of great extent, the principal ſtreets are wide, the houſes large and convenient, eſpecially on the ſouth ſide. It has an academy endowed with eight profeſſorſhips, a muſeum, public library, and arſenal, all of which we had the curioſity to inſpect. In the latter we found arms for 40,000 men (if accoutred in the faſhion of the laſt century) and two curious wooden ſtatues of *Tell* and his ſon; the former in the attitude of ſhooting the apple off the latter's head.

The

The father is dressed in the old Swiss manner, with a coat of different colours, and his countenance resembles that of a highlander; the boy has a fair round face, and seems insensible of the danger. These figures might be called the Dü Penates of the Bernois. The last place that we visited in the town was the great church—a noble building. Our guide would make us climb the tower of it for the purpose of seeing a great bell, but we were more satisfied with the extensive view from the top, which reaches even to the Grison country. The yard of this church is planted with avenues, and laid out in walks. It is supported by a wall, which I should suppose 60 or 70 feet high. On looking over it we were shewn a small square stone below, put there in memory of a horse having leaped down it with his rider, who escaped unhurt. The day after our arrival we walked a mile from the town to see the exercise of some artillery men. At stated times they are ordered by the government to assemble and encamp for that purpose: their tents were well pitched,

and

LETTER VII.

and in good order, but I cannot speak so favourably of their skill as cannoneers, or discipline as soldiers; in the former they but ill acquitted themselves; and for the latter, as the officers and men were upon an equality, I was not surprized at that riot and confusion which prevailed among them as they marched. Berne was begun in 1191 by Berthold, the fifth duke of Zeringhen, and vicegerent in this part of Swisserland, for the emperor Henry, son of Frederick Barbarossa. The foundation of this, and other cities by him and his predecessors, was laid with a design of uniting the inferior nobility and others into society, by way of counterpoise against the great barons. Henry the VIIth of England had the same object in view when he permitted the nobility, &c. to break ancient entails, and alienate their estates. In a short time Berne grew into consequence, and from the tranquillity which it enjoyed during the crusades, obtained partly with money, and partly by conquest, a rich and extensive territory. In 1353 it entered into the general confederacy, and

became

became the eighth allied canton, though firſ in rank, Zurich excepted. The reformation took place here in 1528. In 1536 it conquered, or rather gained poſſeſſion, without ſtriking a blow, of the *Pays de Vaud.*

The city was at firſt divided in four diſtricts, called Abbayes, which contained four companies of trade; each company elected from its own body a banneret as its chief, who were together the firſt military officers, and governed the republic. By theſe were choſen ſixteen of the principal burghers, four from each quarter, who were to aſſiſt at deliberations of importance, and as late as the laſt century, they, with the bannerets, retained the excluſive right of electing the two hundred, or great council. This council, in which all the other colleges are united, under the general title of, *Advoyer Council* and *Burghers* of the *Town* and *Republic* of *Berne,* exerciſes over all ſubjects ſovereign power: enacts and revokes laws: determines on all interior affairs: delegates

to

LETTER VII.

to the other tribunals their several authorities: forms alliances: and judges, in the last resort, on trials of life and death. In the year 1290 it consisted only of 200, but the bannerets, and sixteen, did not keep to any stated period or rule of election, so that through interest and favour, it increased to between three and four hundred, when the abuse becoming too flagrant, it was corrected by law, and the number fixed at 299, which it now is. As a seat in the great council is an object of general ambition, many candidates offer themselves for the vacancies; to obviate any ill consequences from the competition of such pretenders, it has been wisely determined that no election shall take place, until there be a deficiency of at least 80 members, by which means the senate and seizeners, who are the electors, have it the more in their power to satisfy those who are proposed, each of whom must have accomplished his nine and twentieth year. From this delay an election happens only in ten, twelve, or fourteen years. Each member may propose whatever he thinks
conducive

conducive to the general good, and the votes of the council are taken on the queſtion. They ſit three times a week when aſſembled. Their vacations take place in the harveſt and vintage.

The ſenate, or as it is otherwiſe called, the daily council, is choſen from the 299; all civil and political buſineſs, which is to be laid before the great council, is previouſly agitated in this. It alſo expedites the current affairs of the police: preſents to moſt of the livings or eccleſiaſtical benefices, diſpoſes of the inferior charges of the executive government, and judges, as dernier reſort, all criminal proceſs, except ſuch parts of it as are granted by ancient privilege to particular towns or vaſſals of the republic. This council is compoſed of two Advoyers (or great officers of ſtate) two treaſurers, four bannerets, ſeventeen counſellors, and two privy counſellors or cenſors, who ſucceed in priority from the date of their election to the vacant places of the ſenate. Their buſineſs is to watch over the
delibe-

LETTER VII.

deliberations of the councils, that nothing may pafs in them contrary to the national conftitution. The titles of the 299, including the fenate, are, MAGNIFICENT, HIGH and POWERFUL SOVEREIGN LORDS, and when fpoken of individually, they are called their EXCELLENCIES. The public magiftrates are annually re-elected in Eafter week; and the fenate is obliged to demand a new patent of protection from the great council, in token of its dependence on it. Many of the chief officers are elected for a certain time, and fome for life, or rather *quam diu fe bene gefferint,* as the fovereign council referves to itfelf the power of depofing them, in cafe of mal-adminiftration; but all places are confirmed at certain appointed periods.

The principal colleges of government are the council of war: the chamber of appeal for the German part of the canton: the chamber of appeal for the Pays de Vaud, where the language is French: the committees for the management of the public granaries:

granaries: for the forests: for the sale of salt: for the police: for the public buildings: for the customs or duties: for commerce: and the council of health. These, with many other, too tedious to mention, form separate commissions, each of which has a senator as president, and is charged with the execution of the government's orders in their several departments, where they are to discuss preparatorily such matters as are proper to them, and to report their opinions, and the motives of such, to the sovereign council.

As to the ministry of the church, all young men, who are intended for holy orders, go through a course of study, according to a system established in the academies of Berne or Lausanne. After having passed the necessary examinations, the candidates receive consecration by the imposition of hands, and with it the cure of souls. Church benefices, as I have before observed, are given by the senate, except those of the capital, which are reserved for the

LETTER VII.

the disposal of the great council, and the private benefices which depend on the recommendation of the patrons. The German clergy are divided into eight synods or chapters, which assemble separately every year. At their head they have a dean to examine the conduct of each individual pastor, and deliberate on matters of religion. The Pays de Vaud is divided into five classes, in which are comprised the churches and bailiwicks in common, between Berne, Freyburg, and those of Boucheberg in the canton of Soleure, which have embraced the reformation.

The pastors assist at the parish consistories, where breaches of moral duty, and crimes of adultery and fornication are reported, with all matrimonial business and suits of divorce. These are transferred to the supreme consistory of Berne, which is jointly composed of civil and ecclesiastical judges, similar to what it is at Basil.

The military of Berne is formed of twenty one regiments of infantry, each confifting of 2500 men, divided in two great battalions of twelve companies; four regiments of dragoons of ten troops, or five fquadrons each, and three companies of engineers and matroffes. The foldiers provide themfelves with arms and accoutrements, and all the fubjects (the councils, the clergy, and fome public officers excepted), from fixteen to fixty, are regiftered for the fervice. The canton, in virtue of former treaties with France and Holland, is obliged to furnifh recruits for four avowed regiments, two in each country; I fay avowed, as others are privately permitted to be raifed for the fervice of thefe ftates. As it is not my intention to write the hiftory of Swifferland, I wifh this fketch of its government may fatisfy you; to-morrow we continue our tour, and I fhall have more matter for my letter when I refume the fubject.

Freyburg, Aug. 20.

WE found the country between Berne and Freyburg as fruitful and well cultivated, as from Arberg to Berne. This town covers the side of a very steep hill, under which runs the clear river Sane. Though not striking, it contains some fine edifices, and is from its uneven situation, and the care of its inhabitants, remarkably clean. It is divided in four quarters, called the Town, the Isle, the Burgh, and the Hospital. The principal buildings are the cathedral, town hall, fountain, great tower, Jesuits college, with many churches and convents. There is here a commandery of Malta, the religion being that of Rome. The town was bought by the Emperor Rodolph, the first of the Counts of Freyburg. Rodolph was Count of Hapsburg, and Chief of the Austrian family. It continued under his successors above 200 years, and was obliged to take part in their wars against Berne, and the other rising societies of Swisserland.

In 1450 Albert duke of Auſtria, perceiving it impoſſible to ſupport his authority in it, of which indeed his arbitrary and oppreſſive government had made him undeſerving, reſigned it, but in a manner that equally diſplayed the meanneſs of his diſpoſition, and the impotence of his reſentment. His lieutenant Thuring de Hallwyl informed the citizens, that Albert, on this occaſion, intended to appear in perſon at Freyburg; and they, to ſatisfy his vanity for the laſt time, made the moſt ſplendid preparations for his reception. Hallwyl, having gotten into his poſſeſſion their plate, waited a few days for the duke's arrival, and then, ſeemingly ſurpriſed at his delay, went out to meet him, accompanied by the principal citizens, and the treaſure he had collected. On the road they were ſurrounded by a detachment of the duke's troops, and Hallwyl, who had preconcerted the ſurpriſe with Albert, ſuddenly turning upon them, ſaid: " The duke will come no more, but leaves you in full poſſeſſion of that independence which you have ſo

earneſtly

earnestly desired. However, that you may make some return for so generous an action, he condescends to take with him all the plate you have put into my hands for his reception, as a token of your gratitude." After this laconick oration, he turned his back, and left them speechless with astonishment. Some years after this extraordinary acknowledgment of their independence, the inhabitants got into a war with Charles the Bold, duke of Burgundy. This was the epoch of their real liberty, when with their allies they shared the risk and glory of the battles gained over this rash prince in 1476 and 77 at Granson, Morat, and Nancy; in commemoration of which the citizens of Freyburg solemnize two great annual festivals on the 2d of May and 22d of June, the days on which the two former of these victories were won.

The sovereign authority and legislative power belong to the great council of 200, the other tribunals and committees being either subdivisions of, or subordinate to it.

The government is not an aristocracy, but oligarchy, as the right of being admitted into the great council is confined to seventy-one Patrician families. However, the other citizens enjoy all privileges, though ineligible to the magistracy; but the burghers in seven and twenty parishes of the original district, have the right of voting at the election of a new Advoyer, or chief of the republic. The city is divided in four quarters, each of which chuses a banneret, fifteen members for the council of sixty, and twenty eight for the great council, which, together with the twenty-four members of the lesser, make up the 200. The prerogatived families alone can be adopted by any of the thirteen tribes of burghers, and they must be one and twenty years of age before they are eligible into the great council. At thirty a Patrician may be chosen into the body of sixty, and it is necessary that he should be of this order to enter into the twenty-four; but a father and son, or two brothers, cannot sit at the same time, either as bannerets or senators of the lesser council.

The

LETTER VII.

The two Advoyers preside at the different councils, and the stathalter or lieutenant is next to them in precedence. This honour has for the last century been conferred on the senior of the twenty-four. The charges of treasurer, burgomaster, and commissary general follow in rank. The bannerets succeed the members of the lesser council, and preside at the council of state, consisting of twenty-four, selected from the body of sixty. The great council confirms the lesser, and that of sixty, and is confirmed itself by the council of state. Most of the elections are determined by lot, which with great propriety receives the epithet of *blind*, as the names of the candidates are concealed in boxes, into which the electors drop their suffrages. The lesser council judges in dernier resort all civil and criminal proceedings; but should the culprit be a burgher of the capital or ancient district, sentence is pronounced in presence of the great council, which reserves to itself the power of mitigating the punishment, or of pardoning the offence.

There

There are several inferior councils and courts, which I think needless to mention, having already written to you as much as I could wish to remember of this government.

The population is computed at 74,000 souls, the military amounts to four companies of burghers, and eleven regiments of militia.

About six miles from Freyburg is an hermitage, which has very much and very deservedly engaged the attention of the curious. It is worked out of a rock that rises over the river Sane, and encompassed by a romantic wilderness. There are several apartments in it, from one of which the solitary tenant has cut a chimney through the rock—a most laborious work, eighty feet in height. He had also by extreme toil and perseverance formed a plane, on which he laid a sufficient quantity of mould to produce the vegetables that supplied his frugal table, and in the side of the rock had

LETTER VII. 139

had hewn cisterns to receive the clear water that distilled from it; the quantity of which he increased by tracing and opening the veins through which it oozed. This remarkable man, whose name was John de Prè, resided here five and twenty years, cherished and respected by the whole country, particularly by the peasantry; at the end of which in 1708, as he was crossing the river Sane, on his return from accompanying some young people, who had assisted at the consecration of his little chapel, his foot slipped, he fell, and perished. What a subject for pity and reflection!

Yverdun, August 21.

WE continued our journey from Freyburg to Yverdun, and previously to our arrival, enjoyed a most beautiful view of the lake of Neufchatel, or, as it is here called, of Yverdun. On the opposite bank is the village of Granson, famous for the victory gained over Charles the Bold, duke

of

of Burgundy by the confederate Swifs. This country abounds in vineyards, which produce a wholefome and excellent white wine. I will not fay, it is for this reafon that Yverdun is fo much frequented by the Englifh, but really I do not comprehend why it is fo preferred; it furely cannot be for the French language, as the accent is not good. It ftands in a fine country, has many well built houfes, and upon the whole might be called a pretty little town. It was named by the Romans *Caftrum Ebrodunenfe*, and after them fucceffively poffeffed by the kings of Burgundy, and dukes of Zeringhen and Savoy. Under the dominion of the latter it continued until the year 1536, when it was included in the conqueft of the Pays de Vaud. No city of the thirteen cantons has experienced fuch calamities as Yverdun. In the fifteenth century it was almoft deftroyed by fire, and had fcarce recovered, when an inundation of the river Thiele, on which it ftands, laid the whole wafte, carrying away feveral houfes, and the town hall. In 1475 it was befieged and taken by

LETTER VII.

by the Swifs, in confequence of the alliance that fubfifted between the Duke of Savoy, its poffeffor, and Charles the Bold Duke of Burgundy. The miferies that it fuffered during the continuance of this war are particularly ftated in an act of the former of thefe Princes, dated July 13th, 1480, in which it is reported to have been frequently pillaged by the foldiers of each party, and ultimately reduced to afhes by the Swifs, who fometimes appeared as Germans and fometimes as Theotons. The wretched inhabitants wandered about the country for fubfiftence until collected and brought back by the Duke of Savoy, who in compaffion of their fituation affifted them in re-building their town, fupplied them with whatever they wanted, and granted them feveral privileges and immunities. I fhall pafs over in filence the few uninterrefting public buildings that we faw, and mention an inftitution which I am convinced will particularly claim your attention as an active magiftrate. This is a fociety of fome of the principal inhabitants of Yverdun, formed in 1760 for the purpofe of pre-

venting

venting begging, and for the encouragement of labour. The members of it make and receive voluntary contributions, with which they are enabled not only to fupport thofe whom age or accident has rendered incapable of acquiring a fubfiftence, but fo to train the children of the poorer inhabitants, that by their induftry they might be ferviceable to the community. All thefe are employed in the country, and fuch is the effect of this ufeful charity, that not a beggar is to be feen in the ftreets of Yverdun.

Having told you that this place is much frequented by Englifh gentlemen, it reminds me of a circumftance that happened to one of them a few years ago, from whom I heard it. This gentleman had paffed fome months at Yverdun, and had generally dined at a *table d'hote*, in a mixed company of Englifh, French, and Swifs. On going away he called for his bill, and thinking he had been confiderably over-rated, examined the barbook, in which he found the honeft man of

the

LETTER VII.

the houfe had charged the Englifh for each dinner as much again as the other foreigners; being of courfe upbraided for his difhonefty, he replied, "Tout au contraire, monfieur, je fuis plus que jufte en ce que vous, meffieurs les Anglois, foyez *diz fois* plus riches que les autres gens, et je ne vous demande que *le double.*"*

* Quite the reverfe, Sir; I am more than honeft, in as much as you Englifhmen are ten times richer than other people, and I only charge you double.

LETTER VIII.

Lauſanne, Aug. 24th, 1787.

THE morning of our departure from Yverdun, we got into a carriage for the firſt time ſince we had been in Swiſſerland, and aſcended until we came within a few miles of Lauſanne. From the ſummit of the hill we looked over the lake of Geneva and the ſurrounding country, which is as beautiful as language can deſcribe, or imagination conceive it. The view from this town is equally fine, though it ſtands rather lower; but the interior ill accords with its ſituation, being ill built, and ſo uneven, that there is not a ſtreet in it in which the paſſenger does not mount or deſcend. Out of the town is a public walk under an avenue of large trees, which commands the lake: the mountains of Faucignie: the Pays de Vaud: Mount Jura: and the Alps of Savoy. We dedicated the firſt day of our arrival to the Engliſh newſpapers, which we found in a literary coffee-houſe; and never I believe were two creatures happier in the difcovery. The fecond we defcended to the little village of Ouchie, or Port of Laufanne, which lies directly under it on the edge of the lake. Having hired a boat we were carried over to Mellieire in the duchy of Chablais, a part of his Sardinian Majefty's dominion; and oh! what a fudden tranfition from opulence to poverty, from liberty to flavery, from happinefs to mifery! never were the effects of different governments more apparent in two nations than in thefe on the oppofite fides of the lake. On that of Swifferland, nothing meets the eye but what gladdens the heart of the philanthropift; on that of Chablais, nothing but what pains it. Here it is that philofophy may contemplate the oppofite confequences of a free and defpotick government, and hail liberty, as next to health, the chief blefling that the great Author of Nature can beftow. The more I fee the more I am enamoured of her. Mellieire is a beggarly village that lies along a narrow flip of land between the lake and rocks behind it, which feem as it were to lean upon and force it into the water. The inhabitants are as wretched as idleness, poverty, and superstition, can make them. Their chief dependence for food being upon the lake, I cannot conceive how they exist in a severe winter, when the surface of it is a continued sheet of ice. This place is generally visited for the purpose of seeing Lausanne and the opposite shore to advantage, particularly, as the whole of this country has been so pleasingly painted by the lively description of Rousseau in his Nouvelle Heloise; from the rocks of Mellieire St. Prieux wrote that letter to his Julia which is so generally admired as descriptive of the many sensations that arise in the breast of an absent lover on seeing, or thinking he sees, the distant habitation of his mistress; and which Rousseau himself considered as the masterpiece of the whole: I don't know what your sentiments may be of this novel, but I am so unfashionable as to think it extremely exceptionable, and the characters out of nature, particularly that of Julia the heroine; nevertheless I am charmed with the style and language,

LETTER VIII.

guage, which unite two qualities seldom found in similar compositions of the French language, sweetness and energy. Rousseau has done more in this respect, than Marmontel, De la Fontaine, or even Voltaire *in prose.*

From this place we re-crossed the water to Vevay, the most delightful town in Swisserland. This upper part of the lake is, I must confess, equal to any thing we have seen on this tour. Pocock thinks it superior, and calls it one of those complete prospects to which no ideal beauty can be added; my opinion is divided between this and the environs of Lucerne; they are both rivals, but which is the most beautiful I really cannot determine. We lay one night at Vevay, and returned the next morning by water to Ouchie, and thence to Lausanne. This city is famous for the council held here in 1448, when Amadeus the Eighth, Duke of Savoy, then Pope, under the name of Felix the Fifth, resigned the pontificate for the generous purpose of terminating a schism in the church of Rome. Berne, on the reduction of the Pays de Vaud, not only confirmed Lauſanne in all its ancient privileges, but granted many in addition. It enjoys its own magiſtracy, compoſed of a burgomaſter, five bannerets, and three councils, beſides other ſubordinate officers. The academy, when founded in 1537, conſiſted only of two profeſſors in Greek and Hebrew; but has now two paſtors, two profeſſors of Theology, and others in modern Philoſophy, Greek, Hebrew, Belles Lettres, Mathematics, Civil Law; and about fourteen years ago, the government of Berne eſtabliſhed a new profeſſorſhip in Medicine for their modern Æſculapius M. Tiſſot, a gentleman much known by his writings.

Among the excluſive privileges which this town poſſeſſes, one is very ſingular. In a certain part of it, the inhabitants may acquit or condemn any of their own body in affairs of life and death, and at theſe trials every individual has the right of voting, which has conſiderably enhanced the rent of houſes in that diſtrict.

Lauſanne

LETTER VIII.

Lausanne is the favorite residence of the celebrated Mr. Gibbon. We wished much to have seen him, but he was gone to publish the two last volumes of his Decline and Fall of the Roman Empire, in England.

To-morrow we shall make an end of our Swifs tour.

Geneva, Aug. 27.

ON leaving Lausanne we passed through the towns of Morges, Rolle, and Copet, which are pleasingly situated near the lake. The former carries on some trade, and has a commodious port, built by the government of Berne. Great will be your surprise when I tell you I was much disappointed with the celebrated *Pays de Vaud*. That it is one of the finest and most fruitful countries of Europe I am ready to acknowledge; and indeed as beautiful as a great variety of villas, intermixed with pastures and vineyards, can make it; nevertheless, there being little wood,

wood, few rivers, and no mountain, it by no means anfwered my expectations. It feems to me bare of that varied fcenery, which makes Swifferland the moft picturefque country of Europe. I know that I am very fingular in opinion, but I have promifed you on thefe occafions to think for myfelf, and you fee I perfevere in the refolution.

To make up for the deficiency of my former letters on the Swifs cantons, permit me to conclude this with a few neceffary addenda, which I fhall beg leave to introduce by the following fummary account of their general union and alliance.

I have before obferved that in 1315, Uri, Schweitz, and Underwalden, entered into * a perpetual league for their mutual defence, being fearful of incroachments by the houfe of Auftria. In 1332 Lucerne joined this alliance in oppofition to a defign which had

* There was an alliance which had fubfifted between thefe three cantons ever fince the year 1291, but it was not made perpetual till 1315, after their victory over the Auftrians at Morgarten.

been

been formed by the Austrian party to prevent it, and get possession of the town. In 1351, Zurich from similar motives (a conspiracy of its banished citizens) made the fifth confederate canton; and from its superior power, and wealth, was considered as the first of the association. The following year Glaris and Zug acceded; and in 1353, Berne, though a previous alliance subsisted between it and the three first Waldstætt. Before this period the cantons allied themselves for their mutual protection; but we find from experience that the love of freedom is so closely connected with ambition, that no sooner have we acquired our liberty than we are desirous of increasing our dominion at the expence of our neighbours. Thus it was in the present instance, though with more appearance of justice, as the enemies of the Swifs were the aggressors; but it too often happens, that among nations, justice and interest are synonymous. Two circumstances now arose which induced them to take a more active part, and bear arms on the offensive: the first was the restless ambition of the Dukes of Austria,

Auſtria, who by ſecret intrigue, as well as open force, would have reduced them to a ſtate of vaſſallage: and the ſecond, the encouragement of the Emperors, who, jealous of the growing power of Auſtria, perſuaded them, by aſſurances of ſupport, to violate all treaties. For the purpoſe of terminating theſe dangerous factions, the allied cantons in 1370 entered into a convention, which regulated every thing with the Germans, and for the general welfare of the league.

But Lucerne, probably conſcious that the new allies would make its private quarrel a common cauſe, broke with the Houſe of Auſtria, for the purpoſe of exonerating itſelf from a duty impoſed upon its inhabitants at Rothenburg. This brought on a general war, which, after two famous victories gained by the Swiſs in 1386 and 1388 at Sempach in Lucerne, and Nafels in Glaris, was concluded by an advantageous peace; but aware of the dangerous conſequence that might reſult from too great preſumption on their valour and alliance, they entered into a convention

tion at Sempach in 1393, for the purpose of preventing individuals, or even any one people of the triple confederacy from engaging in a war without the consent and approbation of the whole. In 1460 the conquest of Turgovy, or the country that lies between the canton of Zurich and the lake of Constance, occasioned their celebrated war with Charles the Bold, duke of Burgundy, which ended with his defeat and death at Granson, Morat, and Nancy. This quarrel was fomented by that perfidious monarch Lewis the Eleventh of France, who only consulted in it his own interest by the destruction of his rival Charles; however, the event of the war may be considered as the epoch of two important circumstances in Swiss history—their perpetual union with Austria, and an alliance with the crown of France. But this tide of success was not unaccompanied by evil, as it introduced among the conquerors the spirit of pride and licentiousness, which probably would have ended in their disunion, had not Nicholas de Flue, an anchorite, left his

retreat,

retreat, and at a meeting of the deputies in Stanz, formerly the chief place of Underwalden, perſuaded them ſo fully of their real intereſts, in a ſtrain of the moſt animated eloquence inſpired by patriotiſm, and the danger to which his country was expoſed, that they entered into an immediate convention, by which they determined on the following reſolutions : that mutual protection ſhould be granted, as well from interior as exterior violence : that juſtice ſhould be impartially adminiſtered among them : and that the profits of ſucceſsful war ſhould be divided in proportion to their reſpective quotas of troops and money. After this they confirmed their ancient treaties of union, and agreed to ſwear to them every five years. About this period Freyburg and Solcure were aſſociated to the common league, and in 1501 Baſil and Schaffhauſen ; the laſt was Appenzel, which in 1513 made up the whole number.

Whilſt the four Waldſtætt, and the other cantons on that ſide of Swiſſerland, which afterwards

LETTER VIII.

afterwards acceded to the combination, were dismembering the territories of Austria, Berne and Freyburg took possession of the Pays de Vaud, Gex, and Chablais, part of the dukes of Savoy's dominions, who, though incapable of recovering by force what had been stripped from them, could not renounce their superior right to these countries, until through the mediation of Spain, France, and the neutral cantons, the then reigning duke, obtaining restitution of Gex and Chablais, renounced all pretension to the Pays de Vaud, and ceded it to Berne and Freyburg for ever. Since this period the limits of Swisserland have neither been extended nor diminished. What principally disturbed the internal harmony of the cantons, was a difference in religious opinions. On this dangerous subject wars arose between Berne and Zurich for the reformers; and Uri, Schweitz, Underwalden, and Zug, for the church of Rome. However, after various success, they were happily ended, and are not likely to be renewed.

The

The only conftitution that can be faid to have any reference to the national body of the Swifs, is the eftablifhment of a confederate army, determined on in 1688 between the cantons, and their allies. This, however, was adopted only as a plan of defence, fimilar to our militia, * each ftate

* In the contribution of thefe troops the following proportion is obferved, according to the original agreement between the cantons and their allies.

		No. of Men.	Religion	Government
1	Zurich —	1400	Proteft	Ariftocracy
2	Berne —	2000	Proteft	Ariftocracy
3	Lucerne —	1200	Cathol	Ariftocracy
4	Uri —	400	Cathol	Democracy
5	Schweitz —	600	Cathol	Democracy
6	Underwalden	400	Cathol	Democracy
7	Zug —	400	Cathol	Democracy
8	Glaris —	400	Mixed	Democracy
9	Bafil —	400	Proteft	Ariftocracy
10	Freyburg —	800	Cathol	Ariftocracy
11	Soleure —	600	Cathol	Ariftocracy
12	Schaffhaufen	400	Proteft	Ariftocracy
13	Appenzel —	600	Mixed	Democracy

Allies of the Cantons.
1	Abbey of St. Gall	1000	Mixed
2	Town of St. Gall	200	Proteft
3	Bienne —	200	Proteft

Provinces fubject to the Cantons.
1	Lugano —	400	Cathol
2	Locarno —	200	Cathol
3	Mendrifio —	100	Cathol
4	Val Maggia	100	Cathol
5	The free Bailiwicks	300	Cathol
6	Sargans —	300	Cathol
7	Turgovy —	600	Mixed
8	Baden —	200	Cathol
9	The Rheinthal	200	Mixed

Total 13,400 Men

sending its quota of troops according to its extent and population; the whole forms a body of 13,400 men, but in cases of necessity this number would be considerably augmented in the same proportion.

The commerce of Swisserland is very inconsiderable. Its exports consist of linens, muslin, hides, and the produce of their dairies, which are small huts called *Chalets*, built on the mountains, where, during the summer months, their cattle are sent to feed. The Swiss cheese is excellent, and consequently much esteemed in the neighbouring countries, particularly in France, where a great consumption is made of it. Their imports are considerable, though a frugal people, they being in want of corn, iron, and salt; the latter article they draw from France, and according to the treaties of alliance subsisting between the two countries, they receive annually a certain quantity at a much more reasonable price than it is ever sold by the French government to their own subjects. Nevertheless, even in
Swisser-

Swifferland it is a dear article, being retailed by the officers of ftate, who monopolize, and draw a principal part of the public revenues from its fale. The total receipt of Berne amounts to about 75,000 *l.* and of Zurich to a little more than one half. Exclufive of this tax on falt, the revenue is made up by cuftoms and duties on merchandize, the profits of demefne lands, and the tithes of the general produce of the country (the clergy being paid by government) to which might be added the money that the different cantons receive from foreign powers for the hire of their troops. This is a cuftom that has given rife to a difference of opinion among the Swifs, relative to its advantage or ill confequence. They, who oppofe it, maintain that the officers and foldiers of thefe regiments, acquire the vices of the different countries in which they ferve, and on their return to Swifferland, by fpreading them, corrupt the purer morals of its inhabitants. In anfwer to this it is afferted, that as the revenues of the cantons are inadequate to the expences of government
and

and the support of a sufficient army for the national defence, it is necessary to pursue this system laid down by their ancestors, as it gives them all the advantages of a regular army, without the expence of its maintenance, it being stipulated in their treaties that in case of attack from foreign enemy, these troops, which amount to 30,000, should be at liberty to return home and act in concert with their countrymen. Both of these arguments are plausible; but the question is, if they be admitted as fact, whether the morality of a nation should be sacrificed to its policy; but it may be asserted again, that true policy is inseparable from good morals, and still further, the Swifs cannot be apprehensive of the encroachments of any foreign state, as long as they perceive that the general aim of Europe is to preserve an equilibrium of power: this balance is their best and indeed their only safeguard; for though no soldier, I think I might assert that Swisserland with all its force, could never maintain a defensive war against either France or the Emperor. The Swifs and their allies are

supposed

supposed to amount to more than two millions of souls. Their manner of living is much more simple than that of their neighbours, as they are more restricted by their respective governments; sumptuary laws being in full force among them, and no amusement, such as games of hazard, plays, operas, or even dancing, except at appointed times, being permitted. As every citizen is a soldier (the clergy excepted) they on Sundays after divine service go through the military exercise; they are careful of the education of their youth, as is evident from their public seminaries or universities; the principal of which are at Basil and Berne.—In giving you a sketch of the national character I shall confine myself to the popular governments, as I think the people there retain the temper and manner of the ancient Swiss more than the other cantons. Of them I think very favourably, provided I except those of the lower class, who have seen other countries, or have any communication with travellers; as such are not only in this, but I believe in every country of the world, deceitful

LETTER VIII.

ceitful and mercenery; with regard to the general inhabitants of thefe cantons they feem to be frugal without meannefs; brave without vanity; and hofpitable without oftentation: to ftrangers they are courteous and polite, without being either defigning or troublefome. They value but little thofe diftinctions of rank, birth, and fortune, which in the other countries of Europe, and indeed in the other cantons of Swifferland, are fo obfequioufly cultivated, as they meafure the dignity of the fituation by the merit of the individual. Every man here knows the advantages of his own free government; and as he alfo knows himfelf to be a component part of it, is from intereft as well as principle a real patriot. Such is their attachment to their country, that, of the Swifs regiments in foreign fervice, many of the foldiers after a long abfence pine and ficken for their return. Should that liberty be refufed them (which never is from experience of the ill confequence) their death is inevitable; as neither promotion nor emolument can diffipate the melancholy that preys upon them. Home is the only cure of this singular malady, which is called the *Swifs sickness*,* and that infallible In domestic life their private virtues flow from their public character; to their parents they are grateful and obedient: to their families affectionate and attentive: inflexible in friendship: mild as superiors, and benevolent as men.

* They call it in German *das heim wehe*. There is a motive that induces us to recollect the places which we love, more than the *music* we have heard in them; and from this it is, that all songs and tunes that were popular in their country are strictly forbidden among the Swifs regiments in foreign service.

LETTER

LETTER IX.

Grenoble, Sept. 14, 1787.

ON our return to Geneva, we found between forty and fifty English gentlemen, among whom Lord P—— and some others had lately been put in prison, from which, after a week's confinement, they were released through the intercession of his R. H. the duke of Gloucester, but banished the republic for life. I really think the magistrates exerted their authority with extreme rigour; and this indeed seems to be the opinion of all the foreigners with whom I have conversed. The offence for which they were punished was (as I am informed) an altercation and scuffle with the guard for the purpose of getting out of the city after the gates were shut; an act so inconsiderate, that we cannot suppose any men would have been capable of attempting it, if they had not been very much in liquor, which was the case. The commandant of a French city would have laughed at such

such a circumstance as childish, and beneath his attention; and I think the magistrates of Geneva should have been satisfied with reprimanding the offenders, if only in consideration of their being young men and foreigners; but impatient of opposition to their authority, and fearful, lest private disturbance might produce general insurrection, they judged with prejudice, and punished with severity. During our stay at this place we made an excursion to Ferney, formerly the seat and residence of Voltaire. The good which he did here is universally known, and universally acknowledged. He was the friend of the distressed, and the promoter of industry. The population of the village increased during his abode in it (which was but a few years) from eight to twelve hundred persons, and never was there a happier or more peaceful society established, though it consisted of Protestants and Roman Catholics. The castle or seat which he built for himself has nothing very striking in its appearance. We were led into every apartment, and in the

study

study saw fixed over the door a sarcophagus, in which is an urn of silver gilt, that contains his heart; upon it is the following inscription:

Son esprit est par tout mais son cœur est ici.*

Before the house is a church, which he built and consecrated to God; and in front of it put up this motto, DEO EREXIT. You know the sentiments of Voltaire on religion, therefore I need not say any thing on that subject. We examined every thing with attention, and were sorry to find that the present owner neglects the pleasure grounds and buildings. Perhaps he intends to convert the former into a wilderness, and the latter into ruins, for they already border on them.

A few days after this excursion we agreed with an Italian Vetturino, or man that lets out horses, to conduct us over the Alps, and left Geneva on the 10th. We travelled through roads, which, though bad, pleased

* His genius is every where, but his heart is here.

us more than the wild prospect on each side to Remellie, a town of miserable houses, and still more miserable inhabitants. However, I was neither surprized nor disappointed, as I knew myself in Savoy. Remellie stands on a steep rising over the river Arve, the foul current of which is but the counterpart of the general appearance of the country. We crossed it by a bridge, the descent to which on each side is extremely dangerous; but we had the satisfaction to perceive that our postillions, who were no strangers to the place, took all care, and indeed they had every reason to do so, for on our arrival at the inn we found a gentleman and his sister of Geneva, who but a week ago had fallen in their carriage over the side of this bridge, and escaped, as it were, by miracle. The postillion, who drove them, had neglected to chain the wheel, and the horses in descending, being unable to sustain the weight of the carriage, and turn short over the bridge, were forced through a slight rail at the side, and fell at least forty feet. The gentleman,
with

LETTER IX.

with uncommon prefence of mind, finding it impoffible to prevent the accident, caught his fifter in his arms, and probably by fo doing preferved both their lives; for the carriage was broken to pieces, the horfes killed, and the poftillion would have fhared the fame fate (which none could have lamented) had he not thrown himfelf off on the very verge of the precipice. We congratulated them on their providential efcape; and were happy to hear, that though much bruifed, they were entirely out of danger. How ftrongly does this circumftance plead the neceffity of making poftillions ufe every precaution againft danger, for who fo negligent and inattentive? We lay that night in this wretched inn, and the day following travelled to Chamberry, through a country more rude and mountainous than the moft unfrequented parts of Swifferland. This city, the capital of the duchy, and refidence of the ancient dukes of Savoy, has not, in my opinion, any thing to recommend it to the attention of travellers, being upon the whole ill built, and fituated in a country which by no means pleafes my tafte, though I am free to own, that the environs prefent great variety of objects; but the neglected flate of agriculture, particularly in the vines, which trail along the ground for want of attention: the mean appearance of the peafantry: the wild afpect of the impending Alps: and the muddy torrents which run down from thefe mountains—with me an infuperable objection to any country, render the whole one of the moft ineligible places of abode I ever faw. Neverthelefs, we found the city full of people, and a large body of troops in garrifon. While dinner was preparing we procured a guide, who led us to an old caftle, fome churches, monafteries, the Jefuits college, and public walks; all of which had little of our attention, as we thought them but little deferving of it. In the neighbourhood are feveral mineral fprings, which are efteemed very falubrious, and certain remedies for paralytic complaints; but the principal and moft celebrated are at Aix, the *Aquæ Gratianæ* of the Romans, a fmall town between

between this and Remellie, where we found many invalids. The waters of that place are more impregnated with sulphur and allum than any I had ever seen; indeed all who go there merit a return of health, if it be only for the inconveniencies they suffer during their stay, as I think I never was in such a hole of a town, which notwithstanding is honoured with the title of Marquisate.

We left Chamberry on the day of our arrival, and found the country improve as we proceeded; but what pleased us most were the vines on the road side, now heavily laden with their ripe and luscious burdens, of which we did not eat sparingly. A few sous procured us a basket-full, and as many thanks as clusters. Indeed, had we been so inclined, we might have gathered them as we passed along in the carriage; but we knew that the great quantity of the fruit would not extenuate the injustice of such an act. Having again entered France, we lay that night in a village of Dauphiny, the

name

name of which I do not now recollect, and got the next day to its capital Grenoble, which is pleasantly situated on the banks of the river Isere, that divides it from a large suburb. It is not extensive, but to appearance very populous, and full of good company; it once was a place of great strength, being surrounded by high walls and bastions, which are now in the last stage of decay. Its bishops are honoured with the title of princes, but the fee is dependent on the metropolitan of Vienne; its parliament was appointed by Lewis the XIth when dauphin, in 1453. This province, after the general partage of the Roman empire, was possessed by the Burgundians, from whom it was taken by the Franks, and made part of the kingdom of Arles. It then became subject to the emperor of Germany, so that it appears to have been successively owned by the same masters as the town and territory of Geneva. *Guigne le gros Count of Grisnauden*, taking advantage of the disputes between the emperors and the see of Rome, got possession of it in 1101, and by him or his

successors

LETTER IX.

successors it was first called Dauphiny, from the circumstance of their bearing a dolphin as their arms. It remained in this family till the time of Humbert the IId, Count and Dauphin of the Viennois, who, having lost both his sons, the elder in the battle of Cressy, and the younger by an accident, sold the province to Philip de Valois for five and twenty thousand pounds (or 100,000 golden florins) but at the same time stipulated, that the eldest son of the French kings should assume the name of Dauphin, and quarter the arms of the province. This agreement was entered into and signed on the 23d of April, 1343, at Bois de Vincennes near Paris, and Charles the Vth, grandson of Philip de Valois, was the first who bore the title.

The morning after our arrival at this town we set off with the light for the famous Carthusian monastery, about nineteen miles from Grenoble. The two first hours were taken up in ascending a steep hill, after which we traversed a country very similar

to

to the moſt romantic parts of Swiſſerland, though not the moſt beautiful. When we came near the monaſtery we entered a narrow valley, or rather paſſage through the rocks, down which guſhed a torrent of the cleareſt water, and having paſſed under a gate that occupies the whole entrance, aſcended one of the moſt woodland and pictureſque countries I had ever ſeen to the place of our deſtination. Of the convent I ſhall only obſerve, that it is a large pile of building, with every convenience for its monaſtic ſociety; but it is the *ſituation* that is ſo remarkable, being every thing that the moſt melancholy enthuſiaſt could wiſh as the ſecluded ſeat of prayer and retirement—rocks and woods, and everlaſting ſolitude: yet how frequently does it happen, that we perceive the moſt admirable deſign counteracted by the very circumſtance that is intended to produce the deſired effect? as in the inſtance before us. The country, in which this monaſtery is ſituated, was choſen on account of its romantic appearance, and diſtance from all ſociety, as beſt adapted to devotion;

LETTER IX.

devotion; but it is this very fituation that makes it a place of general refort. I believe few convents fee fo much company, and fure I am, that none treat their guefts with more good breeding and hofpitality. On our arrival we were moft politely received by one of the order, whom we fuppofed mafter of the ceremonies for the brotherhood. He firft fhewed us the houfe, and then conducted us near a mile higher to the hermitage and chapel of St. Bruno. If you fhould be unacquainted with St. Bruno, I muft inform you, that about the year 1100 he was a canon of Rheims, and founder of this order and monaftery; but before he built the latter he had retired to his hermitage, which to us appeared an habitation more congenial to the nature of a toad than to that of man, where he paffed many of his latter years in prayer and fevere penance. Poor maniac! Our companion faid not a word either of him, or of his cell; indeed *he* was quite a man of the world, and converfed fo liberally on what paffed in it, that had it not been for his

habit,

habit, I should never have guessed at his profession. On our return to the monastery we entered a large room, and were honoured with the company of the principal, who was to the full as polite and entertaining as our first acquaintance; indeed, all the fraternity we saw were in possession of these engaging qualities. Female society was the only enjoyment wanting to make it a most charming community; but women are to all appearance excluded. Whilst dinner was preparing we diverted ourselves with a book called the Album, in which all who visit the convent are desired to write their names, and whatever else they please. We found on inspection many of our acquaintance, and such a medley of poetry and prose, as never was collected before. Oh that some wag would transcribe these books, and publish the copies of them in England! Then would you see invocations to the Muses, addresses to the Dryads, odes to the Monks for a dinner, descriptions of the place, and sentiments, oh what sentiments! grave and philosophic, tender and elegiac; but the

best

LETTER IX.

best is, you would also see who were the authors of these inestimable compositions, as their names are written in full length at the bottom. I will answer for the sale of such a book, and must again say, I wish somebody would undertake it. When we had amused ourselves near an hour in examining this magazine of Belles Lettres, our attention was called off to table, where we found an excellent service of fish, roots, eggs, cheese and butter, dried fruits, and good wines. What noble fellows are these monks! they accused our appetites, though we ate like two aldermen, and were sorry their wine was not good, when we were deep in the second bottle: never did I make a better dinner, never met with more agreeable company; but, alas! friends must part. They pressed us very much to take another bottle at supper; but no. We, like Shylock, had an oath to return that evening to Grenoble. Therefore shaking very near the whole convent by the hand, which took up at least a quarter of an hour, we bade farewell, mounted our horses, and

arrived

arrived in good time for Tartuffe, one of the inimitable Moliere's beft comedies. In the theatre we renewed acquaintance with an officer of the regiment de Saintonge, who had been our fellow-traveller from Challons to Lyons. He introduced us to many of his corps, all of whom fpeak a little Englifh, having ferved part of the laft war in America. I cannot exprefs to you my aftonifhment at finding thefe gentlemen, and thofe of another regiment, in violent oppofition to the meafures of government, and advocates for an affembly of the States-general, who they fay fhould alone determine on the taxes and contributions of the kingdom.* What reafon have I now to admire the declaration of the gentleman with whom I converfed with at Nifmes four months ago. Pray examine my letter dated from that place. I then looked upon his opinion as nothing more than the refult of his wifhes. I now difcover that it was founded upon the intimate

---

* This alludes to part of a letter not publifhed.

know-

LETTER IX.

knowledge of his countrymen. The French *will be free:* and it is the example of Britain that has given birth to this bold spirit. The fermentation is high, the cry general, the remonstrances firm, hardy and determined. I believe I might so far risk an opinion, as to assert that Louis the XVIth must accede to every thing which they may think proper to demand; for when a government, which has been supported by a military establishment alone, hears the voices of the people and *army* insist on certain privileges, how can it refuse? The king must call an assembly of the states, and their power will be superior to his. All this is the consequence of having supported the Americans; for not only the officers who were sent to assist them caught the flame of liberty, and naturally asked themselves why they had it not; but it having involved the nation in such debts, the king was thrown upon the desperate expedient of having recourse to a National Assembly, which I am persuaded will reduce his authority to

Vol. I.   N   a shaa shadow. When a people are thus united for the purpose of examining the abuses of their government, the consequence, depend upon it, is liberty; but let us wait, and be attentive.

LETTER

LETTER X.

Turin.

HAVING passed two days most agreeably at Grenoble, we left it on the 14th, and travelling back part of the road we had come, arrived in the evening at Montmellian, a town situated immediately under the Alps, and at the entrance of one of their deep and narrow valleys watered by the river Isere. I can say nothing favourable of the place, as it consists of wretched cottages for the most part in ruins. Above the town are the mouldering remains of a citadel, which seems to have been erected for guarding this pass into Italy: The soil of the valley is rich, but neglected; were the inhabitants but half so attentive to the cultivation of the vine, as the husbandmen of Burgundy, I am satisfied they might make an excellent wine, as they have choice of soil and climate. But here is no incentive to industry and improvement, the return of the peasant's labour is swallowed up by

tithes

tithes and taxes, and should he be unfortunate enough to have a little family, which every where but in Savoy is esteemed a blessing, he is constrained, even by parental affection, to drive them out when children, that in other countries they may gain by menial service that subsistence which their own denies; hence it is that *Chimney-sweeper* and *Savoyard* are synonymous in France, as are *Swifs* and *Porter* for the same reason. On the 15th we continued our journey up this winding valley, and entered the hollow regions of the Alps. I suppose the present appearance of their inhabitants is very similar to what it was in the time of the Romans, particularly with regard to their long and shaggy hair, which gives them a wild aspect, though in manners they are easy and simple. We found the roads much better than we expected, but the bridges very dangerous for a carriage, as indeed you will perceive, when I tell you that they consist of two fir trees, which extend from bank to bank, and some smaller timber laid crosways, and loose from one beam to the other.

LETTER X.

other. It frequently happens that many of these bridges are swept away, and travellers delayed six or eight days in these miserable villages, where I suppose they seldom encounter so happy an adventure as the family of Fonrose did—you have read Marmontel's Shepherdess of the Alps. After a tedious journey we arrived at St. Jean de Maurienne; which, though the seat of a Prince Bishop, and governed by a commandant, is like all the towns of Savoy, as vile and beggarly as can be imagined. We here met a Frenchman on his return to his own country from Turin, who, as we were standing at the inn door, entered into conversation with us, and begged leave to offer some advice for our conduct on going into Italy; "though the best I can give you,
" gentlemen (added he) is not to go at all,
" for it is a country of beggars, pickpock-
" ets, and assassins. I have lived there two
" years, and believe that during that time I
" have seen at least forty people stabbed in
" the streets; but God be praised, I have left
" the miscreants, and am now going into
France,

"France, the best country in the world." Our Vetturino, little Bouchon, who is a native of Turin, happened unfortunately to be present at this *panegyric* on his countrymen; I could perceive, that as the picture went on, his countenance changed, and his eyes glistened with rage. However, he with much difficulty contained himself till the whole was finished; when advancing a few steps, he gave our monitor not the retort courteous, but the lie direct, adding, as he turned off with a sneer of contempt, "This fellow is some French thief, who has escaped from the galleys." This you may be sure produced a reply; when mutual abuse rose to that height, that Bouchon, forgetful of the original charge against the Italians, drew out a large case knife; and now bloody deeds would have ensued, had not Monsieur fled with a precipitancy that fear only could have effected. I suppose he made the best of his way home, for we often inquired after him, but he was not to be seen at the inn, though on his arrival there he had ordered a little supper a la Françoise.

As

LETTER X.

As I by no means approved of this difpofition in our poftillion, I afked him how he could attempt fo bafe an action. Oh, Sir, faid he, I only did it to frighten him a little, but yet he is a Frenchman, and what harm is in killing a Frenchman? The next day we reached Lannebourg, having feen on the road fome fpots that pleafed us much, and which might be made agreeable places of refidence, were it not for the idea of being fhut up on all fides in this Alpine prifon. We alfo paffed fome rich mines of filver, lead, and iron, which were difcovered about twenty years ago by fome Spaniards, moft of them are neglected merely from want of enterprize in the proprietors; but how can we expect enterprize in Savoy, where the fovereign is abfolute, and commerce confidered as a ftain upon nobility? Lannebourg is fituated under Mount Cenis,—a vaft Alp that terminates the valley, and divides Savoy from Piedmont. Early the next morning our guides took the carriage to pieces, which they put on the backs of fome noble mules, and flung the body be-

tween

tween two of these animals; in this manner they proceeded two hours before us. We had each a mule, but having determined to walk all the way, left them to the postillions, and began our journey on foot. Travellers are frequently carried over by men in a chair, something similar to a sedan, but much lighter (as you will suppose) for such a journey, and covered with oilskin, or in winter, when they descend to Lannebourg, the guides have at the top a kind of sledge, in which they conduct passengers with inconceivable velocity to the bottom. These machines slide on iron keels down the icy sides of the mountain, and may be stopped or guided at will. So agreeable too is the swift passage, that many English gentlemen, as they informed us, have taken the trouble to reascend Mount Cenis for the purpose of sliding down a second time. We were about an hour and a half in gaining the summit, as we followed the road, which is made in a winding direction for the purpose of easing the ascent. Having sat some time to refresh ourselves, we continued our journey
on

LETTER X.

on foot over a large plain, which extends in an oblong form between two ranges of mountain; and something more than half way over arrived at two or three houses called the Hospital, built for the reception of the poor pilgrim, who travels over the Alps for the purpose of kissing St. Peter's toe, or saying Ave Marias to our lady of Loretto. Opposite this place is a lake about two miles and a half in circumference, which produces the most exquisite trout I ever tasted; those of our boasted Usk being so inferior in flavour, that I will not even bring them in comparison. Bouchon, who had left nothing unattempted to expiate his conduct at St. Jean de Maurienne, plumed himself on directing us to this luxury, and indeed the merit of the action was so great, that had I been a minister of the Roman Catholic church, I should immediately have pronounced his absolution; for on our arrival at the Hospital they were taken out of the lake, fried, and served up in a clean dish of earthen ware, and Pocock, who was if possible more pleased than my-

self,

self, declared he had never tasted any thing so delicious. But they must be eaten on the spot, or they lose much of their flavour, as indeed we experienced the same day; for having carried some of them to the place where we dined, they seemed to be a different species of the trout. Having waited some time at the Hospital, we again went forward, and on the brow of the hill called the Great Cross, came within sight of Italy. From this place the descent into the vale of St. Nicholas is so rugged, that in some author I have seen it admirably compared to a winding and broken staircase. At the bottom we crossed a small brook, and entered Piedmont, of which we were soon made sensible by the change of language; having dined at Novalese, we got into the carriage put together again, and arrived about sun-set at St. Ambrose.

Since our departure from Montmellian, my attention has been principally occupied in attempting to ascertain the rout of Hannibal over the Alps. The historical account

of

of this celebrated expedition is, that he marched from Carthagena in Spain at the head of 100,000 men and 40 elephants: croffed the Pyrenees near their eaftern extremity: traverfed that part of Gaul which extends from thefe mountains to the banks of the Rhone near the Pont St. Efprit, over which river he tranfported his army, and routed the Gauls, who oppofed him on his landing. Here finding that the Conful Publius Cornelius Scipio was at Marfeilles, he was apprehenfive that he would intercept him on his march, and by a battle diminifh the number of his troops; he therefore led them northward up the Rhone, until he came to the fpot where the Ifere forms a junction with that river. At this place he turned off through the country of the Allobroges, or modern Dauphiny, and arrived at the foot of the Alps. Having entered their deep vallies, he had to encounter not only the difficulties of the road, but the attacks of the fierce and favage people, who inhabited thefe hitherto impenetrated regions (as few will give credit to the fabulous

lous march of Hercules.) However, these he overcame, and in nine days arrived at the fummit of the mountains. But now ftill greater obftacles impeded his defcent; over thefe, however, his genius and perfeverance triumped, fo that he brought his army, though reduced to one fifth of their original number, into Piedmont, or that part of Italy which is watered by the Po, and began the campaign with the capture of Turin. Such are the principal circumftances recorded by Polybius, the friend and companion of Scipio Africanus the younger. He had converfed with officers, who had ferved againft Hannibal, and had himfelf travelled for the purpofe of reconnoitring his march. Neverthelefs, I muft fuppofe his paffage to have been as Livy defcribes it; that is, more to the fouth;— by Briançon to Feneftrelles, where he defcended into Italy. My reafons for being of this opinion are thefe; firft, becaufe if the * remarkable anecdote is believed, that he

* Per omnia nive oppleta quum fignis primâ luce motis fegniter agmen incederet. Pigritiâque et defperatio in omnium

he raifed the dejected fpirit of his troops, by fhewing them from the Alps the fruitful plains of Italy; there is only one part of all thefe mountains from which Piedmont, &c. can be feen by an army, which is near the Col de Feneftrelles; and again, if he croffed the Durance, which feems to be the general opinion, he muft, in coming from the mouth of the Ifere, have taken this rout; for had he gone by Grenoble and Mount Cenis, he would have left the fource of that river confiderably to the right hand, as you will perceive by examining a chart of the country. With regard to the ftory of his having cut through a precipice with fire and vinegar, it does not merit attention, not being mentioned by Polybius, and indeed undeferving of a place in the Decades of Livy. There are, who fuppofe he paffed by the great St. Bernard, or *Alpes Pen-*

---

nium vultu emineret. Prægreffus figna Annibal in promontorio quodam, unde longè ac latè profpectus erat, confiftere juffis militibus, Italiam oftentat, fubjectofque Alpinis montibus circum Padanos Campos. Mæniaque eos tum tranfcendere non Italiæ modo, fed etiam urbis Romæ.
LIV. lib. 21. cap. 35.

ninæ,

ninæ,* which received their name from the Carthaginians or Pæni, but the laſt mentioned hiſtorian completely refutes this opinion. Not only then, but even now, this paſſage would be altogether impracticable for ſuch cumberſome animals as elephants; and ſtill farther, had he effected it, inſtead of taking Turin in his way to Rome, he would have left that city at a diſtance on the right. This opinion therefore is fundamentally erroneous.

Such, my dear Sir, is what I have been able to collect of the famous expedition of Hannibal over the Alps, and I hope the peruſal of it might afford you ſome little amuſement.

We ſet off early from St. Ambroſe, and having travelled a few miles, got into a road that runs in almoſt one continued ſtraight line to Turin, and ſhows one of the nobleſt avenues of trees imaginable, much beyond any thing of the kind in

* Penninus is a word of Celtic etymology. It means lofty. Pên is in the Welſh language a head.

Flanders

LETTER X.

Flanders or Brabant, the land on each fide being naturally fertile, and having, as I fhould fuppofe from its low fituation, the advantage of being occafionally overflowed, is laid down in pafture; the vines are trained from one tree to another, as they are in Spain, and according to the ancient cuftom of Italy, *ulmis adjungere vites.* On our entrance into this charming country, I gazed on every object with an eye of affection; and indeed how fhould it be otherwife, fince almoft from my infancy I have been taught to admire it, for who can read the Roman authors without acquiring the ftrongeft partiality for Italy? What friend to patriotifm, to magnanimity, to fcience, would not be enraptured at his firft view of the land that has produced a nation fo eminent for thefe? Every ftep we take is upon claffic ground, and the further we proceed, the more the objects of our regard multiply and pleafe. To the lovers of antiquity it is not the mere face of a country that makes it interefting, but the people who have poffeffed, or the authors who have defcribed it; for believe me, me, I would sooner dwell a month in a cottage on the naked plain where Troy once stood, than inhabit the most picturesque part of Swisserland, or view the falls of the Niagara. But let me dismiss these reflections, which are perhaps a little too romantic, and tell you that we are arrived at Turin, pleased with all we have seen, but infinitely more with the anticipation of all we shall see. What happiness there is in anticipation!

Turin, Sept. 24, 1787.

THIS noble city, which stands on the northern bank of the river Po, is perhaps, if taken all in all, the best built, best fortified, and the most uniform in Europe. Its form is oval, the streets are wide, and extend in strait lines from one end of it to the other. Through the middle of which the clear stream of the Doria is made to flow in little channels that keep them clean, and supply the inhabitants with good water. As I had never read any description of of Turin, I was agreeably furprized on our arrival. The fronts of the houfes in every ftreet are fimilar to each other, being built of hewn ftone, three ftories high. The late king, who was really what kings fhould be, the Father of his country, began thefe improvements, and might be called the fecond Founder; for fo great is the alteration, that it would be impoffible for any perfon, who had feen it before the new plan was executed, to know it in the prefent time. But although the appearance of the whole is particularly grand and ftriking, its uniformity foon tires the eye, which requires variety; and thus it is with numberlefs objects, whofe beauties vanifh with their novelty. Before I fay any thing more of Turin, you will fuffer me to obferve, that it is by no means my intention to give you a regular and minute defcription of the public buildings; for if I judge of your tafte by my own, I am fure it would be more tirefome than pleafing. Whatever I think interefting, you may be affured I fhall not fail to mention; but on the dimenfions of a column, or the mouldings of an architrave, I muſt beg leave to be ſilent. Whilſt the venerable appearance of the royal palace makes it look like the great anceſtor of the city, its heavy and ill-proportioned ſtructure ſtands as a memento of the rude and barbarous ages of Italy. It occupies one ſide of a ſquare called the Piazza Caſtello, and behind it are gardens, which, being ſliced into a variety of ſquares, parallelograms, and triangles, are by no means ſuited to the Engliſh taſte. But the inſide of the palace makes ample amends. It has a noble ſuite of rooms richly furniſhed, and hung with a fine collection of pictures of the Italian and Flemiſh ſchools; of the latter, one by Gerard Douw, the ſubject of which is a dropſical woman attended by her phyſician, her daughter, and maidſervant, is, I think, one of the moſt highly finiſhed pictures I ever ſaw, perhaps too much ſo. It is conſidered as the moſt valuable of the collection, placed in the beſt light, and carefully ſhut up in a ſmall cabinet, or caſe of (I believe) ebony.

We

LETTER X.

We here had a very good opportunity of studying the manner and colouring of the different painters, whose productions were shewn to us; but this is a science that requires much time, and more discernment. However, we shall have leisure for improvement before we leave Italy. The same day we visited the citadel, which is called by military men the first thing of the kind existing; but as I am no judge of counterscarps, glacis, covered ways, curtains or bastions, you may be assured that I shall not attempt a description of this fortification, but only say that it has a very noble and formidable appearance. The foundations were laid in 1564, by Emanuel Philibert, duke of Savoy; but as fortification was little known at that early period, the citadel must have assumed quite a new form to be what it is at present. The great theatre, or, as it is here called, Il Teatro reggio, is a much finer house than we have in London, being built on a plan very different and superior to that of our opera. It is lofty enough to admit six rows of boxes, which continue round the body of the houfe, or theatre, there being no galleries to obftruct and deaden the mufic. The depth of the ftage alone, is, (as I am informed) 126 feet by 96—an immenfe allotment of fpace for theatrical exhibition. As this theatre is only ufed during the carnival, we faw it in the day-time, confequently to great difadvantage. The only theatre now open is that of Carignano, where we found an admirable comic opera—an entertainment to which, by the way, I think I fhall be very partial, when better acquainted with Italian. The fhow of company did not anfwer our expectations, but I find the boxes are feldom full, except on the firft and fecond nights of performance, when the theatre is illuminated, and with the audience makes a very brilliant appearance. If I except fome favourite airs, the opera is entirely difregarded by the parties in the boxes, who are engaged either at cards, or in converfation. In fhort, it is only a public manner to receive vifits, except on the firft or fecond reprefentation, when the

whole

LETTER X.

whole house is silent. This inattention is very natural, when we consider that the same opera is repeated successively for a month or six weeks Among the private palaces that we saw (for you must know that every gentleman's house in Italy is called a palace) the most superb is that of the Marquis del Bergo; and never did I behold any thing so extravagantly magnificent. The furniture is of the richest materials that can possibly be procured, and the ceiling ornamented with garlands, festoons, and fancy work of bands and twist of solid gold enamelled. I assure you the apartments of the royal palace are mean in comparison of them. But what pleased us more was a cabinet of antique gems, the property of the Commandanté del Gialousé. This gentleman, of whose politeness it is impossible to say too much, seemed happy in the opportunity of shewing us their exquisite beauties; and I can truly affirm, that I am indebted to him for making me acquainted with a pleasure, to which I was before a stranger. We expected magnificent churches here, but have been very much difappointed. However, we vifited that of Superga, fituate on a high hill, about four miles from Turin. Having gained the top with fome difficulty, as the afcent is fteep and rugged, we came rather fuddenly on the church, which prefented a handfome portico, and above it a dome and cupola flanked on each fide by fteeples. Within it is quite circular, and in all refpects correfpondent to the exterior beauty. We much admired its marble columns; they are of a colour between blue and grey, and exquifitely polifhed, but I think rather too low. Under the church is the royal vault; the magnificence of which, though ftriking, does not in any degree take from the folemnity; but the whole poffeffes an equal proportion of each, and is moft awfully grand. In the center is the coffin of the late king, where it is to remain till replaced by that of his prefent majefty, at whofe funeral it will be configned to the tomb which now awaits it. Thefe tombs are formed in the walls of the vault for the

de-

deceased of the royal family. But we were less pleased with Superga, than with the rich, the extensive, and varied prospect that it commands; we looked back with exulting pleasure on the Alps, those vast barriers that shut in Italy from the more northern countries of Europe, and divide not only the land, but climates. Below us was Turin, and eastward we beheld the plains of Lombardy, as far as Milan; through which the fertilizing Po winds its long course, and rushes violently into the Adriatic. Thus Virgil:

> Et gemina auratus taurino cornua vultu
> Eridanus: quo non alius per pinguia culta,
> In mare purpureum violentior effluit amnis.*

During the siege of Turin in 1706, Victor Amadæus ascended this hill to reconnoitre the position of the enemy, and then made a vow to erect a church on it, if they did not succeed in their enterprize against the city; in consequence therefore of the vic-

---

* Bull-fac'd Eridanus with gilded horns,
Than which no stream runs through the fruitful lea
With swifter current to the purple sea.

tory gained by prince Eugene, and the total overthrow of the French army, he built Superga nine years after. The expence of it must have been considerably increased by the labour in conveying the materials to the site, which even now, though much better than at that time, is most difficult of access. Another excursion we made in the vicinity of Turin, was to the royal palace of La Venerie, the most noble of the king's country residences; but I cannot say that I much admire it. The situation is low and flat: the buildings (if I except the chapel) heavy and irregular: the apartments gloomy: the furniture crowded and ill arranged: and, finally, the gardens (so much admired in this country) are laid out in the French manner, consequently tasteless and unnatural. There are three rooms in the palace that particularly engaged our attention, as they were hung, or I would rather say, wainscoted with pictures of the crowned heads of England, the German empire, and Savoy—all in my opinion very ill done. You know how nearly allied the Sardinian

blood

blood royal is to the Stuart family. About two miles from La Venerie is a large elm, held in univerſal veneration, and I leave you to judge how much more deſervedly ſo, than the oak that afforded an aſylum to our weak and worthleſs monarch Charles the IId, when I inform you that under this elm, Victor Amadæus, duke of Savoy, prince Eugene, and two other generals (I believe the prince of Anhalt, and the marquis de Prie) held a council of war, and came to the reſolution of attacking the French army then before Turin. This happened on the 5th of September, 1706. On the 7th they forced the enemy's lines, and gained a moſt deciſive victory, which not only raiſed the ſiege of the capital, but reinſtated the duke in all his dominions, and ruined the French intereſt in Italy.

Two days after our arrival at Turin, we delivered our letters from L—d Carmarthen to Mr. Jackſon, who is Chargé d'Affaires in the abſence of Mr. Trevor, the Britiſh miniſter; in conſequence of which, after
certain

certain indispensible preliminaries, such as a visit to the prime minister, and leaving our cards with all the corps diplomatique, we were presented by M. de Choiseul, the French ambassador (as the etiquette of the court will not admit of this ceremony being performed by any one who is not vested with the full powers of a foreign minister) to the king and royal family at Montcallier, a palace on the banks of the Po, about four miles from Turin. We were received by each in separate apartments; the first was the duke of Chablais, the king's brother; from him we went to the two youngest princes, the dukes of Aost and Montferrat; then to the princess of Piedmont; to her consort the prince; and, finally, to his majesty. The time we remained with each was but short, for after a few general questions they bowed, and we retired. The king, who is in the sixty-second year of his age, is much more personable than either of his sons; he conversed in French, observing, among other things, that the English, like birds of passage, appeared in Italy

all

LETTER X. 203

all at a certain season. The prince of Piedmont is an invalid, if I may judge by his appearance. He kept us longer than either of them, and spoke in high terms of England, mentioning the obligations of his family to it. His Consort is a Bourbon, sister to Louis the XVIth. It happened to be her birth day, and in consequence the court was full and brilliant. All military officers, as in England, appear at it in their uniforms; at Versailles you know it is quite the reverse. After the form of presenting ended, there was a levee, at which the king and princes conversed, I think, with every individual in the circle; an act of no small difficulty, as the majority were foreigners. Having thus gone through all the ceremonies of this court, which you know has been long esteemed one of the politest in the world, we returned to Turin, and dined with the French ambassador, a gentleman every way qualified for his high situation, and finished the evening with a converzatione at the Spanish ambassador's, to whom we were introduced by Mr. Jackson. Of

these

these converzationi I will write you some future description when I know more of them. We yesterday went a few miles from Turin to see the king review a regiment of dragoons lately come from Savoy. He was attended by his three sons and brother, the duke of Chablais, besides many of the foreign ministers and noblesse of his court. About ten o'clock they all appeared in the field, on which were three tents pitched for their reception. The king seemed much pleased with the military appearance of the cavalry, which, as far as I can judge, well deserved his approbation. During the evolutions one of the troopers was thrown off his horse, and I could not but with pleasure mark the sovereign's compassion, who, on seeing the accident, immediately dispatched an aid de camp to his assistance; and finding that the poor fellow was much bruised, ordered him to be carried in a litter to the hospital, and all care to be taken of him.

Humanity

Humanity is a virtue of so much lustre, that we are enamoured of it in whatever aspect it assumes; but in monarchs it appears to double advantage, they being less exposed to calamity, are consequently less able to judge of the misery of others by their own misfortunes.

LETTER

LETTER XI.

Turin, Sept. 28, 1787.

ON looking into my journal, I find the subjects of my two last letters were our passage over the Alps, and a description of Turin and its environs. By the same journal I perceive also, that I have a good deal to crowd into this; I must therefore be as concise as possible, and to begin, shall say something more than what I have said of the dominions of his present majesty Victor Amadæus the IIId. They consist of Sardinia, Piedmont, Savoy, Montferrat, and part of the Milanese. Never was a sovereign in possession of two countries more opposite to each other than Savoy and Piedmont; the former is a wild tract of mountain and hollow vallies, which require every aid that art and labour can bestow to make the produce adequate to the consumption, though no people can be more frugal than its inhabitants, frugal indeed in consequence of their poverty. The sides of these mountains

tains are in many places so very steep, as to be inacceffible to beasts of draught or burden, and the plow is there an useless instrument of agriculture; the peasants break up the hungry soil with the pickaxe and spade, and to improve it, carry up mould and dung in baskets. For the purpose of preserving it from drought in the spring and summer, they cut small reservoirs above it, the water of which may be let out at will, and to prevent the earth from giving way, break the declivity of the mountains by building walls on the side for its support, which frequently assume the appearance of ancient fortification, and are a very pleasing deception to travellers. The Savoyards carry their better sort of cheese into Piedmont, as the flavour is much esteemed there; but they gain more by their skins of bears, chamois, and bouquetins (a species of the wild goat) or by the sale of growse and pheasants, which they carry in great numbers to Turin.

Piedmont

Piedmont is part of the plains of Lombardy, which extending from the north weſt boundaries of Italy to the Lagune of Venice, conſtitute one of the moſt fertile and valuable parts of Europe. A quotation in my laſt letter from Virgil, will ſhew you how highly it was thought of in the Auguſtine age. It abounds in fruits and grain of almoſt every kind in our quarter of the world, and its paſtures are as rich as thoſe of Holland. Novara is celebrated for its fine rice, millefiori for his majeſty's tobacco plantations, whilſt the vineyards, in every part of Piedmont, produce a ſweet red wine of an excellent quality. But what the owners of land moſt encourage is the feeding of cattle, and culture of the mulberry tree for ſilk worms; of the former they ſend annually to foreign markets from ninety to a hundred thouſand head, beſides great number of hogs and mules. The laſt of theſe animals are very fine in this country, as I have before obſerved; but the inhabitants have other beaſts, or rather *monſters*, which they find very ſerviceable, though vicious and obſtinate.

LETTER XI.

rate. These are produced by a cow and an ass, or mare and bull, and called Jumarres or Gimerri; I cannot say that I have ever seen any of them, but I am told they are very common. The silk worm thrives so well, that many peasants make above * 100 lbs. of silk annually; and it is not only abundant, but universally known to be stronger and finer than any in Italy. The land-owners divide the profit with their tenants. The duchy of Savoy and principality of Piedmont are, I find, more populous than I thought they were; by the last returns, the number is found to amount to 2,695,727 souls, of which Turin contains about 77,000.

I might almost say, that the authority of his Sardinian majesty is as absolute as his will, being neither controlled by parliaments, nor conditions of government. The succession to the throne is determined by the salique law, so that females are excluded. He is marquis of Italy, and a prince of the

* Each pound is valued in Piedmont at 18 shillings, the little village of La Tour, in the valley of Lucerne, makes above 50,000 lb annually, and the exports every year to the single city of Lyons amount to more than 160,000 l.

empire,

empire, at the diet of which he has a feat. During a vacancy in the imperial throne, he is grand vicar for the empire in Italy, and chief of the two orders of the Annunciada and St. Lazarus. His great council is compofed of eight minifters of ftate, among whom are the viceroy of Sardinia, his ambaffador at Rome, and two fecretaries of ftate. The principal officers of his court are a great almoner, a high chamberlain, three gentlemen of the bed-chamber in the firft order, a grand mafter of the ceremonies, another of the houfhold, a principal maggiorduomo, an honorary keeper of the wardrobe, and mafter of the ftag hounds, all whofe falaries would be thought little in comparifon of what, as Mr. Burke facetioufly called them, the k—g's turnfpits received in England.

The public adminiftration of juftice is entrufted to certain provôfts and intendants nominated by his majefty, who judge in the firft inftance. Appeals from their determinations are carried before the fenates,

of

LETTER XI.

of which there are three, at Turin, Chamberry, and Nice; the firſt is compoſed of three preſidents, and twenty-one ſenators; the ſecond of two preſidents, and ten counſellors; and the third of one preſident, and ſix counſellors. The law, though changed in many inſtances by the king's ordinances, is founded on the Roman code, or pandects of Juſtinian. With regard to the finances, I learn that they are adminiſtered by the grand chamber of accounts, eſtabliſhed ſince 1563 at Chamberry by Emanuel Philibert, duke of Savoy, which is compoſed of two preſidents, ſix counſellors, the ſame number of auditors, two ſecretaries, and an attorney general. As a proof how much the pope's influence is diminiſhed, I muſt obſerve, that no bull, brief, or papal letter, can be publiſhed in the dominions of his Sardinian majeſty without his permiſſion; his ambaſſador at the court of Rome is generally a cardinal, and it is he (the king) who preſents to all vacant benefices within his territories, deducting one third of their revenues for his penſions. All theſe benefices are subject to taxes, except the ancient patrimony of the church, or such property as the clergy possessed before the year 1600; but even this in time of war contributes the twentieth part of its income, which certainly is much too little. All causes, in which ecclesiastics are concerned, are determined by secular judges, and finally to destroy that power by which they so frequently made the interest of religion a pretext for the gratification of their vengeance. The king put himself at the head of the inquisition, so that no person can be seized, but by his order. In conformity to the general system of Europe, and to defend his territories from the incroachments of his neighbours, his Sardinian majesty keeps up an army of 40,000 men, viz. four regiments of body guards, twenty-two of infantry, ten of cavalry, and twelve of militia or provincials. Among these troops are also some Swiss regiments. The marine is so inconsiderable, as to be unworthy of attention, being composed only of two frigates, and as many gallies, out of commission.

miffion. The royal revenues amount to 1,041,666 l. They are principally made up by a land-tax, poll-tax, tax on cattle, gabelle or duty on falt and tobacco, of which I believe each family is obliged, as in France, to take annually a certain quantity; another on ftamped paper, on inns, butchers meat, leather, candles, gunpowder, and a tax on Jews.

I readily fubfcribe to the opinion contained in your laft letter, that a traveller fhould not be unacquainted with the revolutions and memorable events of the countries he vifits; and to prove the fincerity of this affertion, I fhall conclude this with an abridgement of the hiftory of Savoy and Piedmont, more efpecially as from reading it I am led to believe, that there is no where to be found a ftronger inftance of what a wife and prudent fucceffion of princes can do in raifing a fmall territory into a powerful ftate, than what the former prefents in its firft counts and dukes. Berthhold, of the illuftrious Houfe of Saxony,

was in the year 1000 made count of Savoy and Maurienne, by Rodolph the IIId, king of Burgundy, in recompence for the military fervice he had rendered him; and from this nobleman is defcended the prefent fovereign of Sardinia, who may reflect with fatisfaction, that the dominions he has inherited from his anceftors are not the acquifitions of blood and conqueft, which however warranted by cuftom, muft to the philofophic eye appear no better than public robbery fupported by power. Through purchafe, marriage, and fucceffion, the territories of the counts of Savoy became confiderable. Otho, the grandfon of Berthhold, united Piedmont to his paternal inheritance; but thefe countries were again divided by Thomas the Ift between his two eldeft fons. Amadæus the IVth, who fucceeded to Savoy, having efpoufed the intereft of the Gibbelins againft the Guelfs, was recompenfed by the emperor Frederic the IId, who, in 1246, erected Chablais and Aöfte into a duchy, by which the ducal dignity entered into the Houfe of Savoy. For the four firft centuries
it

it may be said, that there were few princes of the race of Berthhold that did not add to their dominions; but far greater than any of his predecessors was Amadæus the VIth, or the Green Count, so called from his appearing with all his retinue at a tournament in Chamberry cloathed in that colour. These appellations, which seem to have been the prevailing fashion of those rude times, arose from the most trivial circumstances, and were lavished on many, whose virtues entitled them to more honourable distinctions; such as Edward the Black Prince, and Amadæus the VIth, who was certainly one of the most illustrious of his family; for during a reign of forty years he supported the character of a wise prince, and an able commander, while fortune, as the reward of his merit, proved favourable to whatever he attempted.

Having established his reputation so much at home, as to make his alliance and mediation sought by the emperor and all the Italian states, he carried his arms into the east,

east, delivered John Paleologus the Ist from the captivity of the Bulgarian king, and replaced him on the imperial throne of Constantinople. He succoured the island of Rhodes, routed the Turk in a great battle, and to make memorable the victory, in 1362 established the order of Annunciada in honour of it. He was also the founder of many convents.—You will probably laugh at this remark, but surely must allow, that although to this enlightened age such an act will appear the least beneficial of his life, it displayed a piety, which, however ill-directed, was the result of a grateful and laudable intention. He died of the plague at Capua in 1383, whither he had carried his veteran army to assist Lewis of Anjou in the conquest of Naples. The character of Amadæus the VIIIth seems to be held in as much esteem as that of the last mentioned duke. In his reign Piedmont, for want of issue from its own princes, was reannexed to the duchy of Savoy. After a series of good and useful actions, he resigned his dominions to his son Lewis in 1434,

1434, exchanging his diadem for the monastic habit and profeſſion; but he again appeared to the world in a character as ſingular as unexpected. In 1439 the council of Baſil, depoſing Eugenius the IVth, choſe Amadæus as the moſt proper perſon to fill the vacant chair of St. Peter, which nothing could perſuade him to accept, but a belief that his acquieſcence in the choice of the council would put an end to the ſchiſm of the church; in this however he was miſtaken, for during nine years after his election the papacy was continually diſputed; when at length, worn out with oppoſition, and deſirous of repoſe, he again retired to the convent, which he had firſt choſen for his aſylum, where he ſurvived his abdication of the papacy only two years. Savoy, and the other ducal dominions, which had hitherto been governed by princes who exerted themſelves for the welfare of their ſubjects, fell into anarchy and weakneſs from the ſucceſſion of Philibert, the infant ſon of Amadæus the IXth, and the diſtraction occaſioned by the various pretenſions

to

to the regency, there being no lefs than six competitors, moft of whom confulted only their own intereft in the claim, but happily the death of the young prince put an end to the difturbances; for he being fucceeded by his younger brother Charles the Ift, who was confequently a minor, his uncle Lewis the XIth, king of France, affumed the regency as it were by force, and dying in the following year, Charles, though but fifteen, took upon himfelf the management of his own affairs, and was found every way deferving of it. At nineteen the kingdom of Cyprus was given to him by Charlotte, daughter of John the IId, king of that ifland, as next heir in right of his grandmother Anne, John's fifter. Charlotte being depofed by her natural brother James, and unable to recover poffeffion, though powerfully fupported, retired to Rome, where fhe made this donation to Charles; but the ifland being feized by the Venetians, as heirs to Catherine Cornâro, relict of the ufurper, Charles and his defcendants faw the futility of putting in a claim,

claim, which, from their want of naval force, could not possibly be supported; so that this gift has been productive to the House of Savoy of nothing more than useless pretensions to the thrones of Cyprus and Jerusalem, with a royal title and additional quarter to their arms; happily so, for could this prince and his successors have supported their rights, they would have sacrificed many thousands of their subjects in gratifying their ambition; nor can I but condemn the continuance of such claims, which for the most part are but a satire on the injustice of former times, and the vanity of the present. During the invasions of Italy by the French kings Charles the VIIIth, Lewis the XIIth, and Francis the Ist, the dukes of Savoy generally espoused the stronger party, and by so doing prevented their country from being exposed to the ravages of war; but, as I have observed in a former letter, their attempts on the little republic of Geneva were always fruitless, and frequently followed by unsuccesful war, particularly in the reign of Charles the IIId, who, on

that

that account, drew upon himself more enemies than he could resist, but principally Francis the Ist, and the canton of Berne; the former had won the greater part of Piedmont, and the latter the Pays de Vaud. In this unfortunate situation Montfort, governor of Nice, displayed an example of valour and fidelity, that was calculated to raise the drooping spirits of his countrymen under the calamities which oppressed them. The Duc d'Enguien, commander of the French forces, with his ally Horuc Barbaroſſa, the Turkish admiral, disembarked their armies at Villa França, a small distance from Nice, and commanded the surrender of the city. The governor, having heard the herald, replied: " Qu'on s'etoit mal " addresſè a lui pour rendre la place, parce " qu'en son nom il s'appelloit Montfort, " qu'en ses armes il portoit despals, et que sa " dévise etoit : Il me faut tenir ; et qu'il ne " falloit attendre q'une vigoreuse défense."*

* " That he had ill addressed himself to him, for his " name was Montfort, in his arms he bore balls, and that " his motto was : I must hold out ; and that he might " therefore expect an obstinate defence."

Barba-

LETTER XI.

Barbaroffa, whose haughty temper was little calculated to admire virtue in an enemy and a Christian, was indignant at this gallant answer, and invested the city on the 10th day of August, 1543. He battered it till the 22d, when a general assault was given. In this, however, he was repulsed with loss; but the heroic Montfort, finding that he could not maintain the place against such superior force, abandoned the city for the castle, which he had previously stored with ammunition and provisions. There he was invincible; for after many desperate attempts, the besiegers considerably reduced by the successful sallies of the garrison, and fearful of its being reinforced, gave up the attempt, after the loss of much time, and many thousands of their best troops. Emanuel Philibert, who succeeded Charles the IIId. in 1553, warmly espoused the side his father had taken, and engaged personally in the war against France; for being nursed as it were in arms, he possessed a thorough knowledge of tactics in those times, and all the valour of his ancestors.

ceſtors. In the famous battles of St. Quintin and Gravelines between Philip and Henry, the ſucceſſors of Charles the Vth and Francis the Iſt, Emanuel Philibert very much contributed by his perſonal atchievement to the victory; it was after the former of theſe, that Philip, whoſe hands the duke would have kiſſed in compliment of his ſucceſs, haſtily prevented him, exclaiming with more generoſity than I ever thought that monarch poſſeſſed: " It is rather my " duty to kiſs your hands, who have gained " for me ſo glorious a victory at the ex- " pence of ſo little blood." Though France was very unwilling to reſtore all the places that had been taken by Francis the Iſt from the late duke, yet it finally took place, and a treaty to that purpoſe was ſigned at Turin on the 14th of December, 1574. Philibert is remarkable alſo for his pretenſions to the crown of Portugal, vacant by the death of Henry the Cardinal in 1380; but in theſe he had no greater ſucceſs than his predeceſſor Charles the Iſt had in thoſe to Cyprus. He was ſucceeded by Charles Emanuel, who

ſeems

LETTER XI.

seems to have inherited the enterprising spirit of his forefathers without their virtues. Covetous of dominion, and regardless of the means by which he acquired it, he took advantage of the civil commotions in France, and seized Provence; but for this act of injustice he was severely chastised by Henry the IVth, who reduced him to the situation of sueing in person for part of his conquered territories. Finding that he was not likely to succeed against a monarch of Henry's heroic temper (who, as I have seen it observed, was supported by his rights, his virtue, his sword, and Sully) he attempted to surprise the city of Geneva by night, in doing which he only increased the infamy of his character; but you have already had a description of this attempt in a letter from that city. After a long life of political intrigue and perfidy, he died of an apoplexy on the 26th of July, 1630. From this time to the reign of Lewis the XIVth, Savoy occasionally took part with France or Spain, as most conducive to its interest. In 1653, the advantage was so much on the side of France,

that

that Charles Emanuel the IId thought of allying himself to that court, and in confequence went accompanied by his duchefs, his mother, and the princefs Margaret his fifter, to meet Lewis the XIVth at Lyons, between whom and his fifter he was defirous of effecting a marriage, which would probably have fucceeded to his wifhes, had not Spain, fearful of the confequences, propofed at the fame time the Infanta Maria Therefa, and peace between the two kingdoms, as the ratification of fuch alliance. This offer, through the intrigue of cardinal Mazarin was preferred, which broke off all connection between France and Savoy, and induced the latter to unite itfelf to the enemies of the former. The firft opportunity that offered was in 1690, when Victor Amadæus the IId. acceded to the grand league that was formed by almoft all the powers of Europe to check the inordinate ambition of Lewis the XIVth; but this junction, which had fo promifing an appearance, was near producing the moft fatal event. Catinat, the French general, ftript the duke of

almoft

LETTER XI.

almost all his dominions in two campaigns, and would have completed his ruin, had not Lewis, who deemed the expences of the war much greater than the advantages that would finally refult from it, ordered Catinat to act only on the defenfive, and in the mean time, for the purpofe of detaching Victor from the alliance, propofed terms of accommodation more fuited to the condition of a conqueror, than to that of the vanquifhed. Thefe were immediately accepted, and a treaty of peace figned at Turin on the 29th of Auguft, 1696. It continued, however, but a fhort time; for the famous war of fuccellion breaking out at the beginning of this century, Savoy became a party concerned. The duke againft his intereft, and indeed againft his inclination, was firft obliged to fight for the execution of the king of Spain's will, and unite his arms to thofe of Lewis the XIVth. Four years before this he had found himfelf almoft difpoffeffed of his dominions by the rapid fuccefs of the French arms; and fhould he now have efpoufed an oppofite

VOL. I.   Q   intereft,

interest, he was more likely to be so than before, as Lewis had filled the Milanese with his troops. However, his interest as well as inclination soon induced him to join the imperial army under count Stahremberg, who commanded in Italy during the absence of prince Eugene, and then he declared war against Lewis, when the French generals acted with such vigour, that he soon found himself dispossessed of all his territories, except the two cities of Turin and Coni, the former of which they had invested, and were on the point of taking, though gallantly defended. In this hopeless situation Victor began to despair, when unexpectedly the allies, who were every where victorious, sent a powerful army to his relief under prince Eugene. This great man triumphed over all the obstacles that were thrown in his way by the duc de Vendome, and arrived near Turin in August, 1706, where he forced the enemies lines, gained a complete victory, and in consequence saved Victor Amadæus from what a few days before seemed inevitable ruin. At the

peace

LETTER XI.

peace of Utretcht in 1713, his fidelity and perseverance were amply rewarded by England, whose ministers insisted, that the House of Savoy should be acknowledged as next in succession to the crown of Spain, in default of issue from Philip, and by way of indemnification for the expence which the duke had incurred during the war, the island of Sicily should be ceded to him with the title of King. In 1720 he was compelled to exchange Sicily for Sardinia with the emperor, and from this island we find he has assumed the present title. Victor, at length tired with a long reign of fifty-years, and desirous of repose, resigned his throne to his son Charles Emanuel the IIId. in 1730, and retired to Chamberry, where he published his marriage with the countess of St. Sebastion, daughter of the marquis de St. Thomas, one of his former prime ministers, and relict of his first equerry the count of that name. It is supposed that his abdication was an act of policy, to avoid the resentment of the Emperor which was excited by his having privately con-

certed

certed measures with Spain for the introduction of Spanish garrisons into Parma and Tuscany; be that as it may, certain it is, that he attempted to reassume the regal dignity the year after his resignation of it, but was prevented by his son. He died at Montcallier the 31st of October, 1732. In consequence of a treaty of alliance at Worms, on the 13th of September, 1743, Savoy was again engaged in a war against France and Spain, to support the inheritance of the late Empress, Queen Maria Theresa; Charles Emanuel, the late King, proved himself every way worthy of his illustrious progenitors. He commanded his own armies in person, and displayed the talents of an able general, the valour of an hero, and what is much more rare, a mind superior to corruption; for his enemies, eager to detach him from the Imperial alliance, offered him the Milanese as the reward of his revolt. This he rejected with all the indignation of insulted virtue, for the only answer he ordered his minister to make to the proposal, was to inform the count de Maillebois, sent to conclude this bufinefs, that he might return to his army, as the campaign had already begun two days. This noble action found its recompence in his fubfequent triumph over the French and Spanifh armies, and at the peace of Aix la Chapelle in 1748, by which he received all that had been ceded to him by the emprefs queen in the treaty of Worms, except the marquifate of Final, which, as it before belonged to, was beftowed on the republic of Genoa.

Such is an epitome uf the moft interefting events recorded in the hiftory of thefe countries. You receive it in confequence of my early return laft night from the Spanifh ambaffador's converzationé, and my rifing this morning full two hours fooner than ufual.

LETTER XII.

Genoa, Oct. 4, 1787.

THOUGH highly entertained at Turin, both of us were completely tired before we left it, which I can attribute only to the uniform appearance of the place, and its unvaried repetition of amusements. We travelled through a dead flat, than which nothing can be more uninteresting, as the objects of sight are confined to the hedges on each side, and to the horses before us; the latter of which generally present a spectacle of the most unpleasing nature, especially if we heighten it by reflection; for what existence is more wretched than that of a post-horse, kept up from fainting, under excess of labour, by the continual torture of an unthinking and merciless postillion? Unhappy animals! they chearfully administer to our pleasures and necessities, and are known even to have an affection for their masters; but too often (I am sorry for human nature to say so) too often are they

they recompenfed by the moft capricious feverity; for even neglect of what is fo entirely dependent upon us, is cruelty in the extreme, and thefe I know from experience are your fentiments. Having reached the Tanaro, we continued our journey on the banks of that river to Aleffandria, a town that has nothing in it deferving of attention, but the citadel, which is much admired by military men. We departed early the next morning very diffatisfied with our landlord, who had made a moft exorbitant demand upon us, that is, about fix times more than what he would have charged a noble Piedmontefe, and all the cargo of his coach, or family and fervants: but indeed we fhould only blame ourfelves for this impofition, as we neglected to make a previous bargain for fupper and beds—a precaution univerfally taken in France and Italy. About mid-day we arrived at Novi, the frontier town of the republic of Genoa; and on leaving it, found the country both hilly and naked. A few miles further we began the afcent of the Appennines, and gained the summit at a point called the Bochetta, whence we had a view of the same kind, but superior * to that from the Vise near Marseilles: below us lay that part of Italy which was the ancient Liguria washed by the Tuscan sea; on the shore of which we viewed the distant city of Genoa, and its environs. Our road from the village of Campo Marone, at the bottom of these hills, was along the broad channel of the Polcevèra, which, though generally dry, is sometimes overflowed by a deluge that rushes from the Appennines, laying waste or sweeping away whatever lies within its reach. The entrance into Genoa by the suburb of San Pietro d'Arena is most magnificent. The city is built in form of a crescent round its beautiful port, and as we came suddenly to one horn or extremity, we beheld the most striking scene of the kind that can be imagined. There being a regular ascent from the water, we caught this noble amphitheatre of buildings at one glance. Within the mole are the merchant

---

* This alludes to a former Letter not published.

ships,

LETTER XII.

ships, and further out in the port a small fleet of Dutch and Neapolitan men of war, which added very much to the grandeur and majesty of the whole. We were so pleased, that we both at the same instant expressed our surprize and admiration on our unexpected arrival at this point of view.

Genoa may be called a city of marble palaces, but unfortunately it stands on such a confined slip of land between the sea and the mountain behind it, that these noble edifices press upon one another. Add to this, the streets are so narrow, as to prevent the passenger from seeing their style of architecture to advantage. The two principal are La Strada Nuova and La Strada Balbi; the first consists of fourteen superb palaces, that contain a profusion of marbles, and a fine collection of paintings, among which are many most admirable pieces of Titian, the Caracci, and Guido Rène; but I was not quite satisfied, as I did not see a single picture of Raphael, with whom I long to be better acquainted. In the Sara Palace

is

is an apartment even superior to any of those we saw in the Marquis del Borgo's at Turin; the carving, gilding, and painted cieling; its inlaid floor, glasses, marbles, damask hangings; and, to crown all, the view over part of Genoa, the port, and the Mediterranean, make it an object of general admiration; not but I think had the materials been collected in London they would have been arranged with more taste. The Doge's palace, or, as the Genoese call it, La Signoria, is an extensive building. The ascent to it is by a large stone stair-case, at the bottom of which are two marble statues of the famous Andrew Doria and his nephew; the former hath this inscription:

> Andreæ Doriæ quòd rempublicam diutius oppressam, pristinam in libertatem vindicaverit, Patri proinde Patriæ appellato, Senatus Genuensis, immortalis memor beneficii, viventi posuit. *

* In honour of Andrew Doria, because he hath restored to its ancient liberty the republic long oppressed, whence he is called the Father of his Country. The Senate of Genoa, mindful of this immortal benefit, hath erected this statue to him when alive.

To the other is:

Jo. Doriæ, patriæ libertatis confervatori.*

We waited fome time the adjournment of the leffer council, when we faw the Doge cloathed in his crimfon robes, and afterwards the two State Chambers, in which the public bufinefs is tranfacted. Thefe apartments are ornamented with feven ftatues of illuftrious Genoefe, and paintings that reprefent fome of the moft memorable events contained in the hiftory of the republic; but I cannot fay that I admired either the one or the other. The churches are magnificent, and poffefs fome capital paintings: that of the Annunciada, in my opinion, ftands firft, both for its architecture and ornament. After it the *Santa Maria Carignano*, built by the family, whofe name it bears, on the moft elevated part of this noble city. From the top we had a bird's eye view of Genoa, &c. and on defcending examined the church, where a ftatue of St. Sebaftian, by Puget, principally engaged

* To John Doria, the protector of his country's liberty.

our attention. This ftatue, the production of a French artift, is one of the beft in Genoa, which very much excites my aftonifhment, as no nation has had more opportunities of enriching itfelf with Grecian fculpture than the Genoefe; but I fufpect, that whatever they acquired, their avarice turned into money, as the whole city cannot boaft of one ancient ftatue that has any merit. In going to this church we paffed over the celebrated bridge built by the fame family, and diftinguifhed by the fame name; it croffes a narrow valley 140 feet deep, which runs through the city to the fea. On looking over the parapets we faw houfes below us at leaft five ftories high. The bridge Carignano is certainly one of the moft curious objects of regard in Genoa, as well for its fingularity of fituation, as for the merit of its architecture; but our time was better employed at a building, that reflects greater honour on the Genoefe, than the endowment of all their monafteries and churches. This is the Albergo, erected for the truly charitable purpofe of bringing

up

LETTER XII.

up foundlings, orphans, natural children, and the offspring of such parents as are unable to bring up their families, to be honest and useful members of society. It is also used as a place of confinement and labour for women of ill fame, and for wives whose husbands have complained to the inquisition of their incontinence; it affords a comfortable asylum to the old and indigent, who are no longer able to support themselves by labour; and food and lodging to the pilgrim. All the inhabitants (amounting to more than a thousand) are kept in separate divisions; the men upon one side, and the women on the other. It is supported by legacies, which amount to a very considerable sum. At the head of this admirable institution are two noble Genoese—a lady and gentleman, for their respective sexes. I was so pleased with the Albergo, which is the best institution of the kind that has fallen in our way, that I got every possible information relative to its inspectors, inferior officers, government, manual labour, provisions, &c. &c. for
which

which I refer you to my journal on my return to England. In regard to the building, it is well planned for its purpose. The chapel too we visited, where we found the best piece of sculpture in Genoa, a bas relief, by that extravagant and universal genius Michael Angelo Buonarotti; the subject is a dead Christ, and Virgin who weeps over him; though I think it uncommonly fine, yet it comes not up to my ideas of the Grecian school; but I dare say no more on this subject till I reach Florence. How changed, how fallen, is the arsenal from its former condition, when Genoa furnished so many potentates of Europe with fleets, and by its naval strength so long kept possession of one of the divisions of Constantinople! The whole of its maritime *force*, if I might use the expression, is now confined to four rotten gallies, which serve as prisons to the galley slaves. These men consist of Mahometan captives, Genoese assassins, and robbers, who, like those of Toulon, are, with some few exceptions, chained together in pairs. On entering the

arsenal

arſenal we walked along a range of ſheds or ſmall ſhops, where ſome of the ſlaves are permitted for money to ſell different articles to the reſt, as bread, ſoup, meats, &c. while others have the liberty of ranging the town to diſpoſe of ſlippers, purſes, &c. but theſe I believe are always Turks. I was aſtoniſhed at the little order kept among them by the overſeers, for the uproar was general and exceſſive. One thing I had almoſt omitted mentioning to you, and that is the Roman prow or iron roſtrum which is put up over the door of the arſenal, *perhaps the only one exiſting*, and therefore an object of curioſity; it was found in cleaning the port, where it had probably lain a long time, as it is now nearly conſumed with age; its form is that of a *boar's head*, or ſome ſuch animal. Having done with this place (the arſenal) which I think would encourage no ſecond viſit, we took oars, and rowed out to ſea for the purpoſe of ſeeing Genoa to the greateſt advantage; and indeed this view of it is magnificent, comprehending the city, the ſurrounding hills,

hills, and the numerous villas that occupy every part of them.

These are the objects which have principally engaged our attention at this place, and as they appeared to me, so have I described them to you.

The Genoese are said to inherit the character of their Ligurian ancestors; but I rather think, if they retain any part of it, it is the worst, as they certainly are the most turbulent, most superstitious, most vindictive, and most mercenary race in all Italy. Of the first charge the history of their country affords a variety of instances; of the second and third the frequency of religious processions and assassinations. To prove the last, I need only relate a circumstance that would be incredible, if it were not sufficiently vouched by the testimony of all travellers who have visited Genoa; and that is, their voluntary servitude on board the gallies after the term of their sentence is elapsed. Examples of this are

very

LETTER XII.

very frequent, the contract is generally for twelve months, and the price of their liberty eighteen shillings in Genoese money. I am really at a loss to account for such depravity, but my surprize yields to my indignation, not so much against the wretched slaves, as against the more wretched government that permits and encourages so infamous a compact. Though the condition of the galley slaves be better here than in France, nevertheless it is so bad, that was I not assured of the fact, I never had given it credit. Chained one to another, exposed to all weathers on board the gallies, subject to severe and arbitrary correction, ill cloathed, worse fed, and finally eat up by disease and vermin; who would have imagined it possible? *but so it is*, and such is the imbecillity, the infatuation, the misery, or whatever you may call it, of human nature at Genoa.

The character of the nobles too has a leading feature in it, that is seldom found in other countries. They pretend to be superior to those prejudices, which so frequently and so foolishly exist against commerce; yet this mask of wisdom is only the effect of avarice, as no race of men is prouder and more ignorant. But the commerce, carried on by the noble Genoese, is that of money, or in other words usury, as they supply the needy of France and Italy with sums at the most exorbitant interest. They are in possession of this money from the exercise of the most rigid œconomy in domestic life; for instead of making use of the noble palaces, which they owe to the ostentation of their ancestors, they inhabit only the attic stories; fathers, uncles, brothers, with all their female relatives and servants, are stowed in different apartments, and their tables, instead of being served in a style adequate to their opulence, are (as I am well informed) most pitifully supplied. In the article of dress, as they always wear black, they incur but little expence; and for hospitality, it is a virtue unknown to them, even among each other. Their general amusement is conversazioni, where they

LETTER XII.

they entertain themselves at cards, and are refreshed with coffee, lemonade, and biscuits. The women are pretty, but their sable dress, and manner of wrapping up their heads in a veil called Il Meſſero, are in my opinion very unbecoming. Their whole time is taken up in play, intrigue, and the observance of church ceremony. They never appear from home either *with* their husbands, or *without* their *Ciciſbèi*, the latter of whom are always the objects of their choice, and often the fathers of their children. From the general imputation which the Genoese lie under of ignorance, I am not at all surprised to find no university here; but from that partiality to music which they entertain in common with all the Italians, I did not expect to see so vile a theatre. The singers were what I should have been out of humour with, even at such a place as Novi, and the band was still more despicable: I am informed that this is the consequence of parsimony, as the managers, from the little encouragement they receive, are not able to employ the best voices and music.

Commerce at Genoa is reduced to its lowest ebb, having declined in proportion to its rise at Leghorn. Few of these noble usurers would risk a cargo in a vessel of their own state, as they know how entirely their flag is unprotected, and therefore make use of British bottoms as their best security. In these they export their velvets, silk, oil, dried mushrooms (which are famous) wines, Parmesan cheese, and Carrara marbles. Their imports are various, English cloth is a considerable article, their chief trade however is with Spain. But that on which the existence of this republic as an independent state, as well as the properties of many of its citizens have long rested, is the celebrated *Bank of St. George*, established since the commencement of the fifteenth century. It is less dependent on government, than government is on it, being managed exclusively by its own laws, and separate directors; its capital is immense, its credit universal,

LETTER XII.

versal, and the security as firm as the defenceless condition of Genoa will admit. In 1746 it supported the republic in its distress, by advancing 750,000 *l.* the whole of which (as I am informed) has been reimbursed. The interest it gives for money is two and a half per cent.

I shall conclude this letter with an anecdote related to me by a French gentleman who resides here, which will give you a much better representation of the national character, than any thing I could otherwise write upon the subject.

Some months ago two Venetians (whose countrymen and the Genoese still keep up that inveterate hatred to each other, which distinguished their ancestors) were present at an Osterìa, or wine house, where the conversation of the company arose, not as it would in England, on politics or pleasure, but upon the merits of St. John, the Protector of Genoa, who, it was asserted, had worked innumerable miracles, and was the greatest of all faints. If nature be so much the parent of patriotism, as to create in us an affection for those minuter objects in our native land, which the citizen of the world would regard with an eye of indifference, how much more powerfully must she operate on our passions, when we remember that on which the prosperity of our country is supposed to depend? The two Venetians were precisely in this predicament. They probably knew as little of St. John, as they did of St. Denis; but St. Mark was the guardian of Venice, and consequently their all in all. Resolved therefore to maintain his honour in opposition to this provoking eulogium of the Genoese on their patron, one of them observed, that the bones of his saint had worked more miracles, *particularly in healing diseases*, than all the apostles and saints; that in heaven he was next in rank to the Virgin and popes, and as much superior to their St. John, as the patriarch of Venice was to the archbishop of Genoa. To prevent any reply to this, he and his friend left the room, but

were

LETTER XII.

were soon followed by one of the company, who had the honour of bearing the great crofs of a religious order in their church profeſſions. This deſperate enthuſiaſt on overtaking, ſtabbed the Venetian, who had ſpoken, to the heart, crying out with the blow, Ti manda queſto San Giovanne che ti guariano le oſſe di San Marco.* His friend, aſtoniſhed at a deed ſo bloody (tho' an Italian) applied to a magiſtrate for juſtice, who, having heard the particulars, told him, that had a Venetian murdered a Genoeſe in Venice, no notice would have been taken of it, but that his complaint would probably be conſidered in a few days;—and ſo indeed it was, even ſooner than he had promiſed, for early the next morning he too was found aſſaſſinated at the door of his lodgings, and the bearer of the great crofs ſtill maintains his poſt of honour. Now determine on the character of a people, among whom ſuch crimes are committed with impunity.

* St. John ſends thee this, that the bones of St. Mark may heal thee.

LETTER XIII.

Genoa, Oct. 6th, 1787.

WE shall leave Genoa in a few hours, and therefore I must conclude what remains to be said of it with as much expedition as possible. You wish to hear what English gentlemen we know in Italy. As we were among the first that passed the Alps, we have hitherto seen but few, a Mr. Dundas, son of Sir Thomas Dundas, met us at Turin, and has been of our party here. Yesterday we all dined with Mr. Braham, the British consul, at his villa near this place, and concluded the evening with him at his house in town. But to proceed in my account of Genoa, I must observe to you, that the republic is about 140 miles in length, and from twenty to thirty in breadth. The soil is not as grateful as the climate is favourable. If I except the country near the gulphs of St. Remo and Spessa, together with the valley of Polcevèra, which are fruitful in olives, grapes, truffles, mushrooms,

rooms, figs, oranges, and lemons. The wines are of two sorts, an ordinary, and rich muscadine. The mushrooms are so much admired in these parts of Europe, that their annual importation into Spain alone amounts to 5000 *l.* but what the Genoese find most profitable is their oil, which is only inferior to that of Lucca. The mineral productions principally consist of salt, slate, and marbles; the last are beautiful and various, particularly those of Sestri di Ponente, which are the most esteemed. Near the suburb of San Pietro d'Arena is a species of black sand, that possesses a strong magnetic quality, evident from its influence on the compass. This sand has very much engaged the attention of the naturalist, as also a source of fresh water that rises in the gulph of Spessa, and occupies a space of about thirty feet in circumference.

The government of Genoa, which is confined to the nobles, was new modelled by the celebrated Andrew Doria and his associates

ciates in 1528. Having determined on such families as were eligible to state employments, they declared, for the purpose of preventing jealousies among the citizens who were excluded, that they would aggregate to the number then named ten families annually, which was accordingly done; but it was found that the nobility first chosen assumed privileges incompatible with the equality that should subsist among the members of an aristocratic government. This was violently resented by those of subsequent creation, who in 1579 obliged the former to renounce all claim to exclusive power, and to declare the whole of the nobility on an equal footing.

It was then determined that every male patrician should, at the age of twenty two years, have a seat in the great council, or body wherein the supreme authority resides. This council enacts or abrogates laws: imposes taxes: elects a Doge or chief magistrate, with the great officers of the republic: makes war and peace: ratifies treaties: and,

LETTER XIII.

in a word, exercises or delegates all the superior functions of government. The number is generally from three to four hundred, but as it has been found difficult to assemble so large a body, they draw annually by lot 200 of them, which they call the minor council, who in reality govern the republic. In affairs brought before either of them, it is necessary to have two thirds of the voices to carry the question, a rule that I think must be attended with confusion and delay. The Doge, or chief officer, of the republic, is chosen from the councils of which he is president, and vested with the exclusive power of proposing whatever is submitted to their consideration. No person is eligible until he has attained the age of fifty. He remains in office only two years, but may be rechosen at the expiration of ten. His place of residence is the Signoria or Ducal Palace, where he is constantly attended by two senators, who are in fact *spies*, and guarded by 100 Swiss soldiers. During his term of office he has the title of Serenissimo, and ever afterwards that of Excellentissimo,

with

with the honorable charge of perpetual Procurator; but so carefully does this jealous constitution provide against his abuse of power, that on quitting his office, he is responsible to the supreme Censors for his administration. Every Doge must be lawfully born, and not the adopted son of nobility. Their manner of election is as follows. The great council assemble and draw by lot out of their own number 50, who propose 20 as worthy of the dignity; out of whom the great council again select 15; this number is reduced by the 200 to six, from whom the Doge is chosen by a majority of voices. The other officers of state I shall pass over in silence, as I have already put more into my journal on the subject than I can even review with patience, much less transcribe. The law of Genoa, I mean that which determines on the property of the subject, is as I believe in all Italy founded on the Roman, and the criminal has nothing in it to engage the attention of an Englishman. The first (whatever might be its merit,) is generally subservient to interest; and

the

LETTER XIII.

the second very seldom put in force; as you may perceive by what I have said on the frequency of assassinations, that crimes pass with impunity; which I partly attribute to the supineness and immorality of the magistrates, partly to the fear they are in of the common people or mob. The ecclesiastical state is governed by an archbishop and six suffragans; besides these are the bishops of Sarzana and Savona; the first dependent on the see of Rome, and the second on the Metropolitan of Milan. The inquisition they say is no longer formidable, but as I find a dominican friar at the head of it, I do not give the most implicit faith to this declaration. The soldiers of the republic, for I cannot say military establishment, are about 1500, principally Germans and Swifs; as they have a noble at their head, who is never seen in an uniform, you may conceive what sort of an appearance they make *individually*, for *in a body* I believe the government is too compassionate to expose them to view.

The

The population of the republic is eſtimated at 350,000 ſouls, out of which number 90,000 are inhabitants of the capital.— The revenues amount to 153,264 *l.* and the expence of government is only 98,407 *l.*; ſo that there ſhould be annually a ſaving of 54,857 *l.*

The hiſtory of Genoa has little in it deſerving of more than general attention, previous to the new modelling of the government by the elder Doria. It belonged to the Romans, the Goths, the Eaſtern Empire, the Lombards, to Charlemagne and his ſucceſſors. In 1096 the inhabitants revolted, and declared themſelves independent, making choice of ariſtocracy as their form of government. In 1257 they elected a Captain or Doge, one Simon Bocca-negra, whom they veſted with abſolute power. Inſtead of tracing the ſeveral forms of political adminiſtration (of which I believe no country ever had a greater variety) I ſhall remind you that about the commencement of its independence the Cruſades broke out, and ſet

all

LETTER XIII.

all the fanatic ſtates of Europe in a blaze.—
In the ſhort ſpace of thirteen years, Genoa
furniſhed the princes, who embarked in this
expedition, with ſeven large fleets, one of
which alone, was compoſed of 68 gallies.—
By ſuch valuable contracts it ſoon became
the moſt opulent and powerful city in
Europe, and got poſſeſſion of the iſland of Sardinia and principal commerce of the Mediterranean. The firſt of theſe was the ſubject of thoſe bloody and obſtinate wars between it and Piſa, which ended in the deſtruction of the latter. But its moſt formidable rival was Venice.

The intereſt of theſe ſtates claſhed no
leſs in their commerce than in their conqueſts, and the wars, that were the conſequence of their hatred, have been a principal cauſe of their preſent mutual inſignificance. But to paſs over theſe times to the period when the politics of Genoa became more interwoven with thoſe of the leading kingdoms of Europe, I ſhall take up its hiſtory at the time that Charles the fifth and
Francis

Francis the first contended for superiority in Italy.

The holy league of Cognac, formed for the express purpose of opposing the ambition of Charles, absolved Francis from the oath he had taken to fulfil the treaty of Madrid; in which, among other things, was the cession of Genoa to the emperor. In consequence therefore of this league of absolution, &c. a detachment of 2000 men under the command of Lautrec invested this city by land, whilst the celebrated Andrew Doria blocked it up by sea, and soon compelled the garrison to surrender it to the arms of France.

Doria had been attached to the French interest from his youth, and had rendered the nation the most essential service. As an admiral his reputation was unrivalled, nevertheless, being of a disposition entirely dissimilar to the pliant and subtle humour of those with whom he served, and accustomed to speak his sentiments with more freedom

freedom than courtesy, he drew upon himself the ill-will of those who surrounded the king, and they represented him as proud, turbulent, and disaffected. Francis, whose mind was of a nature the most open and unsuspicious, gave little attention to this general imputation, till hearing that Doria had so violently resented the clearing and fortifying of the harbour of Savona, intended as the rival of Genoa in commerce, as to menace a revolt. He commanded Barbisieux, one of his admirals, to sail immediately for Naples (in the siege of which Doria was then employed) and seize him and his gallies; but it was too late. The Genoese admiral, having received early intelligence of his intention, had already formed his plan of leaving him: and was determined on giving liberty to his country. By the persuasion of the Marquis del Guasto, a Spanish nobleman, whom he had taken prisoner in a sea combat off Naples, he sent a messenger to the emperor, by whom he proposed to put himself and his republic under his protection, and to serve him with eleven

eleven gallies for a certain monthly sum. Charles, who well knew how to value so great an acquisition to his arms, sent him *Carte blanche*; in consequence of which he sailed to Genoa, and took possession of it almost without resistance, expelling the French garrison commanded by the Mareshal Trivulcio, the very governor whom he had left there on taking it from the Imperialists. Having thus delivered his republic, he new modelled the government; and then proved the sincerity of his patriotism, by not assuming the sovereignty of it; he retired to private life, in which he received a reward more desirable and more glorious to a noble mind than universal empire,—the love and gratitude of his country.

These he enjoyed undisturbed for nineteen years, with the additional satisfaction of seeing his system of political administration firmly established; but suddenly the whole was on the very point of being overturned by the ambition and abilities of an indi-

individual. John Lewis Fiefco, Count of Lavagna, a young nobleman, head of one of the moſt ancient and illuſtrious families in Genoa, determined on attempting that, which Doria, from a love of liberty, had rejected,— the abſolute dominion of his country. Though only twenty-two years of age, he poſſeſſed all thoſe qualities which made him equal to ſo dangerous and ſo difficult an enterprife. Under the appearance of being entirely devoted to pleaſure, he concealed his real character, and avoided the ſuſpicion that his great talents and popularity might otherwiſe create; for his unbounded generoſity had gained him the affection of the common people; which, though ever governed by caprice, or the ill-directed liberality of the opulent, is very neceſſary in ſuch deſperate attempts. When every precaution had been taken, it was determined to put the plot in execution at midnight, between the firſt and ſecond of January 1547. This was accordingly done; the conſpiracy had ſucceeded; and even deputies were appointed to treat with the leaders

leaders of it, when an accident rendered the whole ineffectual. Fiefco, having allotted to his partizans the different quarters of the city which they were to fecure, referved for himfelf the leffer port or d'Arfena, as the moft difficult and important. There alfo every thing had happened to his wifhes, and he was on the point of departing, when a tumult arofe in one of the great gallies that lay neareft the fhore; fearful of fedition among the flaves at a time fo critical, he turned about fuddenly, and haftening on board, ftepped on the plank which reached from the wharf to the deck, his foot flipt, he fell into the fea, and from the weight of his armour funk and perifhed.

The protection which Genoa received from the emperor Charles the Vth, in confequence of Doria's revolt, attached her to the intereft of Spain, with whom fhe was engaged in three wars againft France. The firft broke out in the reign of Henry the IId, who was invited by the Corficans to take poffeffion of their ifland, and receive
them

LETTER XIII.

them as his subjects. This war continued from 1553 to 59, when peace was concluded at Chateau Cambresis between all the belligerent powers. The second commenced in 1624 during the reign of Lewis the XIIIth, to whom Charles Emanuel, duke of Savoy, allied himself, in hopes of recovering the marquisate of Zucarello, of which he had been dispossessed by the emperor Ferdinand, in consequence of a claim laid to it by the Genoese as a fief of the empire, formerly granted to them. The rapid success of the duke of Savoy threatened the entire conquest of the republic, when it was unexpectedly relieved from several quarters, the enemy driven back, and in 1673 a peace concluded, which restored every thing that Genoa had lost. The last war with France, which happened in 1684, was more destructive than either of the two former.

Lewis the XIVth, intoxicated with the adulation of a splendid court, and the abject servility of an entire people, was piqued at the attachment of this republic to Spain.

For the purpofe of giving the blow he meditated againſt it ſome colour of juſtice, (a condeſcenſion to which he ſeldom ſtooped in his career of inſolent proſperity) he demanded ſatisfaction for certain inſults put upon the ſervants of his reſident St. Olon by ſome inferior officers of juſtice, and what is ſtill more extraordinary, for the councils not having reinſtated the baniſhed family of Fieſco. The Genoeſe, perceiving his deſign, and confiding in the protection of Spain, refuſed his demand; on which he ſent a fleet of fourteen men of war, twenty gallies, two fireſhips, with many inferior veſſels, under the command of Du Queſne, who anchored before Genoa in May 1684, and bombarded it from the 17th to the 28th. The wretched inhabitants, to ſave what remained of their city, were obliged to obey the commands of the haughty monarch, who ordered them to ſend their Doge Imperiali Leſcaro, and four ſenators, to Verſailles, to ſue for pardon at the foot of his throne. An act of ſuch inſolent, ſuch ungenerous reſentment, to a city in compariſon of his power so pitiful as Genoa, and which his arms had already reduced to ruins, must long ago have excited in you a thorough contempt for the character of Lewis, sir-named the Great by the very ancestors of these men, who are now so violently opposing the power of the crown; and you will in consequence enjoy all that triumph which virtue feels in the humiliation of powerful despotism, when you reflect that this monster of pride and ambition, who would have reduced all Europe to his controul, was humbled to the very dust, and sued to England for peace, offering concessions more disgraceful than those by which Genoa appeased his indignation.

What a lesson for despotic princes!

The republic having suffered so severely by this war, and having so fully experienced the inability of Spain to protect her, grew cautious by misfortune, and wisely pursued the most rigid neutrality, as the system that could alone keep up its independence.—

This prudent conduct however was interrupted by the war for the succession of Austria, as Maria Theresa had in the treaty of worms ceded the Marquisate of Final, which the Genoese had purchased of the Emperor Charles the Sixth, to the King of Sardinia. In this war, during the year 1746, they were dispossessed of all their territories, and finally obliged to surrender their capital to the Imperialists, commanded by General Brown. Thus, to all appearance, there was an end of the republic, when the Marquis di Botta, Brown's successor, suffered himself to be surprised and driven out of Genoa, by the populace,—perhaps by money. However, it would have been very soon retaken, had not the peace concluded at Aix la Chapelle re-instated the Genoese in all their possessions.

The last thing that happened to disturb the tranquillity of the state, and convince it if necessary of its oppression and weakness, was the Corsican revolution.

The inhabitants of that ifland had ever been impatient of the Genoefe dominion, having been always treated with contempt, rigour, and injuftice—the charaƈteriftic features of hereditary republican government. The revolt in 1768, under the celebrated Pafcal Paoli, would (as you well know) have had all the fuccefs that thefe gallant Iflanders merited, had not Genoa, feeling its own want of power to reduce them, fold the fovereignty of Corfica to France, whofe ftrength was too great to be refifted with fuccefs.

LETTER

LETTER XIV.

Milan, Oct. 11, 1787.

THE road from Genoa to Pavia was in general the same as we had travelled in coming from Turin to Genoa. As Pavia has no monuments of its ancient grandeur, when it was the residence of a long race of monarchs, nor any thing of more modern date that merits attention, we made but little stay there. Adjoining to it we surveyed those plains, where in 1525, Francis the first was routed and taken prisoner by the Imperialists; and then pursued our journey to Milan, about fifteen miles further.

This city, which of all in Italy is in point of size inferior only to Rome, appears to disadvantage after Turin and Genoa, being upon the whole ill built; yet far from uninteresting, as it contains many objects highly satisfactory to the attentive traveller.

The cathedral or (as here called) Il Duomo, is of the kind the most magnificent building

building I ever beheld. The whole is coated with slabs of white marble, and on the outside are six hundred statues of the same; some of which, though not many, have great merit. The aisle of this church is ample and grand. The choir full of sculpture, which seems admirably finished; but there is so much of it, that I should suppose six months would be insufficient for the contemplation of its beauties, there being, as they informed us, no less than 15,000 figures; but in my opinion far more deserving attention than the Duomo, is the new opera house, reported to be (and I readily believe it) the largest modern theatre in the world. Judge therefore of my surprise and admiration, on going into it!— The boxes are as so many parlours, with every convenient appendage, and being fitted up with furniture and hangings by the families to whom they belong, are magnificient in the extreme.

The citadel or castle of Milan is a mass of heavy fortification, which once was almost

impreg-

impregnable. This, however, you will suppose, has decreased in proportion to tactical improvement; as now its resistance could be but very feeble against the operations of a regular siege, though Elliot himself should defend it. We also visited the Ducal Palace, where we were shewn a noble ball or gala room, and some English furniture, but no good statues or pictures. However, our guide, or as here called, *cicerone*, made us ample recompense for our disappointment in this respect; by taking us to the churches of Santa Maria delle Grazie, and Santa Maria presso San Celso; in the first are two famous paintings by Titian and Leonardo da Vinci; the subjects of which are Christ crowned with thorns, and the last supper.— The portico of a church, called San Lorenzo, seems to have been part of the peristyle of a temple, built in honor of Hercules, by Maximian, the associate of the Emperor Diocletian; it consists of sixteen marble columes beautifully fluted. The Ambrosian library and museum, of which Milan is so proud, did not answer my expectation.—
They

LETTER XIV. 269

They certainly contain a noble collection of books, paintings, &c. but from the hyperbolic defcription I had heard of them, I looked for fomething more than I faw.— This library was founded by the Cardinal Frederick Borroméo, and what is rather fingular for a building of this kind, was dedicated to St. Ambrofe, from whom you perceive it is named. It is faid to contain 40,000 volumes, and in the mufeum are many good pictures. I was particularly pleafed with a drawing or cartoon by Raphael, called the School of Athens, the painting of which (they tell me) is at Rome.

I believe few travellers come to Milan who are not foon after their arrival taken to a place called La Cafa Simonetta, an uninhabited feat, two miles from the city, remarkable for its echo, which repeats the human voice 38, and the report of a piftol 57 times; as we found by experiment. It is at the back part of the houfe, and feems to be produced by the projection of two wings from the body, that form a kind of

court

court yard, but I think there muſt be ſome other unknown cauſe for ſo ſingular an effect. As the nobleſſe of this place have the character of being the moſt hoſpitable and polite in Italy, we much regret the abſence of the Marchioneſs Caſtiglone, who is here what the Ducheſs of Polignac is at Paris, the friend of foreigners, and the model of faſhion. Among the letters we were honored with from Lord Lanſdowne, one was for this lady.

The manufactures of Milán are, for an inland city, very conſiderable. One houſe alone, called la Caſa Clerici, employs above 700 men in making glaſs, earthen-ware, goatſkin leather, woollen cloths, &c. and another the Caſa Penſa, near 600, who work only in ſilk—the handkerchiefs made there are much the beſt I ever ſaw, of which I cannot mention to you a ſurer inſtance than the generality of their wear. Excluſive of theſe are many other works of importance in velvets, brocades, Indians, gold, ſilver, copper, chryſtal, and paper.

We

LETTER XIV.

We learn from the history of this country, that after the conquest of Lombardy by Charlemagne, it continued subject to the emperors of Germany till the league of Mosio, concluded in March 1226 by all the principal cities that lie between the Alps and the Appennines, the confines of France, and the Adriatic sea, under the appellation of Societas Lombardorum. The sovereignty was then disputed by the Visconti and Torriani, two powerful families of Milan, and obtained by the former, who held it till 1447, as long as there was any legitimate issue to succeed, when Francis Sforza, bastard of the celebrated general of this name, who is so frequently mentioned by Guicciardini in the wars of Naples, having married Bianca Maria, the natural daughter of the last duke Visconti, got possession of the dutchy. His second son was the celebrated Lewis Sforza, sirnamed the Moor, whose character strikes me, as similar to that which is generally given us of our Richard the IIId, ambition, courage, cruelty, and hypocrisy, being the distinguishing qualities

of

of both. Lewis, like Richard, was uncle and guardian to a young prince, and like him alfo did he afcend a throne by the murder of his nephew. Though the fates of the two ufurpers were not exactly the fame, yet they feem equally the effect of divine judgment, as punifhments for their crimes. The king of England loft his crown and life in battle; the duke of Milan was difpoffeffed of his dominions by Lewis the XIIth of France, and fhut up in the caftle of Loches, where he died after eleven years of clofe confinement, aggravated by neglect, and probably embittered by reflection. It might not be improper to obferve to you, that thefe princes were contemporary, tho' the ufurpation of Sforza happened ten years after that of Richard. The laft of this family was Francis the IId, fon of Lewis the Moor, who dying without iffue in 1535, the emperor Charles the Vth feized the dutchy of Milan as a fief efcheat to the empire. It continued in his family till the demife of Charles the IId, king of Spain, when in the war of fucceffion to the Spanifh monarchy,

monarchy, it was taken by prince Eugene, and reannexed to the empire, in which it now continues, having been confirmed by the treaty of Raſtadt in 1714: by the quadruple alliance two years after: by the peace of Vienna in 1725: and, finally, by that of Aix la Chapelle in 1748.

The government of the Auſtrian Lombardy is abſolute, there being no conſtitutional law that limits the authority of the ſovereign. Like that of Brabant, &c. it is principally carried on by a governor and miniſter of ſtate, who, on affairs of moment, receive inſtructions from the court of Vienna. The preſent governor is the reigning duke of Modena, who will be ſucceeded by the emperor's youngeſt brother, the archduke Ferdinand, now reſident at Milan.

The military eſtabliſhment of the country is from 16 to 20,000 men, the population 1,000,000, including the capital, which is ſaid to contain 116,000.

We have not been at court, as the archduke is absent. He is very partial to England, which (you may remember) he visited two years ago, where he was magnificently entertained by the king at Windsor castle.

I shall conclude this letter at Bologna.

———

Bologna the 19th.

WE left Milan on the 11th, and soon reached Lodi, a town remarkable for the best Parmasan cheese. It is made entirely of cows, not as I had heard in England of goats milk; the cattle are brought lean out of Germany to graze on these plains; so that its rich and peculiar flavour is altogether dependant on the pasture. From Lodi we came to Placentia, or, as it is here called, Piacenza, a city subject to the duke of Parma. We ascended the tower of its cathedral for the purpose of viewing the country, where Hannibal routed the consul Sempronius; but to ascertain the exact spot is impossible, though we know the two armies

armies were encamped on each fide of the river Trebia. The equeftrian ftatues of Alexander, and his fon Ranuzio Farnefé, did not give us the fatisfaction we expected; therefore on that fubject I fhall be filent. Early the next morning we arrived at Parma, having (according to Pliny) travelled either over or very near the Æmilian way. I fhall fay no more of Parma than that it is an extenfive city, and on the whole not ill built. What principally engage the attention of the traveller are the theatre, and academy of fculpture and painting; the former of thefe built by Vignola in the reign of Ranuzio (whofe ftatue I have juft noticed) is much admired and ftudied by the lovers of architecture; it is upon the ancient model, and remarkable for the full effect which found has even at the moft diftant part of it from the ftage, that is, about 310 feet. This circumftance is attributed not to the defign of the architect, but to fome accidental caufe, hitherto undifcovered. In the Profcenium is a kind of bafon, that by pipes might be occafionally filled with water. In it they reprefented naumachiæ, or fea-fights, for which the gallies are ftill fhewn in the theatre; but I think a fcene of this nature under cover, and in fo confined a place, muft at the beft have been infipid, and uninterefting. In the academy is fome mutilated Grecian fculpture, the drapery of which is admirable; but the grand object is Corregio's famous picture of the holy family—a wonderful production of the pencil. It has been afferted, that the figures of this fine piece are too homely; but I think the objection fcarcely deferves attention. Corregio was too great an artift to be inobfervant of character, and to facrifice confiftency to complexion.

The dutchies of Parma and Placentia are governed by an infant of Spain; the Spanifh royal family being defcended in the female line from the Farnefi, the illegitimate offspring of Pope Paul the IIId. Anthony, the laft duke of this houfe, died in 1731 without iffue. From Parma we came to Reggio, and from Reggio to Modena, where I was

delighted

delighted with the architecture of the ducal palace built by Avanzini. The collection of pictures is still capital, though a hundred of the best were purchased for Auguftus king of Poland. In four hours after our departure from Modena we arrived at Bologna, which is said to contain 55,000 people. Though in the churches and palaces we had some specimens of noble architecture, its general appearance is unpleafing, from the prevailing custom of building all the houses with piazzas or porticoes before them, which however useful against the inclemency of the seasons, close up and disfigure the streets. Bologna is above all other cities, Rome excepted, remarkable for its collection of paintings. It was (if you recollect) the birth-place and school of the Caracci; but instead of crowding my letter with a catalogue of these performances, I shall only observe, that * a Saint Cecilia by Raphael, † a picture of the Virgin, Child, and little St. John, by Cor-

---

* In the church of Giovanne in Monte.
† Caprara palace.

regio, * two by Guido René, one known by the name of St. Peter and St. Paul, the other fuppofed to reprefent Liberty and Modefty; a † St. Jerome by Ludovico Caracci, &c. gave me the greateft fatisfaction.

There are alfo many mafter-pieces of modern fculpture, but the moft ftriking, and in my humble opinion the beft executed, is the Coloffean bronze ftatue of Neptune, by John of Bologna. It is the principal figure of a noble fountain; the attitude, the afpect, and anatomy of which are inexpreffibly fine, and I think reach even Homer's defcription of this *earth-fhaking* god. The famous towers of this place Là Garifenda and Affinelli, we have frequently feen. The former is 142 feet in height, and leans eight over its bafe; the other 300, and inclines fomething, though little, out of its perpendicular; but one view of fuch objects is quite fufficient for me.

* Palaces Zampieri and Monti.
† In the Monti palace.

LETTER XIV.

The public Museum, or Istituto, founded by Pope Lambertini, who was a Bolognese, is a noble collection of almost every thing proper for the study of the arts and sciences; a library of 100,000 volumes, apartments for chemistry, botany, and surgery, full of anatomical preparations in wax: a cabinet of natural history: an observatory: schools for the polite arts: a collection of genuine and counterfeit medals for that study: in short, it is a complete practical encyclopedia, with appointed professors for each respective branch. A committee of twenty-four directors assemble there every Thursday to superintend the whole. I should have omitted mentioning the opera, but for the singular illiberality of the managers, which indeed reflects disgrace upon the city, and I believe you will adopt this opinion, when I inform you, that they exact of foreigners a sum nearly double to what Italians pay for entrance. We did not perceive this imposition till we had been twice at the theatre. The third night we were determined not to submit to it, and being refused admission for the common sum, returned to our inn, where we had not been five minutes before they sent to apologize, and begged us to come back; but with this request we did not think proper to comply. The last places that we visited were the churches of San Petronio and San Michaele in Bosco. In the former is the famous Meridian of Cassini, engraved on copper, and inserted in the pavement 222 feet in length. By the admission of the sun's rays through a small aperture on the top of the church, it marks the equinoxes and solstices. From San Michaele we enjoyed a most pleasing prospect of Bologna, and the extensive plains of Lombardy.

I have little to observe on the history of this city. Since the reign of Charlemagne it has been governed by the holy see, some revolutions brought about by the Pepoli and Bentivogli excepted. In 1462 John Bentivogli seized and exercised the sovereign power until 1506, when he was driven out

out by that bold and enterprising church militant Pope Julius the IId.

The citizens apparently possess great privileges, being governed by their own senate of sixty, from which are chosen a Gonfaloniere, or president, and eight Anziani, or counsellors: the people are subject to no duties, but one on wine: their properties are secure from confiscation. They send an ambassador, and auditor of the rota, or supreme court of justice at Rome, to that city; and, finally, have no citadel or fortress to overawe them. But from farther enquiry I am induced to believe that this is mere pageantry, as the senate is nominated by the pope, who governs as despotically through his cardinal and vice-legate at Bologna, as in any other part of his territories.

One morning we happened to be present at the infliction of a punishment that was quite new to us. I believe they call it La Corda; it is as follows.

A large

A large pulley is fixed to an iron crane, about 40 feet high, which projects from the side of a house. Over this pulley is a rope, to which the culprit's wrists (being previously tied together behind him) are fastened. He is then drawn up slowly to a certain height, when the rope being suddenly loosened, he drops within a few feet of the ground. This torture is repeated a second and a third time, the last fall being made higher than that preceding it; but the second never fails of producing the desired effect, that is, of dislocating the shoulder bones. On enquiry into the offence of the criminal whom we saw, I was told that he had undergone this punishment three times in seven months, for giving the coltellata, or stab, with a knife to three different persons, the last of whom was his mother. Had he robbed the church he would have been burnt alive.

The people of this place seem to have all that partiality for music which I expected to find in Italy. I mention this from the many serenades we hear every night. One of of thefe marching concerts is rather curious; it confifts of eight old men, who are all blind, all coufins, and all natives of Bologna. They never fail to attend us in the afternoon.

We are again joined by Mr. Dundas, who is a charming companion. He is very fond of fculpture and painting, and will before he leaves Italy be a true virtuofo. We all think ourfelves extremely fortunate in not having any acquaintance here, which would but divert our time from that we moft wifh to cultivate—a knowledge of the polite arts.

Though we expected to find novelty in almoft every object, I was much furprized on enquiring the hour to hear the waiter reply twenty-three and a half; I have fince learnt that in moft parts of Italy the laft hour ends, and the firft begins, at funfet; fo there being four and twenty between thofe periods, the anfwer was proper: yet I fear it will be long before this manner of computing time becomes familiar to me.

LETTER

LETTER XV.

Florence, Nov. 10th, 1787.

A Few miles south of Bologna we again ascended the Apennines; which are so much steeper than on the confines of Genoa, as to make it necessary to assist the posthorses with yokes of oxen; and yet these mountains have not that rude and naked appearance which I expected to have seen; but, on the contrary, are covered with brushwood, the foliage of which, now mellowed into a variety of shades and tints by an Italian autumn, present a most pleasing appearance; for though it remind us of the coming winter, yet, as we shall pass it in the softer climates of Italy, I have not to apprehend such storms and chilling mists as sail over you from * Bwlch y Van. We lay the first night at a small inn on these hills, and the day after arrived at Florence, having stopped some time on the road for the purpose of seeing La Pietra Mala, a spot

* A high mountain over Brecknock.

of earth and ſtones on the ſide of a mountain, that takes fire from the application of lighted ſtraw and wood; but we had not the good fortune to ſucceed in the experiment, though attended by people of the place, and all the neceſſary apparatus. From the road our view of Florence in the vale of Arno was noble; but yet, believe me, this boaſted valley, whoſe very ſound has ever created in me the moſt pleaſing ideas of rural ſcenery, has not half the beauty of many I could name on your ſide of the Severn; and the Arno is not that limpid ſtream, which I thought could be ſecond only to the Peneus, but a muddy and ſhallow river, the exact counterpart of the Seine at Paris. However, the city is much to my taſte; its ſituation is agreeable; its ſtreets for the moſt part wide; and its edifices, both public and private, remind us of the Medici, and revival of the liberal arts.

The palace of the grand duke was built by one Pitti, a private citizen, from whom it was named. Its architecture is the rudeſt

ſpecimen

specimen of the Tuscan and Ionic orders I ever beheld; yet I cannot but think its appearance grand and magnificent. The apartments were, as we expected, rather too dark for their numerous and valuable collection of paintings by Titian, Guido René, Salvator Rosa, Paul Veronese, Pietro da Cortona, and Raphael, whose celebrated picture of the Madonna della Sedia, even infidels would worship. It represents the Virgin seated (thence called della Sedia) and the infant Jesus on her lap. The choice of attitude in holding the child to her bosom, her complaisant look, beautifully pensive, and the happy countenance of her son, are treated in a manner peculiar to this wonderful artist, which, as it never has, I much fear never will be equalled. Behind the palace rises a steep hill laid out in pleasure gardens, called Boboli, which are ornamented with statues, and basons of water. From its summit the view of Florence, the river, and the vale of Arno, is extremely rich.

The

The city is divided by the river in two unequal parts. One of its bridges, called Il Ponte della Trinitá, is much admired for the cycloidal turn of the arches; but I am less partial to this than to the semicircular form. Of the churches the most remarkable is the Duomo; more, however, as an object of novelty than admiration, from its being coated with various coloured marbles, which gives it an appearance not dissimilar to a harlequin's jacket. Besides the architecture is a medley of all the orders, heaped and crowded together in confusion; but from this general censure I must except the dome or cupola, which is admirably raised. Near this cathedral is a building called, Il Battistèrio, where all the Florentine children are baptized; the bronze gates of which are sculptured with such art by Lorenzo Ghiberti, that the great Buonarotti is said to have exclaimed on seeing them: " Queste son degne di esser presentate a Giove per farne le portelle del paradiso." * In the

---

* These are worthy of being presented to Jupiter, and made the portals of paradise.

church

church of San Lorenzo is the superb chapel of the Medici Family, and some fine sculpture by Michael Angelo. We visited also that of St. Mark, not as dilettanti, but to provide ourselves with liqueurs and perfumes, made by the Dominican friars of this convent, and generally esteemed the best in Europe. And now let me draw your attention to the gallery of this place, which, for its various and valuable collection, is eminently distinguished above all other. However, as so many ample descriptions have been given of it by ingenious travellers, I shall be as concise as possible, only taking notice of what I received the greatest pleasure from contemplating. It stands on the banks of the Arno near the ancient ducal palace, and was begun and finished by the Medici, originally a family of private citizens, to whom succeeding ages are more indebted for their refinement, than to the most powerful monarchs of Europe. In 1564 Cosmo the Ist employed the celebrated George Vasari as architect, with intention of uniting under the same roof the different

chambers

chambers of the magistracy. But Francis, who succeeded him, altered the design of it to its present purpose; so that instead of being appropriated to courts of law, and a noisy bar, it was more happily converted into an elegant and peaceful asylum for antiquity and the muses. It is composed of three corridors, similar in form to a Greek Π; the two longest are about 404 feet, and the other 140, with sixteen or seventeen noble apartments on each side. In the former are antique busts of the Roman emperors, from the first Cæsar to Constantine, with many of their wives, &c. the portraits of several of the most remarkable men from Hanibal to Paoli; statues both modern and ancient, and a noble collection of pictures: in the latter are also paintings and sculpture, but of a higher order: ancient and modern medals: precious gems, whose exquisite engravings remind us of the age of Alexander, and of the art of Pergoteles: sacred, domestic, and military utensils of the ancients: specimens of their porcelain: Etruscan vases: ancient and modern

dern bronzes; and antique pictures: but of this numerous catalogue I am sure you are too charitable to wish me to write you a description; I shall therefore, as I have before said, confine myself to those pieces with which I was most pleased, such as the statues of two wolf dogs in the vestibule, both antique, and highly finished: the busts of Julius Cæsar, and a dying Alexander the Great. At the upper end of the eastern corridor, a horse, the anatomy and proportions of the head and body most admirable; but the legs the work of some modern stone-cutter: the statues of Æsculapius and Mercury, both antique: that of Bacchus, by Michael Angelo: a bronze statue of an Etruscan Haruspex, robed and in the act of speaking. This was found in the lake of Thrasimene, and is so perfect a figure, that the very attitude and countenance seem to carry with them persuasion: a copy of the famed Laocoon in the Museo Clementino at Rome, by Baccio Bandinelli, than which I can scarce conceive the original to have greater merit. These are all in the corridors.

dors. What I most admire in the cabinets are a bronze statue of Mercury, by John of Bologna, the design of which is singular, the artist having introduced this felon deity, as wafted to heaven on the breath of Zephyrus, whom he represents by a head with the face upwards, and from the mouth issues a strong blast on which Mercury seems to rise: the Hermaphrodite, a divine Greek statue, that is exactly what it ought to be. You recollect the story of the fond Salmacis, who clasped her lover Hermaphroditus in her arms, and prayed, not ineffectually, that the gods would make them one body: Hercules subduing a centaur, but what centaur I know not, never having heard that he had slain any other than Nessus, who perished by his arrow, not club, in attempting to force Dëjanira on the banks of the Evenus. This is an admirable piece of antique sculpture: finally, the unhappy Niobe and her children, the exact number of which it is impossible to ascertain, as so many ancient authors have differed in that respect. The sculptor, or rather sculptors of this group (for it is attributed to more than one) have followed Ovid's account, and made them fourteen. The different attitudes, and expreffions of grief, terror, and defpair in the fons and daughters, are wonderfully given; but the principal figure is that of Niobe; fhe appears bending over the laft and youngeft of her children, who clings to her knees for protection, whilft her right hand is fpread over the child, her left is lifted up to ward off the fatal fhaft, and her countenance, beautiful and majeftic, though in extreme anguifh, is raifed towards heaven, feemingly to fupplicate the offended offspring of Latona. In a word, fhe appears to be in the very moment of change, when

"Nullos movet aura Capillos:
"In vultu color eft fine fanguine; lumina mœftis
"Stant immota genis : nihil eft in imagine vivi.
"Ipfa quoque interiùs cum duro lingua palato
"Congelat; et venæ defiftunt poffe moveri.

"Nec

LETTER XV.

" Nec flecti cervix, nec brachia reddere geſtus,
" Nec pes ire poteſt *.

OVID. METAM. lib. vi. line 311.

But I was ſurpriſed to find theſe fine ſtatues ſo ill placed. Inſtead of being (as they ſhould be) grouped in confuſion, they are ranged in rows, and ſeemingly equidiſtant round the noble ſaloon, which the Grand Duke has built for their reception. Near this room are two apartments, which contain, what I am ſure is in no other place aſſembled, a collection of between 300 and 400 of the moſt celebrated painters portraits, done and preſented by themſelves to the Florentine gallery. I rather exulted in perceiving that none of the modern had equal merit with that of Mr. Moore, an

Imitated.

* Not a hair
Moves to the wind. Her crimſon beauty flies
Her lifeleſs cheeks, and fixed are both her eyes.
Now cold and petrified her veins ſhe feels,
Her palate ſtiffens, and her tongue congeals;
Neck, arms, and feet, the fatal influence own,
And all the woman hardens into ſtone.

Engliſh

English landscape painter resident at Rome: but the pride I felt in the skill of a countryman, was severely wounded by being shewn the faded daubing of Sir ———, which, unfortunately, is hung near some of the oldest portraits in the room, remarkable for their strength of colours. How is it to be lamented that this gentleman, who undoubtedly ranks among the first of modern painters, should have so long persevered in this error? I sincerely hope, however, that he will replace this his present disgraceful representative, by another in his best manner of colouring. And now let me conclude this article with the tribune, an octagon cabinet, which, for its collection of sculpture and painting, is, I should suppose, unequalled. Though the corridors and other apartments had prepared me for this scene, I assure you, that my surprise on entering was a more violent emotion than I ever felt of the same nature. Nor did it, as it generally does, die away into indifference, from the frequency of beholding the objects that had raised it; but was succeeded by

the

LETTER XV.

the mildest sensations of delight, which I have since experienced many an hour when sitting, silent and alone, to contemplate these works, that I can hardly conceive human. On advancing a few steps into the room, I found myself in the middle of five statues: a dancing fawn: a pair of wrestlers, or, as I would rather suppose, Pancratiastæ *: an Apollo: the Arrotino, whom some call (though I see not with what reason) the slave that discovered Cataline's conspiracy, and the Venus di Medici. In the four first, few faults and innumerable beauties appear. But thou, parent of love! how shall I describe thee, who art all beauty and all perfection?

Suppose her in a state of nature just risen from a bath, and, as Thomson says,

> "Shrinking from herself,
> "With fancy blushing; at the doubtful breeze
> "Alarm'd."

* See Pliny, Book 34. Chap. 8.

Her face turned over the left shoulder, presents an assemblage of features lovely in the extreme. Her body rather inclines forward, whilst her right hand is spread over her bosom, and the other somewhat lower. She rests upon her left leg, which is consequently straight; whilst the right bends gracefully, and leans upon the toe. Such is the attitude of the Venus di Medici; and let me add, that the magic sweetness of her countenance: the proportion and delicacy of her limbs: the softness and fleshy semblance of the marble, together with that fascinating grace that sits upon the whole figure, make me no longer wonder at the idolatry of the ancients; for if such were their images, I should, had I lived in those days, have deemed it wisdom to adore. But think not that these, though inestimable, are the only treasures of the tribune; the walls are hung with pictures by a triumvirate of painters, who, since the revival of the liberal arts, have never had their equals. First and alone Raphael, then Corregio and Titian. We beheld the three

manners

manners of the former; in the last is a St. John, of which I shall say nothing, as I am really at a loss for expression. By Corregio is a little Madona on her knees, and by Titian, the famous painting of his naked wife, called his Venus. Instead of expatiating on the merit of these pictures, I have done well in naming the artists who painted them, by whom it is almost impossible that any thing should be otherwise than excellent.

The dutchy of Tuscany, after the destruction of the Roman empire, fell under the dominion of the Ostrogoths, who were succeeded by the kings of Lombardy. After a series of years, and a variety of revolutions, through which the form of government continued republican, the celebrated family of the Medici took possession of it. In 1531 the emperor Charles the Fifth, created Alexander di Medici, Grand Duke of Tuscany, though violently opposed by the noble families of Florence, whose republican spirits could not easily brook the absolute

absolute government of a man raised from their own order. A long line of princes succeeded Alexander; most of whom seemed to possess an hereditary taste for science and the polite arts, and greatly encouraged their growth. The last of this illustrious race was John Gaston, whose conduct was very dissimilar to that of his ancestors, being extremely immoral. After his death Tuscany devolved on Francis duke of Lorrain and Bar, in lieu of his dutchies which were granted to the unfortunate Stanislaus king of Poland. Francis was succeeded by the reigning duke Peter Leopold, brother to the present emperor of Germany.

Much as I respect those of the Medici, who were the patrons of learned and ingenious men; yet I am free to own, that I look up with still greater veneration to * the wise prince that now fills the ducal throne of Tuscany. On his accession in 1765 he found every thing in that disorder and confusion,

---

* Since emperor of Germany, having succeeded his brother Joseph the IId.

which

which is the natural confequence of a long and diffipated reign. Commerce was languifhing: manufactures at a ftand: agri-. culture neglected: the nobles ruined by imitating the vices of their prince: the commonalty haraffed: and crimes of every nature fo increafed from impunity, and the total fubverfion of law, as to threaten confequences of the moft dangerous and deftructive nature to fociety. Tufcany was at that time the moft oppreffed and deplorable of the Italian ftates. To tell you that it is now the happieft would be faying but little; I fhall go much farther, and obferve, that there is no country in Europe, in which the prince rules abfolutely, that is governed with fuch policy and moderation. Leopold knew that the licentioufnefs of his people was the main obftacle to their well-being, and refolved to make that his primary fubject of reform; true it is, that in the arduous attempt he loft many of his fubjects, who migrated to other countries, and has not perhaps as yet fucceeded among the higher order to his wifhes; but of the

common

common people he has almost changed the very character. As I know your sentiments on penal laws, I am persuaded you will much admire him as a legislator, when I inform you that he permits no man to suffer death, whatever be his offence; but by the most rigid slavery (the extreme labour of which is converted to the public benefit) wisely inflicts a punishment far severer and more dreadful. His encouragement of the useful arts has increased the population and riches of his dutchy to a great degree unknown before; and though his people be lightly taxed in proportion to those of the other Italian states, I believe there are few princes whose treasuries are so full as his. The domestic profusion of his subjects he has put a stop to, by holding out an example of œconomy in his own household; and the nobility can appear at court in no other than the plainest and most simple habits. His chief pleasure is the discharge of his duty by promoting the national welfare. Though there be several departments of government with their respective officers,

the

the Grand Duke seems to direct the whole; or, in other words, to be his own minister, for he suffers no measures of consequence to be transacted without his knowledge and approbation.

I shall conclude this letter with a few cursory remarks on the country over which he rules.

The vegetable productions are similar to what they are in other parts of Italy; the principal being corn, vines, olives, and mulberry trees for the silk worm.

The mineral are most various and valuable, consisting of beautiful and different coloured marbles: transparent alabaster: agate: amethysts: chalcedonies: chrystal: allum: salt: saltpetre: earth for colours: silver and copper mines: (none of which however are worked) and a great variety of mineral waters.

Along

Along the Mediterranean lie tracts of marſhy plains, which comprehend no leſs than 1800 ſquare miles, where numerous herds of oxen are fed during the winter and ſpring; but as a noxious vapour exhales in the ſummer months, they make an early retreat (conſcious of the approaching evil) to the hills up the country. I think this breed of cattle much larger than ours in England. They are all of a dark cream colour, and being very tractable, are more uſed for draught than horſes.

The ſwine alſo of Tuſcany I ſhall beg leave to mention, being remarkable for the flavour and delicacy of their fleſh, which I attribute to the cheſnuts they feed upon. But the moſt lucrative buſineſs of this country is the anchovy and tunney fiſheries. They begin on the firſt of July, and end about the middle of Auguſt. The beſt anchovies are found off the iſland of Gorgona; and though the fiſhermen take annually from ten to fifteen thouſand barrels, that weigh 40 lb. each, this does not amount to

LETTER XV. 303

to half the quantity that the English ships demand. They must be very attentive to cure the fish immediately on their being taken out of the sea, or they spoil. The tunney is caught off the isle of Elba, to the amount of 450,000 lbs. every season that proves favourable.

In addition to the many agreeable things at Florence, I cannot but mention to you our hotel; it is kept by one Meggit, an Englishman, and is, in my opinion, equal to any I ever entered, either in or out of England. We find every thing served up in the English manner, which I am unfashionable enough to prefer to all other. Meggit is not only a good innkeeper, but very moderate in his charges.

As I have no more to say to you, adieu.

LETTER

LETTER XVI.

Leghorn, Nov. 15, 1787.

THREE weeks, three little weeks, that seemed no more than three happy days, did we pass at Florence; and dedicated never less than four out of the twenty-four hours to the grand gallery, and the muses. At length, great ideas of Rome and the capitol roused us from these inactive scenes of pleasure, and persuaded our departure. How restless is the human disposition, how impatient for novelty! Having taken one parting look at the tribune, and Madonna della Sedia, we bade adieu to this charming city, and travelled along the southern bank of the Arno to Pisa. You well remember, that Pisa was once the capital of an independent, a warlike, and a commercial republic, that disputed the dominion of the Italian and Grecian seas with Genoa, and withstood all the attempts of Florence to reduce it, until 1509, when it was forced to capitulate, and become subject to its conquerors. From its present state it would be difficult to believe that fo many large fleets had belonged to it, were it not fufficiently authenticated by hiftory, efpecially as it is no longer a maritime city, the fea having receded to the diftance of twelve miles, and the Arno being (if I miftake not) much too fhallow for gallies. Its noble manfions empty and in decay; its filent ftreets, and general appearance, are melancholy proofs of its altered condition. Perhaps no people of modern date have been more attentive to the embellifhment of their native city than the former inhabitants of Pifa; their commerce in the Mediterranean gave them continual opportunities of enriching it with the fpoils of Greece, which they have moft largely collected; as the profufion of Greek marbles with which they have covered their churches indicates. The cathedral, though Gothic, is one of the moft fuperb edifices I have ever feen; for befides its rich coating, it is in many places fupported by columns of granate and porphyry, fome of which are of one piece. Is it not more than probable that thefe marbles were the ornaments of Grecian temples, long the admiration of the moſt ingenious people that ever exiſted? and now that they ſhould glaze over the defects of this building; which, though admired, has for me no beauty but what it receives from them. Oh! how much is it to be lamented, that the Piſans had not, inſtead of demoliſhing thoſe noble monuments of antiquity for their rich materials, imitated their orders of architecture, and introduced them to the age in which they lived, as the only good models to adopt. But this was not to be expected in the eleventh century, when ſuperſtition was ſo predominant, that ſcience and the polite arts were conſidered as inimical to religion. Near, but not adjoining to the cathedral, is the Battiſtèrio, or Baptiſtery, which is equally remarkable for its rich marbles: its form is circular, and its gates of ſculptured bronze, but the moſt remarkable object is the celebrated leaning tower; of which I well remember to have heard, before I knew that Piſa was in Italy. It ſtands in the ſame ſpacious area as the cathedral and

baptiſtery,

baptiftery, and is, in my opinion, a very noble ftructure, being, as the perfon who fhewed it us juftly obferved, formed like a cylinder. It is in height 180 feet, and projects fourteen and a half over its bafis,—the foundation having on that fide funk under the weight; fo that you fee its inclination is juft three feet more than the tower of Caerfilly Caftle in Glamorganfhire. Near thefe buildings are long and fpacious cloifters, called Il Campo Santo, which the good people of the place regard with a veneration that borders on devotion. During the crufades, the republic of Pifa, as well as Genoa, furnifhed the belligerent powers of Europe with fleets for tranfporting their troops and ftores to Palæftine. Thefe fleets brought back what was confidered an invaluable treafure—heavy cargoes of earth fcraped from near the holy fepulchre at Jerufalem, and carried to the fea fhore on camels backs. The tranfports having fafely landed this facred lading at Pifa, it was immediately conveyed by all defcriptions of people to thefe cloifters, which were in consequence made a burying-place for those citizens who would pay the sum demanded for their interment, which I hear is not inconsiderable. I had the presumption to ask the sexton what was the benefit that dead bodies received from being put into this mould. By way of answer, he stared me full in the face, and then turning to our guide, said, Non son Christiani sti Signori *? Non, non, son Inglesi †, replied the other, and walked on. The only tomb to which I paid any attention, was that of Algarotti, the inscription of which tells you it was written by his royal patron, the late king of Prussia.

Algarotti, Ovidii Æmulo,
Newtoni Discipulo,
Fredericus ‡.

In returning from this place to the inn, we were met by a large troop of galley

---

* These gentlemen are not Christians.

† No, no, they are Englishmen.

‡ Frederic, in honour of Algarotti, the rival of Ovid, the disciple of Newton.

slaves, whose condition is so extremely severe, that I think the most timorous would seize with transport any opportunity of putting an end to his existence; and yet, instead of pitying, I rather exulted in their misery, as most of them have perpetrated crimes that merit even this, the worst of tortures, which is indeed much too mild, for the monster who is the subject of the following anecdote. In the year 1769 one Rossiter, a young Irishman, came to Leghorn in search of adventure, with no other recommendation than the deportment of a gentleman, added to a fine figure and countenance. Soon after his arrival, a lady, whose personal property was considerable, saw, and became violently enamoured of him; which was soon succeeded by a direct proposal on her part (no uncommon thing in Italy) to live with her. As he had been previously informed of her circumstances, and was pleased with her person, he immediately closed with the offer; and they in consequence resided together in all the warmth of love and intimacy of marriage.

riage. Her paſſion for him had at firſt prompted her to difregard the common law of modeſty; after cohabitation it grew to ſuch exceſs, as to trample on all prudence; for not ſatisfied with having purchaſed for him a lieutenancy in the Tuſcan army, ſhe anticipated his every wiſh, more than ſupported his profuſion: and on being obliged to viſit her relations in a diſtant part of Italy, intruſted him in her abſence with her jewels, her money, and, in ſhort, every thing ſhe owned. Can you ſuppoſe that a man ſo cheriſhed, and ſo relied on, could betray a confidence of this nature? Should you wonder at it, how much greater will be your ſurpriſe, when I tell you that he not only robbed her of her property, but of her life. She returned to Leghorn ſooner than ſhe had intended, being pregnant by this monſter, who received her with every mark of unaltered affection, but that ſame night murdered her in the very bedchamber that had ſo often been the guilty ſcene of her weakneſs and affection, a place that ſhould of all other have been inviolable.

The

The deed was soon discovered, and Rossiter apprehended, judged, and condemned to the gallies for life. Previously to the execution of this sentence, he was led out before the troops of the garrison, where his sword was broken over his head, his uniform stripped from him for the coarse habit of a galley slave; and thus, with a halter about his neck, was he delivered over to his punishment, under every mark of degradation and infamy. Yet even this wretch, thus stigmatized, could create affection in the female sex, who took every opportunity of supplying him with food; and one, a woman of condition, exerted all her interest to obtain his release for the purpose (as it is said) of marrying him. But the good Leopold rejected the petition with horror, declaring that he should look upon that man as a disgrace to his court, who could intercede on so wicked an occasion. How more than brutal was the affection that could attach itself to such a monster as Rossiter?

Pisa seems to be the hospital of Italy, from the salubrity of its climate, and the virtues of its baths; but as our object there was happily not the re establishment of health, we departed early on the morning after our arrival, and in less than two hours got to Leghorn; a city that for commerce and population has far exceeded my expectations. The streets quite swarm with busy faces, insomuch, that I think few commercial towns in England are more alive. The ground on which it stands was ceded for Sarzana, a place almost unknown on the frontiers of Tuscany to the family of Medici by the republic of Genoa; which would now most willingly regain it, even by the sacrifice of half its magnificent capital, for the purpose of re-establishing its ruined commerce. How powerfully does experience convince us, not only in this, but in various other instances, of the inability of our understandings to calculate future events from present action. Had the Genoese foreseen the consequences of this cession, not Florence itself would have been

accepted

accepted in exchange for the marſhy and unwholeſome ſpot on which this celebrated city now ſtands. The decline of the one, and the riſe of the other, may be dated from the time that Robert Dudley, duke of Northumberland, perſuaded Ferdinand di Medici the IId. to declare it a free port. Since this epoch it is, from great encouragement, wife regulations, and treaties of amity between Tuſcany and the pirate ſtates of Barbary, become the moſt conſiderable emporium of the Mediterranean, Marſeilles not excepted; nor do its advantages flow altogether from its immediate commerce, as the greater number of ſhips employed by Britain, Holland, and the northern ſtates of Europe in the Levant trade, ſtop here for the purpoſe of performing their quarantine on their return, which is moſt admirably regulated, and rigidly obſerved. No nation frequents it more than our own. We import Britiſh merchandiſes, and carry away anchovies, oils, wines, marbles, Parmeſan cheeſe, dried fruits, &c. but the moſt lucrative branch of trade is that of coral, the fabric

of

of which (principally managed by the Jews) is the moſt conſiderable of the kind in Europe. The quality of this petrified marine vegetable is ſo various, that they reckon no leſs than fourteen ſpecies of it. The beſt is brought from the coaſt of Africa, Sardinia, and Corſica; but the largeſt quantity is fiſhed up at Leghorn. They grind it into different forms; the round is ſent to America, the oval to the coaſt of Africa, and the larger pieces to Conſtantinople, where the Turks make uſe of them for buttons, &c. It is no wonder that I meet ſuch crowds, when I find the population of this town, which is far from large, to be above 60,000 ſouls. Though the general appearance of the houſes be not ſtriking, yet many of the ſhops vie for ſize and brilliancy with thoſe of London, and the coffee-houſes are the moſt ſuperb I have ever ſeen. The port is ſo crowded with ſhipping, that it was with difficulty I examined it in a ſmall boat. It ſeems very commodious, but is ſo ſhallow in the middle, that ſhips are obliged to enter on each ſide. The quay that defends it from

the

the sea is the nobleſt I ever beheld. You will readily ſuppoſe that a place of ſo great population, and ſuch extenſive commerce as Leghorn, contributes largely to the revenues of the Grand Duke, which amount to five or ſix hundred thouſand pounds ſterling, a very moderate ſum when compared with thoſe of England. We can ſay little of the ſociety of this place, as we have been here ſo ſhort a time; but the hoſpitality of the Engliſh inhabitants is very great, particularly of Mr. Darby, a gentleman in the banking and mercantile buſineſs, whoſe entertainments are moſt ſplendid. We have official letters from Lord Carmarthen for our conſul Mr. Udney; but hear he is abſent in purſuit of paintings, in which he deals very largely. His place is extremely lucrative. I am told that Sir John Dick, one of his predeceſſors, cleared no leſs than 50,000 l. by a commiſſion for victualling the Ruſſian fleet in the laſt Turkiſh war, given him by Count Orlow, who made uſe of his houſe when he lay at Leghorn. His mode of obtaining this is ſtill repre-

ſented

sented here as a fine stroke of policy. It was in a manner determined that one Fraink, a German merchant, should have this employment; but Sir John, knowing the fastidious and vain character of Orlow, fitted up a large house in the most elegant English style, dividing it into summer and winter apartments. The bait took; the Russian gave it the preference to Mr. Fraink's, and its owner the very lucrative commission to which I have alluded.

Good bye,

LETTER XVII.

Rome, Nov. 25th, 1787.

WE were much pleased with the country between Leghorn and Sienna, which is hilly and cultivated; but the prospect did not compensate for the disappointment and delay that we experienced on the road. Our countrymen at Florence had gone for Rome on the morning that we left Pisa, and as their carriages were numerous, they did not leave a single post-horse; we were therefore obliged to creep on part of the way with a melancholy pair just taken from the plough, which retarded our arrival at Sienna to ten at night. The next morning we were delighted with the situation and general appearance of the place. The cathedral (as it usually happens in provincial towns) is the most interesting object, being coated with slabs of black and white marble, and ornamented with columns of porphyry, verde antique, &c.

It

It seems to be a received opinion, that every country has a particular city in it, eminent above the others for the purity and just pronunciation of its language. I know not that this is so in England, but in Italy, Germany, and France, it certainly is. In the first Sienna is distinguished on this account. Indeed, except in Tuscany and at Rome, the Italian language is so corrupt, that the best educated people of one state would not, without difficulty, understand those of another. At Florence it is correctly spoken, but ill pronounced; for the letter *C* is generally founded as a guttural, in the same manner as the Greek χ *ought* to be. A Florentine would pronounce the two first lines of Tasso, as if written

    Χanto l'arme pietofe c'l Χapitano
    Χhe'l gran fepolχro liberó di Χriſto.

But at Sienna they speak the language of Florence with the Roman utterance, or La lingua Florentina in bocca Romana. There the conversation of the *common* people seems, as it were, formed on the model of the best

LETTER XVII.

authors. It would confequently be a more proper place for the academy della Crufca than the capital, in which all the refident members of that once refpectable fociety adopt the local pronunciation.

We were two days and a half on the road between Sienna and Rome. The firft night we lay in the palace of Radicofani, which is precifely what credulity and fuperftition would call a haunted houfe,—a lofty and extenfive building, fituate near the fummit of rocky mountains almoft bare of vegetation. In it are long and difmal paffages, and a labyrinth of naked rooms, through which reigns continual filence, unlefs when interrupted by the hollow roar of winds, or the clattering of fhutters. I wandered over the whole, and each dreary chamber feemed

"By many a foul and midnight murder fed."

The accommodation of this caravanfcrais was, as we expected, correfpondent to its appearance; however, we happily found a large quantity of dry wood, which made a good

a good fire, and after a moſt infufficient ſupper of hot water ſoup, an animal which I would hope, if not believe, was a ſtarved rabbit, and macaroni, we bolted the door of our apartment, dragged our beds to the fire, and ſlept in our cloaths till daylight. Near this place is the little village of Chiuſi, formerly Cluſium, the capital of Porſenna's kingdom. We found no object that particularly engaged our attention between Radicofani and Viterbo, except the Volſinian lake, now Il Lago di Bolſena. This pleaſing piece of water is thirty miles in circumference, and at preſent, as in the elder days of Rome (when frequented for its cool and ſilent retirement from the noiſe and hurry of the forum) overhung with groves of oak and ilex. We lay that night at Viterbo, and proceeding the next morning, travelled through a country that was not beautiful, but highly intereſting, from having been the ſchool of Roman patriotiſm and enterprize, wherein that republic, from the conqueſt of theſe little ſtates, learnt to ſubdue the world. Over the ſame
ground

ground as we paſſed, how often have the legions, when virtue and ſimplicity were their characteriſtic qualities, returned from victory? and, on the contrary, when univerſal conqueſt had introduced corruption, luxury, and effeminacy, how often have their degenerate ſons waited in fearful ſuſpence the approach of the northern world, marching by the ſame rout to the plunder of the capital? Every hill, from its vicinity, ſeemed to indicate, that on its ſummit had been ſtationed horſemen to watch the progreſs of the Barbarian invaders, increaſing by their report the panick of the defenceleſs city. With theſe, and many other reflections of the ſame nature, did we amuſe ourſelves, when looking forward, at length the gilded croſs of St. Peter (which from the ſun's radiance ſhone with all the luſtre of a meteor) appeared. The nearer we came to Rome, the more our attention was engaged with the ſurrounding objects, and every thing pleaſed us; though on ſober reflection, I believe, our imaginations more than once raiſed buildings that

that never had exifted, and converted the remains of a cottage into the ruins of a temple—a trifling fault, if attributed to no fmall ftock of enthufiafm. On paffing the Ponte-mola, or Pons-milvius, we looked down upon the fame Tyber that Conftantine faw, when he purfued Maxentius over this bridge, and in a few minutes entered Rome by the Flaminian gate, now called Il Porto del Popolo.

The modern city, which ftands on the Campus Martius, &c. is thirteen miles in circumference, and fuppofed to contain 160,000 inhabitants. To facilitate the attempt of giving you a curfory defcription of it, and the remains of ancient Rome, I have arranged the many fubjects which have principally engaged our attention, and fhall prefent them to you in the fame order as they appeared to us. We began with things of modern date; but to confefs the truth, though thefe were inexpreffibly interefting, we could not withftand the temptation of our vicinity to the feven hills,

but

but occasionally wandered among their auguſt and venerable ruins. I think no city in its general appearance can unite more magnificence and poverty than this; as adjoining the moſt ſuperb palaces, we ſee the meaneſt habitations; and temples, the boaſted ornaments of antiquity, choked up by ſheds and cottages. From the drawings I had ſeen of this place, I expected to find the ſtreets at leaſt as broad as in London, but was diſappointed. Il Corſo, the principal and moſt admired, is little more ſo than St. Martin's lane; but this mode of building their ſtreets ſo narrow, is done with the view of intercepting, as much as poſſible, the ſun's heat; it is a cuſtom tranſmitted from the ancient Romans, and I believe (even in deſpite of ſuch authority as Homer to the contrary) that the Greeks and all the ſouthern nations adopted it, as the conſequent of neceſſity, not choice. The ſquares are neither numerous, nor well-built, but the public fountains have great beauty and grandeur; the moſt remarkable are thoſe of Navonna, Pauli, Trevi, and St. Peter's.

The superb basilick of St. Peter's is the largest building that ever existed; as neither the temple of Jerusalem, nor those of Ephesus, Eleusis, or of Olympian Jupiter at Athens, could (from what history has recorded of them) be ranked with it in this respect.

The semicircular colonnades that inclose its spacious court: the Egyptian obelisk in the center brought from Heliopolis to Rome by Caligula: and the before-mentioned fountains on each side, which continually throw up columns of water sufficient to fill the bed of a small river, are the grandest objects of the kind I ever beheld. The front of this edifice is generally thought less noble than that of St. Paul's in London, which was built in imitation of St. Peter's, and indeed I am of this opinion; but when I view the whole crowned with its majestic dome 617 feet in circumference, I am so convinced of its general superiority, that I would not derogate from St. Paul's, by an injudicious comparison of their appearance.

ance. The pediment of the portico is supported by twelve columns, over which is an open gallery, where the Pope in paffion-week pronounces, during a fhort and awful interval of filence from the din of cannon, bells, drums, and mufical inftruments, his folemn benediction to the multitude before him. Though we gazed with fingular aftonifhment and delight on the exterior of this auguft temple, yet we were, if poffible, more charmed with its infide. In its different parts, though of immenfe magnitude, the moft exact proportion is obferved. The form is that of a right-angled crofs, on the interfection of which, and immediately under the dome, ftands the high altar, covered with a fuperb baldachin, or canopy of bronze, which is fupported by four twifted pillars of the fame metal. This, though ninety feet in height, feems low, from the very fuperior elevation of the roof; before it is the defcent to the facred grottos, or ground-work of the old church. There, in long and gloomy alleys, they fhewed us by torch-light the tombs of former Popes;

but thefe caverns were fo little interefting, that I believe we fhall not make them a fecond vifit, and yet I received fome pleafure in contemplating an urn of oriental granate, that holds the afhes of Adrian the IVth, *becaufe he was an Englifhman,* and the only one that ever afcended the apoftolical throne. His name was Nicholas Brakefpear, of Langley in Hertfordfhire. He was elected Pope in 1154, the fame year as Henry the IId. was crowned king of England.

The paintings of St. Peter's are not (as we expected) of the firft clafs; but to fupply the defect, they have put up copies of the beft in Mofaic—an art brought to perfection at Rome, as the pictures from Raphael's transfiguration, and the archangel Michael of Guido, fully prove. There are here confeffionary boxes, wherein the priefts of, I believe, every nation in Europe, attend daily at a certain hour, to hear and abfolve all comers. The language of each box is written over it in Italian, as Pella Lingua Tedefca,

LETTER XVII. 327

Tedefca, Spagnuola, Inglefe, &c. The monuments too are remarkable for their defigns and fculpture. Among many we particularly noticed that of Chriftina queen of Sweden (on which is reprefented in bas relief her abjuration of the Proteftant religion) and another of Maria Clementina Sobiefki, mother of the prefent pretender. The epitaph calls her Regina di Inghilterra. But the moft extraordinary object in this place is a brazen image of St. Peter in a fitting attitude, being an idol of general veneration. The Pope worfhips it every day between twelve and one. I have often been a fpectator of this moft ridiculous ceremony. He enters the church, attended by certain officers of his houfehold, and, having croffed himfelf with holy water, walks up to the ftatue, where in fuppliant pofture he repeats a prayer, then putting his bare head under the foot which projects over the pedeftal, prays again to his metallic divinity; this done, he kiffes the toe, and departs, bleffing the people who kneel around him. I of courfe fuppofed that this

Y 4 miracle-

miracle-working image was a celestial gift, but to my utter aſtoniſhment learnt, that the compoſition was, before it received its faſcinating form, part of the well known ſtatue of Jupiter Capitolinus——would it had ever been ſo!

I am ſo enraptured with this ſuperb building, that I generally viſit it every day; the warmth on going into it from the cold, is one of the moſt agreeable ſenſations I ever experienced, a ſenſation that I ſhould ſuppoſe can be exceeded only by its cool air, during the dog days of an Italian ſummer. I concluded that this change was occaſioned by artificial heat, but am informed to the contrary: however, I do not give this intelligence the moſt implicit credence.

When we had ſeen and reſeen every thing that the aiſles and chapels contained, we aſcended to the top, though not without ſome difficulty and danger. There we had (as you will imagine) the fineſt bird's-eye view in the world, the height from its court being

being 471 feet. In descending we visited the whispering gallery, and a variety of other places into which our guides conducted us.

The next church I shall notice is St. John di Lateran, so called from standing on the site of a palace that belonged to the Laterani, an old Roman family; one of whom, Plautius, was put to death by Nero for a supposed conspiracy against him. In 324 the emperor Constantine erected a church and palace here, and is reported (though with as much truth I suppose, as there is in the assertion of St. Peter having resided twenty-three years at Rome) to have received baptism in it from the hands of St. Silvester. By this circumstance, whether real or fictitious, St. John di Lateran ranks as first of the Latin churches. The Pope, soon after his election, takes personal possession of it, as the cathedral of Rome. It is stiled * Ecclesiarum, Urbis et Orbis,

---

* The Mother and Head of Churches of the City and World.

Mater

Mater et Caput, and held in singular veneration. In the square or place before it, is raised the largest of the Egyptian obelisks in this city. It is one entire piece of red granate full of hieroglyphics, and supposed to have been placed in a temple of the sun at Thebes 1577 years antecedent to the Christian æra by Ramesses-Miamun, who, according to archbishop Usher, was the Pharaoh of Scripture. By the orders of Constantine and his son Constantius, it was with extreme difficulty brought from Egypt to Rome, and erected in the Circus maximus, whence it was removed by that great man Pope Sixtus the Vth to its present situation. It measures without the base 115 feet, but was considerably higher; of such magnitude indeed, that Augustus Cæsar thought it impossible to transport it to Rome [*].

The columns, fonts, and part of the pavement in this church, are of the most rare and precious marbles. The altar is

[*] See Pliny, Lib. 36. Cap. 8, 9.

covered

covered with a canopy of gilded bronze, supported by four channelled columns of the same metal, taken, alas, from the temple of Jupiter Capitolinus. Its treasures were very considerable, but are now no more, yet there is still what is infinitely more valued than the largest masses of gold and silver, namely, a collection of the most wonderful relics. As they were repeated to us, I took the liberty of inscribing them in my pocket-book, and these are the most remarkable.

" The staircase of Pontius Pilate's palace, by which our Saviour ascended to the judgment hall."

" The table on which he ate the last supper with his disciples."

" A tooth (I believe a *jaw* tooth) of St. Peter."

" The skull of a certain Saint Pancratius, who sweated blood three days and three nights during the burning of this church, when set on fire by hereticks."

" A gown

" A gown of the Virgin Mary."

" A cloak of our Saviour."

" The napkin with which he wiped the apoſtles feet."

" The purple garment, in which the Jews cloathed him before his crucifixion."

" A large piece of the *true* crofs, and as many more of thefe rarities as would fill a ſtorehoufe."

The original palace adjoining the church was the pontifical refidence, till the removal of the fee to Avignon in 1305, but is now never occupied as fuch.

The other churches moſt deferving of attention are, the Santa Maria Maggiore, and Santa Maria degli Angeli. The latter belongs to a Carthufian monaftery, and is built where the celebrated baths of Dioclefian ftood, in form of a Greek crofs, defigned by Michael Angelo Buonarotti. If I exclude St. Peter's, there is no church in Rome that pleafes me fo much as this.

It

LETTER XVII.

It is not, as they generally are, gorgeous from a profusion of paintings, velvet hanging, and marbles; but the plan and noble simplicity of its architecture charms me beyond expression, and makes me often revisit its silent walls. Here let me conclude the article of churches; for to proceed would be an endless labour, there being from three to four hundred at Rome, many of which we have visited with pleasure.

And now I shall introduce you to the Vatican, the largest palace in Christendom, said to contain 13,000 chambers and closets. It stands close to St. Peter's, the perspective of which (I should have before observed) loses much of its effect by their junction, as the exterior of the vatican but ill accords with the grand and regular appearance of the church, being an immense pile of building without order, raised by different architects, and at different times. The principal entrance is from the court of St. Peter's, up a noble staircase, guarded by Swifs soldiers,

diers, who, like the beef eaters of England, retain their ancient drefs, which is of fingular appearance. Near the landing-place is a chapel built from a defign of Baccio Fintelli, by Pope Sixtus the IVth, in 1473, from whom it was called La Capella Seftina; it is remarkable for a famous picture by Buonarotti, that occupies one end of it, reprefenting the laft judgment. There probably never was fuch a production of original and extravagant genius as this painting; the defign, various groups of figures, attitudes, anatomy, expreffion, and deep colouring of the whole, are inconceivably ftriking. The eye is weary in examining this fingular work; it therefore raifes my wonder, that Michael Angelo could perfevere to the completion of it; for genius is generally impatient, and unable to dwell long upon the fame fubject.

The library of this palace is fuppofed to contain the moft numerous and valuable collection of books, &c. in the world. On going into it, we looked up an immenfe room,

room, which had little the appearance of what it is, the volumes being shut up in armories. It is said to contain 120,000 in printed and manuscript; but this assertion I disbelieve. We found many of them rare and curious, particularly two bibles, one of the sixth century; and another remarkably large, which had belonged to the dukes d'Urbino, of whom the Jews at Venice would have bought it for its weight in gold: the work of Henry the VIIIth on the seven sacraments, and his original letters to Anne Bolleyn: several literal compositions on Papyrus, &c. &c. There are also Etruscan vases, gems, medals, bronzes, and a variety of other curiosities. I was surprized to find no other people than the librarians here, especially as it is open every morning in the week (Sundays and holydays excepted) for all who wish to read or transcribe.

The next thing I shall mention to you is what I most admire and most lament—the mouldering fresco-paintings of Raphael.

In

In the principal court-yard of the vatican are three galleries, one above another; in the loweſt of which the conclaves are held. Their cielings are painted from the deſigns of this unequalled maſter, and ſome parts he painted himſelf. From the ſecond we entered a ſuite of apartments, three of which were *for the moſt part* done by him, and one *entirely*; wherein we ſaw his ſchool of Athens; which, though in decay, is ſtill the beſt picture in the world.—Do you recollect my mention of its cartoon in the Boromean muſeum at Milan? I have often, on viewing the works of theſe great painters, lamented, that their genius ſhould, from the narrow and bigot temper of their own times, be entirely confined to religious ſubjects, and wiſhed much to ſee the illuſtrious actions of antiquity repreſented by their pencils. The ſchool of Athens, in great meaſure, falls under this idea; for although Raphael, without any regard to time or place, has here introduced philoſophers, &c. who lived in different centuries and countries, yet, the ſubject is, in my humble opinion, as intereſt-

ing

LETTER XVII.

ing as can be chosen. The scene is in a portico at Athens; up a few steps, in the center of which are two of the most venerable and majestic figures I ever saw, intended for Plato and Aristotle, who are reasoning before their respective disciples, ranged on each side of them, and listening with all the attention and wonder that such profound wisdom and eloquence would naturally create. Near this group are Socrates and Alcibiades; the former seems to be winding up his arguments to a conclusion, and the latter charmed and convinced by their simplicity and truth. Sitting on the steps, and alone, is the Cynic Diogenes, intent upon a book before him; and besides these, we discover Periander, Pythagoras, Zoroaster, Empedocles, and many other great men, all in employments or attitudes descriptive of what they professed and taught. As disciples, Raphael has represented Ferdinand the IId, duke of Milan, and Francis di Rovere duke d'Urbino, together with his master Pietro Perugino, and himself. In his face, though simple, I perceived

ceived traits of that divine genius which he poffeffed. Day after day have I examined this picture, and tried to difcover fome defective part, but in vain, every thing I fee in it convinces me that nothing of the kind was ever fuperior, nor I believe equal, fince the age of Pericles. I fhall conclude this letter with the Clementine mufeum, a collection of the moft exquifite fculpture in the world, begun by the great and good Ganganelli, from whofe affumed name of Clement it was called. It ftands at the extremity of a corridor, from five to fix hundred paces in length, and near that part of the vatican called Il Belvederé, from its rich and extenfive view over Rome, the Tyber, and the furrounding country. On entering it, the firft object that prefented itfelf was a tomb of Pub. Cn. Scipio, found in the monument of that illuftrious family lately difcovered near Rome. The characters on it are extremely rude—a ftrong proof of the little progrefs refinement had made among the Romans at that time. Near it is a famous trunk of Hercules, called

called Il torso; which, when whole, must have been a statue of the first class, as the body is one of the finest pieces of sculpture I ever saw, but the Laocoon and Apollo prevented our examining these, and many other statues of the collection as much as we wished; having the same effect on us, as the magnet on the needle. The first Michael Angelo calls a prodigy of art, and so indeed it is. Pliny too speaks of it as wonderful*. But what must the Apollo be? If some convent had got possession of this statue when first discovered, and declared it to have fallen from heaven into their church, the declaration would be received with more faith than the many falsehoods of this nature, which are told of their worm-eaten images, as the perfection of the sculpture would give an air of probability to the assertion. I assure you that since I have seen it, my ideas of

---

* He says it was formed out of one stone by Agesander, Polydorus and Athenodorus,—Rhodians.

See his description of it in the 5th Chap. of his thirty-sixth book of Natural History.

man have been confiderably raifed, to find him capable of reaching fuch excellence in the art of imitation, or I fhould rather fay in forming a marble image that far exceeds any thing human. I am fure the ftatues of Prometheus were never more calculated to excite the jealoufy and refentment of Jupiter than this, as it really appears to be a work beyond the reach of art—fomething divine. The deity is (as I think) reprefented in act of flaying the Cyclops with his arrows. The attitude, proportion, ftature, and countenance, (in the laft of which appear extreme manly beauty, dignity, refentment, contempt, and triumph) are fo rendered, as not only to defy the flighteft objection of criticifm, but that even all the united powers of conception and art could not give it any additional beauty. After this ftatue and the Laocoon are the Meleager, Antinous, and Cleopatra, which you would idolize in England, befides bufts of Jupiter, Homer, &c. and little images of birds and beafts finifhed to perfection.

Such

Such is the Vatican, which contains the beſt ſculpture, the beſt paintings, and the beſt library in the world; to which if you add its ſituation, command of proſpect, and St. Peter's church, will you not, when all theſe, with many ſecondary items are conſidered, allow that few places can be equally intereſting to a *liberal* mind ? but this is an unneceſſary queſtion to one who is ſo fully in poſſeſſion of that bleſſing.

So adieu.

LETTER XVIII.

Rome, Dec. 8th, 1787.

WE have seen so many palaces since I last wrote to you, that I find it as impracticable to enter on their separate description, as it was to send you a detail of the several churches in this city. However, it will be necessary to make some mention of them, because they are in every respect the most magnificent and interesting in the world. The first we visited after the Vatican, was that of Il Monte Cavallo, which the Pope makes his summer residence. It stands on the Mons Quirinus, one of the most elevated spots in Rome, and consequently less within the reach of the noxious vapours, which exhale, in that season, from the marshes and flats of the environs. Though not half as roomy as the Vatican, the apartments are very numerous and well-proportioned; but in their furniture we were disappointed, if I except the pictures, of which there is a very noble collection.

Many

LETTER XVIII.

Many of them were put there by the present pontiff, who is a dilettante of the first order. Before the palace is a large square, in which are the two celebrated Colossean horses and their managers in white marble, each supposed to be a representative of Alexander and Bucephalus, done by Phidias and Praxiteles in emulation of each other; but unfortunately for this conjecture Phidias lived near a century antecedent to the time of Alexander and Praxiteles. I am rather inclined to think them the work of the same artist, who, whether either of the above named, or any other, merits infinite praise for their bold design and beauty of execution. They were brought from Greece by Constantine, and put in his baths, whence they were removed to this place by Pope Sixtus the Vth, and raised on two lofty pedestals under the direction of the architect Fontana. Their forged inscriptions, Opus Phidiæ, and Opus Praxitelis, have propagated the error of their origin: In another place we read

Sixtus V. PONT. MAX.

Colofsèa hæc figna, temporis vi deformata reftituit veteribufque repofitis infcriptionibus, e proximis Conftantineanis Thermis, in quirinalem aream tranftulit.

An. Sal. MDLXXXIX*.

Near this is the palace Rofpigliofi, which contains many valuable pictures, but the moft remarkable is the Aurora of Guido, painted on the cieling of a fummer-houfe. It reprefents the god of day guiding the chariot of the fun up the afcent of heaven, drawn by four celeftial horfes abreaft, preceded by Cupid and Aurora, and attended on each fide by the happy hours, reprefented as beautiful nymphs, whofe hands gracefully linked together are emblematic of the uninterrupted lapfe of time. The whole is fo wonderfully conceived, grouped, and

---

* The Sovereign Pontiff Sixtus Vth.

Reftored thefe Coloffean ftatues injured by time, and having renewed their ancient infcriptions, removed them from the adjoining Thermæ of Conftantine, to the quirinal fquare.

In the year of grace 1589.

finifhed,

finifhed, as to feem actually mounting on
the clouds. The fame fubject has been
painted in a villa near Rome by Guercino,
but the picture is very inferior to this. The
palace Farnesé and Villa Medici have been
ftripped of their invaluable collections by
the king of Naples and the grand duke of
Tufcany, to whom they devolved by fucceffion, but the lofs is fcarcely perceived
in a city fo opulent in every production of
the liberal arts as Rome. The fuperb houfes
of Colonna, Doria, Borghefé, Juftiniani,
Mattei, Barbarini, Spada, and many others,
are full of the moft exquifite fculpture and
painting, befides collections of intaglios,
cameos, bronzes, medals, &c. &c. infomuch, that a houfe, even of the fecond order
here, is more deferving of regard in this
refpect, than the fplendid caftle of Verfailles.
The firft of thefe is fuppofed to contain the
beft private gallery of pictures in the world,
though I muft fay I prefer that of Doria.
As you exprefs a wifh to know the paintings which pleafe me moft, I fhall obferve,
that in the Altieri palace are two landfkips

by

by Claude, the moft charming imitation of rural nature I ever faw. In one, this great artift has introduced the landing of Æneas in Italy, and in the other a paftoral facrifice. If fuch hiftorical fcenes were always reprefented in landfkip painting, how much more interefting would they make the pictures, than what they generally are? They would be (if well done) like the poetry of Milton fet to the mufick of Handel. Among thofe of the prince Borghefé, I moft admired a Macchiavel and Cæfar Borgia by Titian; the Laft Supper by Caravaggio: and a portrait of the fame Borgia by Raphael. In the palace Juftiniani, Chrift before Pilate, by Hundtorft, here called Gerardo delle Notte, from his pictures being generally night-fcenes. In the Mattei collection a St. Peter half length, by Guido: Judas betraying Chrift, by Gerardo delle Notte, and the woman taken in adultery brought before our Saviour, by Pietro da Cortona. Thefe, and at leaft twenty more in the different galleries, &c. are inexpreffibly ftriking, and confequently have engaged

much

much of our attention. In the Spada palace is the Coloffean ftatue of Pompey, under which Cæfar fell when flain by the confpirators—

"Even at the bafe of Pompey's ftatue,
"Which all the while ran blood."

The prince Borghefé is the moft opulent of the Roman nobility; exclufive of his magnificent palace he has a villa near the city, the contents of which are invaluable. It was built by the cardinal Scipio, nephew of Paul the Vth, the founder of the family, and is furrounded by pleafure grounds three miles in circumference. The front is ornamented, or, I would rather fay, crowded with baffo and alto relievos' of Grecian fculpture. As I fhould tire both you and myfelf, were I to go into a defcription of the ftatues we faw there, I fhall only obferve that a Curtius plunging on horfeback into the gulph in alto relievo: a foldier (and not I think, as fome fuppofe, a gladiator) rufhing forward to the onfet of battle: a Silenus holding the infant Bacchus in his arms: an hermaphrodite, and a dying Seneca,

neca, are in my opinion only inferior to the Apollo, the Venus di Medici, and the Laocoon. Nor is the villa Albani lefs remarkable than this. The collection of sculpture, &c. is indeed larger, but I think not so interesting. It was begun and completed by the cardinal Alexander Albani, a man of singular taste, and arranged by that first of antiquarians Winkelman. On seeing it we lamented that so many wonders were assembled in the same place, and wished there had been lefs to examine. The former of these villas is under the direction of Mr. Moore, an English painter, whose picture (you may remember) pleased me so much in the gallery of Florence; and he seems to have set out every thing to the greatest advantage, but unfortunately the prince, who has not the least judgment in things of this nature, frequently interferes, and introduces what he confiders amendments to the collection, but which in reality are only proofs of his utter want of taste. As an instance of this, in the center of one of the apartments is a piece of sculpture by

LETTER XVIII.

by Bernini, reprefenting Apollo and Daphne at the moment that he reaches her, and fhe is metamorphofed into a laurel. In the fame room is a landfkip done by Mr. Moore, in which the prince thought it would be *very clever* to introduce an imitation of this fculpture. Moore (as I hear) not only expoftulated with him on the glaring abfurdity of fuch an idea, but abfolutely refufed to comply with his requeft. This, however, did not prevent the execution of his defign; for he employed a miferable dawber, who has inferted the Apollo and Daphne, and ruined the landfkip. Exclufive of thefe are feveral other villas, which we have feen; but I fhall pafs them over in filence, as I apprehend I have already been rather tedious upon the fubject.

On the banks of the Tyber, and on the fame fide of it as St. Peter's, is the caftle of St. Angelo, built on the foundation of the emperor Adrian's maufoléum, which was once fo remarkable for its columns, its ftatues, statues, and its Parian marble. Now there are no other remains of its grandeur than a ball of bronze in the Vatican, which crowned its cupola, and was suppofed to inurn the afhes of its Imperial founder. The prefent building was firſt ufed as a place of defence by Boniface the IXth, and ſtrengthened by many of his fucceſſors, particularly by Alexander the VIth, who built a gallery of communication between it and the Vatican for his perfonal fafety. It aſſumed the name of St. Angelo, from a circumſtance which you may either reject or credit when told. In the pontificate of Gregory the Ift, ſtyled (I know not why) the Great, that is about the year 600, a moſt deſtructive peſtilence raged at Rome. The pope, the cardinals, and all the clergy had long endeavoured to avert the calamity by prayer; but fo ineffectually, that all the people defpaired of relief, and refigned themfelves to fate. At this crifis an angel appeared with a naked fword on the top of the caſtle, and there ſheathed it, as an indication that the plague ſhould ceafe from that moment, and

fo

so I suppose it did; for a statue of this angel was erected on the same place, and is still there to perpetuate the memory of the miracle. The castle of St. Angelo is used as a state prison. In one of its apartments we saw the armour of the celebrated General Bourbon, who was killed in scaling the walls of Rome, A. D. 1527, and weapons, with which several remarkable assassinations had been perpetrated. I took up a stilletto, and enquiring into the history of it, was told it was the same that the young and beautiful Beatrice Cenci had given to her father's murderers. As you probably have never heard this tale of horror, I will relate the particulars, which I had lately the curiosity to collect. It happened in the year 1598. The father, Francis Cenci, was descended of an illustrious family, and one of the most opulent noblemen of Rome, but of a disposition so depraved, that human nature shudders at the recital of his iniquity, and shrinks from the reflection. He was twice married; by his first wife he had five sons and two daughters. The sons he treated

with

with extreme cruelty; and the elder daughter he would have debauched, had she not petitioned the Pope, who compelled him to bestow her in marriage. Thus disappointed of his diabolical design upon *her*, he determined to attempt the other, before she had arrived at those years, in which reason might operate as an impediment to the deed. He did so, and by persuading her that the action was not criminal, unhappily succeeded. So abandoned was this monster of impiety, that he frequently committed the incest in his wife's presence. By her the daughter was made sensible of her criminality, and ever after refused to comply with his request. Her father then proceeded to exact by beating what he had before obtained by seduction. The unhappy Beatrice, to withdraw herself from his brutality, had recourse to the same expedient which had preserved her sister's innocence, and presented a remonstrance to the Pope—Clement the VIIIth; but had not the same success, it being either neglected or forgotten. In this helpless situation,

tion, stung with remorse for the abominable crime she had committed, and continually urged to a repetition of it, she could devise no other means of avoiding the incestuous commerce, than by taking the life of her seducer. For this purpose she entered into a conspiracy with her step-mother, her elder brother James, and a certain Monsignor Guerra, a dignitary of the church, and hired two assassins, named Olympio and Martin, who were to receive each a thousand crowns for the murder. It was accordingly committed on the 9th of September 1598, at a family seat near Rome. The bravoes were introduced into the old man's chamber (for he was then seventy years of age) at night, where they dispatched him with the dagger I have already mentioned. The next morning it was reported he had died suddenly, and as there was no suspicion to the contrary, he was buried without examination. Some time after the interment the widow of the deceased sent a bundle of foul linen to a washerwoman in the neighbourhood, not having examined the contents, from the supposition that her step-daughter had done it; among these were the bloody sheets in which the late murder had been committed. They were immediately sent to Rome, and in consequence all the Cenci family confined. Monsignor Guerra fled on the first report of this proceeding; but Olympio having given some cause of suspicion was apprehended, and immediately made a deposition of the whole. The judges, however, not satisfied with this, determined to extort confession by torture from the step-mother, the elder son, and Beatrice. With the two former they easily succeeded, but the most racking torments could not overcome the silence of the latter, until confronted by the testimony of Olympio, and the declaration of her relatives, she was at length persuaded to acknowledge herself an accomplice in the crime. On this, the Pope condemned them to be dragged to death at the tails of three wild horses, but deferred the execution of this 115 days, in which time the many powerful applications made in their behalf would probably have

LETTER XVIII.

have procured them a pardon, had not the murder of the noble Roman lady Santa-Croce by her own son, determined him to make an example of the Cenci. He was, however, persuaded to alter their sentence. On Saturday the 11th of September 1599, a scaffold was raised on the Ponte Sant. Angelo, the common place of execution, to which the women were first conducted in funeral procession, and beheaded amidst the tears and groans of thousands. After them the elder brother was led out and deprived of life by the blow of a club; but the misfortunes of the Cenci did not end here; for the younger sons, though innocent, were deprived of their virility *, and the extensive property of their house confiscated by Paul the Vth (a Borghese) to enrich his family, which, as I have before told you, is the most wealthy in Rome. Was this last deed less iniquitous than the parricide? In their possession is the portrait of the ill-fated Beatrice, done during her confine-

---

* This was the only motive that induced his Holiness to extirpate the Cenci.

ment by Guido, and I think I never saw
a countenance less guilty or more beautiful.
Having now done with the modern buildings of Rome, I come, and with extreme
pleasure, to those that were its chief ornament in the days of its greatest power and
refinement. Temples, &c. that drew from
our own Silurian prince Caractacus that fine
exclamation on the ambitious spirit of conquest in the Romans, recorded by Tacitus
in his annals. Of all the squares or places
in the world, the most magnificent was the
Campus Martius. Livy says it belonged
to the Tarquinian family, and was consecrated to Mars, from whom it was named.
Situate between the city and the Tyber, it
was at first used as the Palæstra, or martial
seminary, in which the Roman youth inured
themselves, by bathing and military exercises, to sustain the hardships of war. In
the course of time it was ornamented with
some of the noblest structures of Rome,
such as the mausoléum of Augustus: the
pantheon: the forum and column of Antoninus Pius: the porticos of Europa, Neptune,

LETTER XVIII.

tune, and Pompey: the baths of Adrian and Agrippa: the circus agonis: theatre of Marcellus, and the famous solar obelisk brought (as Pliny relates) from Egypt to Rome by Auguſtus, which meaſured 116 Engliſh feet in height, and ſerved to mark the hours and length of days, on a dial of black marble at its baſe. I think the ſame author obſerves, that in his time (about a century after its erection) the ſhadow of this obeliſk had varied, and was falſe to the figures of the dial, but he does not aſſign any reaſon for this extraordinary change. The ruins of many of theſe edifices are ſtill extant, particularly of the mauſoleum of Auguſtus, and theatre of Marcellus; but they are ſo choked up with modern building, as to preclude any ſatisfactory examination.

Among the columns of this city, the moſt beautiful and intereſting is that of Trajan, now ſeen in a place called from it, La Piazza Colonna. It was erected by the ſenate and Roman people, in honor of that moſt excellent emperor, in the center of his

forum

forum. On it are represented in bas-relief, admirably sculptured, his Dacian expeditions, and indeed all his other public triumphs, sacrifices, &c. I may venture to assert, that Rome never possessed a more magnificent, nor posterity a more useful monument for the increase of science than Trajan's column, as it is a faithful representation of the dresses, arms, processions and ceremonies of the ancients. On the summit was the emperor's statue 18 feet in height, holding a sceptre and globe; in the latter of which were deposited his ashes. The column consists of 34 pieces of marble, in which were cut a winding staircase of 184 steps. It has 43 windows, is 128 feet in height, comprehending a statue of *St. Peter* on the top, six and a half in diameter, and the figures of the relief exceed five thousand. Of the forum, that superb edifice erected by the Grecian architect Apollodorus, there are no remains.

Antonine's pillar, though very inferior to this, of which it might be called an humble

humble imitation, is neverthelefs a very noble object. It was erected by Marcus Aurelius, and Lucius Verus, in honor of Antoninus Pius, whofe fons they were by adoption, as the infcription indicates.

Divo Antonino, Augufto, Pio,
Antoninus Auguftus, et Verus
Auguftus filii *.

The pantheon feems as gifted by all the gods, to whom it was dedicated, with immortality; as neither fire, nor the mouldering breath of time, neither the ravages of barbarian conquerors, nor the bigotry of more barbarian Popes, have reduced it to ruin. Were I the fucceffor of St. Peter I would write on it in golden characters:

> Quod non imber edax, non aquilo impotens
> Poffit diruere, aut innumerabilis
> Annorum feries, et fuga temporum †.
>   Hor. lib. iii. Od. xxx. l. 5.

* Antoninus Auguftus, and Verus Auguftus, the fons,
    To the god Antoninus, Auguftus, Pius.

Imitated.
† Which eating ftorm, or impotent fouth wind,
   With the long lapfe of countlefs years combined,
   Can never wear away.

It was built by Agrippa, the son-in-law of Augustus, and called Pantheon, from the universality of its celestial dedication. The ascent to it was originally by seven steps, but the ground on which Rome stood being raised from 12 to 30 feet by its ruins, for several ages it was entered by a descent of 13 steps; but Alexander the VIIth caused the earth that surrounded it to be removed, so that the exterior surface is now upon a level with its floor. Its majestic portico has 16 columns, with Corinthian capitals; the first of each (one intire piece of oriental granate) is 36 feet in height, and 15 in circumference. On the architrave is the following inscription.

M. AGRIPPA L.F. COS. TERTIUM
FECIT.

The form of this temple is circular; the dome (imitated by all modern architects as the first and best of models) is in dimensions rather less than St. Peter's. I am informed that its diameter is 146 feet, and
its

its height the same. Having no windows, the light enters by a round aperture at the top, under which, on the pavement of the temple, is a sink to carry off the rain. Though I discredit the assertion, that it was tiled with silver, and coated on the inside with the same metal, yet it certainly was immensely rich, particularly in sculpture. Among the statues, that of Venus wore the companion of the celebrated pearl which Cleopatra, to exceed the profusion of Anthony, dissolved in vinegar (as reported) and drank to him at a banquet. The elder Pliny observes, that the prodigal Egyptian was preparing to consume the other in the same manner, but prevented by L. Plancius, who, to save it, declared that she had fully accomplished her design. Augustus had it sawed in two, to make ear-rings for his Venus, and it was valued at 125,000l. * Another remarkable statue in the pantheon was that of Minerva in ivory, the work of Phidias, which was probaby destroyed for its matter. The majestic beauty and solidity of this

* See Pliny, Book 9th, Chap. 35.

edifice

edifice muſt ſtrike the moſt indifferent beholder. Though pillaged of its principal ornaments, it ſtill retains a ſuperb gate of bronze: pillars of Giallo-antico—that moſt precious of marbles, and others from the diſtant quarries of Numidia. It was repaired by Adrian, Marcus Aurelius, and Septimius Severus; the firſt of whom covered the whole with bronze, of which it was plundered by his Holineſs Urban the VIIIth, to ſupply the caſtle of St. Angelo with cannon, the high altar of St. Peter's with its twiſted columns, &c. and himſelf with money. The metal weighed 4,500,273 lb. In the year 607 it was converted into a Chriſtian church by Boniface the IVth, who being reſolutely determined that its new patrons ſhould exceed the number of the old, dedicated it to all the Martyrs, and in conſequence called it Sancta Maria ad Martyres; but Gregory the IVth went ſtill farther, and added to them all the ſaints of the Roman calendar. About the year 630 it was robbed of its ſtatues, &c. by the Greek emperor Conſtantine the IId, ſince which

which period it has fuffered many indignities, one indeed as late as the pontificate of Benedict the XIVth, who white-wafhed its venerable cupola. However, its having been converted into a Chriftian church has certainly preferved it from ruin, for feveral Popes have repaired, and fome enriched it, particularly Boniface the IVth, who collected from the church-yards and charnel-houfes of Rome, twenty-eight waggon loads of relics, and laid them under the high altar.

In it are the tombs of Raphael, Hannibal, Carracci, and other renowned painters. On the monument of the former is the following admirable diftich :

> Hic ille eft Raphael timuit, quo fofpite, vinci
> Rerum magna parens, et moriente mori*.

Adieu.

Imitated.
* Here Raphael lies, who could with nature vie,
 To him, fhe fear'd to yield, with him, to die.

LETTER XIX.

Rome, Dec. 14th, 1787.

WHAT is there, my dear Sir, that can resist the desolation of ages? The capitol, once the seat of universal empire, and fondly deemed co-eternal with time itself, hath now no monument of its former strength and beauty; its proud towers and battlements are gone down to the dust, and the ground which they occupied is no longer the same. So it is with that renowned bulwark, and so it shall be even with the pyramids of Egypt. Future travellers will visit the plains of ancient Memphis, and moralize upon their fallen grandeur. This celebrated rock, now called Il Campidoglo, stands between the ruins of Rome, and the Campus Martius, or modern city. Its staircase and superb buildings, designed by Buonarotti, I should greatly admire any where but here. Instead of them, I expected to find the remains of the Feretrian and Capitoline temples, &c. but

LETTER XIX.

but being diappointed, am quite out of humour, and view all modern ftructure with anger and regret. At the bottom of the ftaircafe are two fphynxes of Egyptian marble, or bafalte, from the mouths of which flow fountains of clear water, and on the top the Colofféan ftatues of Caftor and Pollux, with their horfes, the fculpture Greek; on each fide of thefe are two antique trophies of Marius admirably executed in marble. Having afcended, we entered an area, in the center of which is an equeftrian ftatue in bronze of Marcus Aurelius—an objeƈt of univerfal admiration. The buildings on this area are the fenatorial palace, that of the confervatory, and the mufeum. The two latter are crowded with fculpture and paintings. Out of a thoufand objeƈts on which real virtuofi would gaze for ages, the moft interefting to us were thefe. * The column erected in the Forum Romanum, in honor of Duillius, who gained the firft naval viƈtory over the Carthaginians: a Curtius leaping

* Pliny, Book 34, Chap. 5th.

into

into the gulph in mezzo relievo: a bronze statue of the wolf that suckled Romulus and Remus, which, though a master-piece of art, is less remarkable on that account, than for the very extraordinary anecdote which Cicero in his orations has given of it, viz. that when Cæsar was stabbed it was struck with lightning, the marks of which are as fresh upon it, as if done at the present moment: the bust of Junius Brutus: four antique measures for wine, oil, and corn: a plan of ancient Rome on marble, found in the temple of Quirinus. The altars of the Winds, Neptune, and Tranquillity: a bust of Scipio Africanus: the Mosaic picture of the three pigeons and vase, which * Pliny mentions as the work of Sosus of Pergamos: and the dying gladiator called Il Mirmillone. This statue has infinite merit. The wretched object whom it represents appears lying on the arena mortally wounded, and feebly supporting his weight upon his arm. His limbs are as finely formed as those of the

* Book 36, Chap. 25th.

Belvi-

Belviderian Apollo, but it is the countenance that is so wonderfully striking, for in it, shame, anger, and courage, seem to contend with agony, and struggle against death.

On the right hand side, near the principal entrance of the capitol, and not, as generally shewn, under a small garden, is the Tarpeian rock, the scene of Manlius's glory and disgrace. The Roman people, when they condemned him to be thrown over it, insulted the merit of his former achievement, and did an act of the most flagrant ingratitude. Such service as his deserved pardon for any offence; but had it not, that should never have been the mode of punishment; and Livy was of this opinion, when he says, " Violatum Capitolium esse sanguine servatoris; nec diis cordi fuisse poenam ejus oblatam prope oculis suis, a quo, sua templa erepta e manibus hostium essent *." I should suppose

* The capitol was violated by the blood of its protector, nor was it agreeable to the deities that they should behold the punishment of him by whom their temples had been rescued from the hands of the enemy.

this

this precipice does not now exceed 50 feet in height; it was then confiderably more, for not only the ground below it is raifed by the ruins of the furrounding buildings, but probably on the brink ftood the lofty walls of the capitol.

You may conceive how very ftriking the contraft is between the former and actual ftate of this place, when I tell you, that on the fcite of that famous temple of Jupiter Capitolinus, in which the moft facred and precious depofits of the greateft nation of antiquity were guarded, is now feen a convent of poor friars, who fubfift on alms. The golden ftatues of the prefiding god, and of victory, are now fucceeded by fome paltry image of St. Francis; and the fpoils of the vanquifhed, by the offerings of fuperftition. In the fenatorial palace is a tower, which commands an extenfive view of ancient and modern Rome. Upon this I have remained many an hour in contemplation of the furrounding objects, and enjoying all that indefcribable pleafure, which

minds

LETTER XIX.

minds, enamoured of antiquity, are capable of receiving. Directly under me I looked down upon the Via facra and Forum Romanum; but oh! how changed, how fallen from their former state; neverthelefs, their ruins are still extant, to remind us of their ancient honors. The triumphal arch, erected for the victories of Septimius Severus over the Parthians, is directly below the capitol, and almoft entire, though above half buried in the ground. As I look down on the one fide of this celebrated way, I behold the fuperb portico of a temple built in honor of Antoninus Pius and Fauftina; and a little beyond it the remains of that erected by Vefpafian after the Jewifh war to the goddefs of peace. Near it is the triumphal arch of Titus, the relievi of which are not only remarkable for their mafterly execution, but for reprefenting the tables of the commandments: the golden candleftick of feven branches: and the facred veffels of the temple of Jerufalem: a little further is the arch of Conftantine crowded with figures, many of which were taken from that of Titus, as is evident from the ſtyle and ſuperior excellence of their ſculpture. Within a few paces of this arch is the Flavian amphitheatre, ſo named from its founder the emperor Flavius Veſpaſianus, who employed 30,000 Hebrew ſlaves made priſoners at Jeruſalem in its conſtruction. I believe it to be the largeſt building of the kind in the world, as it contained ſitting room for no leſs than 80,000 ſpectators.

The edifices of ancient Rome have been ſo ſtripped of their materials, that even their ſolid walls were perforated for the metal uſed in raiſing them. To the lover of antiquity it is melancholy to behold the numerous chaſms, which the avarice of a people, who conſidered theſe buildings as monuments of Pagan impiety, have made. The Flavian amphitheatre has not only been ſeverely injured in this manner, but part of the building itſelf, when entire, was taken down by Paul the IId, *a Venetian* (to the diſgrace of his country
be

be it spoken) to erect the palace of St. Mark. The cardinals Farnese and Riario followed his example, and probably by this time there had been no remains of the majestic pile, if Clement the Vth had not fortunately been informed that several Christians were exposed on the arena to beasts of prey. This prompted him to consecrate the place, but I still fear, that so great has been the devastation before this *pious* act, that in another century little more than the foundations will be seen.

To return by the Via Sacra to my station on the tower of the senatorial palace; before me is Mount Palatine*, on which Evander, and in after ages a long succession of Roman emperors dwelt. It was most remarkable for the golden house of Nero, so called from its rich gilding, gems, and precious stones. This royal dwelling (than which antiquity can boast nothing more magnificent of the kind) was continued upon pillars over the

---

* From this hill, the habitations of kings, &c. were named Palatia,—Palaces.

interjacent vallies to the Celian and Esquiline hills. Its grand entrance was from the Via Sacra. Before it stood a marble colossus, the work of Zenodorus, that measured according to Pliny 110 feet; it was raised by Nero in honor of himself, whom it resembled in countenance; but was soon after the death of that monster dedicated by Vespasian to the Sun, and the head encircled with a glory of gilded bronze, the rays of which were seven yards in length. We saw the feet and hands of this remarkable statue in the palace of the Conservatori. The Palatine Hill is now so overgrown with briars, as to prevent our investigating the ground-work as much as we wished. Between it and the Capitoline was the Forum Romanum, which the elder Tarquin inclosed with noble porticos. In it were temples, columns, and statues of illustrious citizens, and also the gulph which is fabulously reported to have closed, when Curtius*, by plunging into it on horseback, gave himself as the most valuable sacrifice

* Livy, Book 7th, Cap. 6th.

that

that could be made to effectuate this miracle. You may probably suppose that I believe all this, when I tell you, that we saw the spot where the pit *was*, or I should rather say, where it is reported to have been. Three pillars are now standing, which belonged to the colonade of the Forum, and these very much surpass in height and beauty any thing we have hitherto seen. How grand the appearance when the whole was extant! how correspondent to the majesty of the Roman people! but alas, this valley, which was the most honorable part of ancient Rome (the capitol excepted) is now the most vile. Here, where not only the ambassadors of powerful monarchs, but even they themselves have sued for protection: where the decrees of popular assemblies have decided the fate of nations; and in short, where every thing of the greatest moment was transacted, is now heard the lowing of oxen. The Forum Romanum is the Smithfield of modern Rome, and the walls of those sacred edifices, which were more revered than any

B b 3   earthly

earthly object, are constantly polluted by the dung of cattle. Even the Temple of Concord, in which Cicero assembled the senate on the discovery of Cataline's conspiracy, and where the sentiments of Cæsar, of Cato, and of himself, were delivered on that subject, is made an occasional beasthouse. I mention this as a striking instance of that change which ever has and ever will take place in all things temporal.

The Cloaca Maxima, which Livy calls "Omnium Purgamentorum Receptaculum," and the elder Pliny so much admires for its solidity and strength (it having remained entire from the reign of Tarquinius Priscus to his time) is still unimpaired, though 2405 years have since elapsed. It is impossible to regard these stupendous vaults without astonishment. Some of them still serve as the common sewers of the city, and will, I dare assert it, exist, when the proud dome of St. Peter's shall have sunk under the hand of time.

West

LETTER XIX.

West of Mount Palatine is the Circus Maximus, famous for the rape of the Sabine women, who not only brought forth a race of heroes for the defence of Rome, but effected an inseparable junction between their countrymen and ravishers. At the southern extremity of the circus were the baths of Caracalla, the ruins of which are still considerable. In buildings of this kind the Romans displayed their greatest magnificence; the known world being, as it were, ransacked for their embellishment. The most valuable gems: the richest marbles, and the best sculpture of Greece, are frequently found under them. They were so very extensive, that no less than 2300 persons could bathe at the same time in these of Caracalla, without seeing each other. Nor were those of Diocletian less sumptuous, or less ample. Exclusive of the ruins already noticed, are the aqueducts, those monuments of the opulence and patriotism of individuals: the catacombs, of which nothing certain can be determined in regard of their origin, as I little believe the idle

tale

tale of their having been formed by the primitive Christians of Rome during their persecution: the remains of many other temples, particularly of that consecrated to the god of ridicule, in memory of the sudden departure of Hannibal from the place in which it was built near Rome: the fountain of the nymph Egeria, from whom Numa Pompilius pretended to have received the religious ceremonies which he instituted: the chamber or tomb of the Campus Sceleratus, in which those vestals, who had yielded their virginity, were buried alive; the last of whom * Livy informs us was Minutia: the ground-work of the Curia Pompeii, wherein Cæsar was killed by the conspirators: the pyramid of Cestus; the tombs of Cecilia Metella, and of the Scipio family: the gardens of Ovid and Sallust: the house of Cicero, and, in short, a long list of other edifices interesting beyond expression. What subjects are these for reflection! how fully do they engage

* Book 8th, Chap. 15th.

LETTER XIX.

the attention, and warm the imagination of the beholder! To me their charms are so irresistible, that I visit them daily, and when there, can hardly persuade myself to leave them. How frequently have I discovered the richest ornaments of architecture in the ragged walls of a vineyard! and broken columns, which once perhaps supported the theatre of Scaurus, used as props to the humble roof of a cottage! I saw them, and lamented their change. But the modern palaces absolutely excite my indignation, as I know their materials to be the spoils of the noblest ruins in Rome. You read that this city has been often sacked and pillaged by the Goths, &c. but, believe me, those Goths who have done it the greatest injury, were its popes and cardinals. Few of the many pontiffs, who have resided here, are innocent of this charge. Alexander the VIth, a superstitious Spaniard, carried this outrage so far, as to destroy the pyramid of Scipio, for its stones to pave the streets. Would that his life
for

for this offence had depended on a jury of antiquarians!

I always view the Tyber with singular satisfaction, because it has retained the appearance it had in the early days of Rome. The foundations of its ancient bridges are still extant, particularly those of the Pons Sublicius, the passage of which Horatius Cocles so valiantly defended against the Etrurian army, until it was broken down behind him, when he plunged with his horse into the rapid stream, and gained the shore amidst the acclamations of his countrymen. The treasures of this river must be immense, from the valuable things thrown into it, at different times, and upon different occasions. Many offers have been made the apostolical chamber to clean it, for the chance of what might be discovered in its channel. But these proposals have been rejected, from the well-founded supposition, that the noxious exhalations of the mud would prove fatal to many of the inhabitants. The climate of Rome is already

LETTER XIX. 379

ready much infected with unwholesome vapour, and this addition would make it insupportable. We have lately made a little tour to Frascati and Tivoli, the former ten, the latter twenty miles from Rome. Frascati was the ancient Tusculum, where, among many others, were the villas of Cicero, of Horace, and of Virgil. In the former (the scite of which they pretend to determine) were written the Tusculan disputations, those admirable compositions of the great orator. Of the country houses we saw here, I have only to say, that they display great magnificence and labor, but little taste; their gardens might excite the admiration of an *Italian*, but an *Englishman* would never make them a second visit.

The situation of Tivoli on a high hill presents one of the most delightful inland landskips I ever saw. The river Anio (now Il Teverone) falling in different channels over the brow, forms two cascades, one of which is singularly bold and striking. We beheld it from the narrow valley below,

rushing

rushing out of the ruins of Mæcenas's villa, which hang, as it were, upon the summit. I had no conception that Italy could produce any spot so romantic and so beautiful as Tivoli; and these charms which I mention are augmented by the addition of Roman ruins, and an Italian climate. On the verge of the steep rocks over the Anio is the temple of the Sybil; a little octagon building, that is, without exception, the most exquisite *morcean* of Greek architecture I ever saw.

This place, so favoured by nature, wants no addition to its beauty but wood, for which it was once so remarkable. Horace, you may remember, says,

> " Et præceps Anio, et Tiburni lucus, et uda
> " Mobilibus pomaria rivis *."
>   Hor. lib. i. Od. vii. line 14.

Imitated.

* And Anios cataracts, and Tibur's woods,
  And orchards, with their many streams——

And again in the same Ode,

> " Sen densa tenebit
> " Tiburis umbra tui *."
> Hor. lib. i. Od. vii. line 21.

Were Tivoli in England, it would have as many inhabitants as when Mæcenas dwelt there; but the modern Roman has no taste for rural scenery. He never visits the country, but when the suffocating heat of the capital compels him to leave it. On our return we were conducted to the ruins of Hadrian's villa, that rich mine of antique statues. The situation appears to me much too low, but I believe the ancients did not consider the advantages of prospect as much as we do. Several of its apartments are still known, particularly those called I cento camarelli, or barracks for the emperor's body guards.

Vale.

Imitated.
* If his own Tibur's shade should keep him hence.

LETTER

LETTER XX.

Rome, Dec. 26, 1787.

THE triumph of reason over credulity and superstition has reduced the sovereign pontiff's authority so low, that he is now much greater as a temporal than as a spiritual prince. In the center and finest part of Italy he possesses a territory of 14,348 square geographic miles, and at present (but how long they may remain I know not*) 520 round Avignon. Though the situation of his dominions be so favourable, they are less productive and less populous than any of the Italian states, in consequence of hierarchy, and that frequent change of sovereigns, whose views and interests are not to enrich, but to impoverish their subjects; for the purpose of raising their families to wealth and distinction. In all the long list of St. Peter's successors, whose history is transmitted to us, I know but few who pre-

---

* Since this letter was written, the sovereign pontiff has lost Avignon and the Comptat.

LETTER XX.

ferred the happiness of their people to the aggrandizement of their kindred; and eminent among these few was the virtuous Ganganelli, but unhappily he was soon poisoned by the Jesuits.

The tracts of rich land, which formerly supported thousands, but now lie uncultivated, are melancholy instances of wretched government, sacerdotal celibacy, and the many religious feasts which the peasants of the Roman Catholic persuasion most scrupulously observe. It is impossible that any country without commerce can become opulent, unless the attention of the legislature be principally directed to agriculture; and this is so far from being the case here, that the spirit of husbandry is entirely depressed by the monopoly of corn. The farmers are (literally speaking) the slaves of government; for they are obliged to bring in all their wheat, which the apostolical chamber buys at its own valuation, and retails at a price exorbitant, in proportion to what it pays. Even the Campagna

pagna di Roma, which was as the neighbourhoods of London and Paris now are, gardens to the capital, has been so neglected, that no animal can exist on it from the fatality of the vapors that its soil exhales. It lies south and south east of Rome, between it and the hills of Tivoli and Frascati. There are in the papal territories several extensive marshes. The Paludi Pontini, which lie on the sea coast between Rome and Naples, still consist of many thousand acres, though the present pope has recovered large tracts of land from them. It is to be hoped (I fear more than expected) that his successors will follow his example in this great and useful undertaking, and carry it on to its completion; as it would not only increase the revenue of the state, by the acquisition of rich and extensive pastures, but no longer infect the Sirocco with its effluvia; a south wind that would be fatal to the inhabitants of Rome, were it during the summer heats to continue five days successively.

LETTER XX.

As I find nothing particularly interesting in the government of this country, I shall be silent on that subject, when I have told you the people are so universally corrupt, that the administration of justice must, according to the constitution, be confided principally to foreigners: three only of the twelve auditors of the rota or chief tribunal, being Romans.

The triple crown of St. Peter has ever been so great an object of ambition among those of the clergy who were eligible to it, that every species of intrigue to influence the voices of the electors may be said to prevail upon this occasion; nor indeed can it be otherwise, when men are thus raised from the condition of a subject to that of a Sovereign, not only of such spiritual but temporal authority, as the Pope. You will remember Woolsey as an example of this. Though the cardinal electors may chuse any clergyman of the church of Rome, their choice (as you will suppose) ever falls upon one of their own body; and fince the reign of Adrian the VIth in 1522, who was a Fleming, it has been confined to Italians, fo that now no other than a native of Italy can be elected; but to compenfate for this exclufion of foreigners, the emperor of Germany, and the kings of France, Spain, and Portugal, have a negative voice in the Conclave, fo as to prevent the election of any cardinal by making previous objection to him.—No great privilege (you will fay) for the firft of thefe princes, who was originally the fole difpofer of the papacy. The mode of election is as follows. Ten days after the pope's death, the facred college affemble in one of the galleries of the vatican, prepared for their reception, where they chufe from their own body three fcrutatori, or infpectors, and three infermieri, or delegates for collecting the votes of the fick electors, to whom they are firft to adminifter the neceffary oaths, and then to receive their written fuffrages in a fmall box, fimilar (I fuppofe) to our charity boxes, as the infermieri cannot open them but in the prefence of

the

the electors. Should either of these invalids be so reduced, that he cannot write the name of him for whom he votes, any cardinal may do it, but he must first swear before the delegates, that he will not divulge the secret. Having received the sick votes, they immediately proceed to the election. Upon a table in the chapel where they assemble are certain papers, printed according to a form prescribed by the master of the ceremonies, each elector in seniority taking one, writes his own name, and that of him whom he supports, upon it, then seals, and carries it to the altar *, at which he swears he has given his voice for the cardinal, whose virtues (in his opinion) intitle him, above the rest, to the vacant throne of St. Peter, and, finally, drops his billet into a large vase. This being done by all, the first inspector mixes the billets together, and the third examines their number. Should more than there are voters

* Were they not cardinals, I should suspect that this election seldom happened without perjury, or something like it.

be found, they are all burnt, and the suffrages again collected in the same manner. The business being so far adjusted, the first inspector takes up a billet, opens, and having seen the name, shews it to the second, from whom the third receives it, and by him it is declared aloud. Each elector has before him a list of all the sacred college, marks each vote as given, and at the conclusion, on casting up the numbers, perceives who has the majority: but it is required that the successful candidate should have two thirds of the voices; when this does not appear on the first scrutiny, they go through the business again, with this difference, that instead of writing on their billets, as the first time, the word * eligo, they put † accedo. The election being made, the master of the ceremonies and secretary of the conclave are called in, and informed of the event, when it is immediately published, and a variety of ceremonies, &c. ensue. I should tell you, that from the time the cardinals are assembled

---

* I elect.   † I accede to it.

LETTER XX.

in conclave, they are forbidden all external communication, until they have chosen a sovereign pontiff: should either of them be obliged to go out, he cannot be readmitted.

YOU will perceive by what I have written to you since we have been here, that much time has been employed in visiting its ancient and modern buildings, and in contemplating with rapture the most admirable sculpture and painting in the world. But this occupation was confined to the mornings, or, I should rather say, to part of them, as on getting up we dedicate an hour and a half to our Italian masters, mine, a certain Abbate Giuntotarde, is a gentleman of singular merit; he is as great an enthusiast in poetry as I am, so that we read little else than Ariosto, Tasso, and Metastasio. Soon after our arrival we left our cards, and a letter of introduction from the marquis of Landsdown at the cardinal de Bernis's. We were in consequence invited to dine with his eminency the next day, when he received us with great ease and politeness, but said he had not the honor of recollecting the marquis of Landsdown. You may conceive how much my friend and I were astonished at this declaration; but I happily soon saw the mistake, and told him, that if he remembered lord Shelburne, he must know the marquis of Landsdown, for they were one and the same person. How (said he) is your letter from lord Shelburne, and has he for the first time in his life now deceived me? However, you are doubly welcome, first, for reminding me of an old friend; and, secondly, for introducing me to a new one; nor were these mere words of course, for he justified their sincerity by his subsequent attention and hospitality. His dinners, conversazioni, and academie or concerts, are the most magnificent in Rome, and I assure you that every thing travellers have said of his liberality, his wit, and amiable manners, is but the bare acknowledgment of truth. During the last war between Great Britain and France, his invitations

to

LETTER XX.

to the English gentlemen at Rome were as frequent as ever; indeed he compelled them to visit him, observing that the political quarrel of two nations so enlightened as ours should never disturb the harmony of societies at Rome. He is much more attentive to the English than the generality of their own ministers, as indeed are all the French ambassadors. But his hospitality is not confined to travellers, it is equally directed to those who have no other recommendation to him than their merit; as a proof of this one day in every week he invites to his sumptuous table the foreign artists who study at Rome. Through him and Mr. Jenkins, the English banker, and I might say Chargé d'Affaires in this city, we have been very generally introduced. The assemblies of the princess Santa Croce are only inferior to those of the cardinal di Bernis. There we found a constant Pharaoh bank, though I believe expressly forbidden by government; you may suppose that this breach of law is not very uncommon, when I tell you that the legislators themselves frequently countenance it by their presence. The common people are remarkable above all the other Italians for their taste in musick, consequently their comic opera is most admirable, though the performers are all eunuchs, no actresses being permitted to sing. However, they have so much the appearance of women when in their dress, that an English gentleman of our acquaintance, who went more to gratify his eye than his ear, was so much in raptures with one of them, that he declared, to the great amusement of his countrymen, who were in the secret, *She was the most beautiful girl he had ever seen*, and the next day wrote *it* a billet deux. This opera is constantly attended by a well-known character, that once set all England in a ferment, but how reduced, how altered from what he was! you will perceive I allude to *the Pretender*. He is the only person in Rome who is permitted to have lights in his box, and indeed I believe this to be the only mark of distinction he now receives. His face is turned to the performers, but he he continually keeps his head down, and seems infenfible to every object that furrounds him. He never appears but with the infignia of the garter, and I have once or twice feen him take up his George, and examine it with great attention. It is (as I hear) the fame that his anceftor Charles the Ift gave bifhop Juxton immediately before his execution. A few years ago he was married to a fecond wife, but fhe, with many of his followers, deferted him for fairer profpects; their place however is fupplied by his natural daughter whom he has created duchefs of Albany. She has the character of an amiable woman. I only know that fhe is not handfome, as the fmallpox has made great havock on her features. We meet her in every company, but never the Pretender, nor the cardinal of York. There is not the leaft refemblance between the brothers, but the cardinal is very like the portraits I have feen of Charles the IId.

It is impoffible to have a numerous acquaintance at Rome without paying a
very

very heavy tax for it, as the morning after you have left your letters or cards at any houfe, and when you take leave, your doors are befieged by a legion of fervants for what they call the *mancia*, or vails. This fcandalous cuftom is peculiar to Rome, and univerfally adopted here; what is ftill more fcandalous, the mafters are not only privy to it, but fhare in the fpoil, as the wages of their numerous beggars in livery are fmall, from the certainty of their being made up to them by the contributions they draw from foreigners, which in many houfes is very confiderable. Should the money given be lefs than they expect, you are liable to fome marked infult in your vifits. Is it not furprifing that the cardinal de Bernis fhould fully his hofpitality, by permitting fuch an infamous ufage? But fo it is, to the difgrace and reproach of all the nobility at Rome. The difpofitions of the people are fo vindictive and fanguinary, that the commonalty are forbidden, under pain of perpetual flavery in the galleys, to carry knives about them; but this prohibition

LETTER XX. 395

hibition has unfortunately not lessened the number of murders. On coming out of St. Peter's the other day, I was addressed for charity by a tall ill-looking fellow in a shabby blue cloak, who told me, by way of exciting my compassion, that he was *a poor assassin.* I had the curiosity to know something of this *amiable* stranger in distress, who, according to the common custom, had taken refuge under the inviolable portico of this church; and therefore put my laquais de place to interrogate him, but all in vain; he would tell me nothing, except that he should be very happy to assist me in his way. I turned from him with horror, which was farther increased by my reflections on the morals of a people among whom murder is professional, and men live by blood.

Great inconvenience is experienced here from the immense quantity of ragged paper money, which is payable only at the Monte di Pietá, or place whence they are first issued; and there you receive no more than

so

so much per cent. in specie; for the rest you must take a fresh bill. An undeniable instance this of wretched government: but fortunately we have not felt the grievance, as our banker Mr. Jenkins is uncommonly attentive to his countrymen.

I bid you adieu, and so I shall to Rome in a few days.

LETTER XXI.

Naples, Jan. 20th, 1788.

WE travelled over the foundations of the Appian way, which with an aqueduct of the same name (in part still extant) were made at the sole expence of Appius Claudius, and arrived in the evening at Terracina, the Anxur of the Volscians. This little town, or I should rather say village, stands at the southern extremity of the Paludi Pontini, of which many thousand acres have been drained by the present Pope, who is indefatigable in forwarding this great work; but I fear it is *too great* to be completed by modern Romans, when the ancient could not effect it. These extensive tracts of morass were probably produced by one of those sudden and violent convulsions of the earth to which this part of Europe is so subject, as the elder Pliny observes *, from the authority of Mutianus, who had been thrice consul, that

* Book 3d, Chap. 5th.

upon the fame ground were twenty-three cities. On leaving Terracina the next morning, we faw Il Monte Circello, which you perceive ftill retains the name of its ancient owner Circe. This celebrated mountain ftands on the fea fide. It was (if the authority of Homer be admitted) an ifland.

Αιαιην δ' ες νησον αφικομιθ' ενθα δ' εναιε
Κιρκη ευπλοκαμ۞ *.   Od. B. 10. lin. 135.

But I rather fuppofe that he, thinking an infular fituation a more fuitable refidence to his inchantrefs than the main land, gave up his knowledge of geography, in this inftance, to his poetic mufe. A few miles from this place is Gaeta, a city named from the nurfe of Æneas, who died there.

Tu quoque littoribus noftris Æneia nutrix
Æternam moriens famam Caieta dedifti, &c.†
    VIRG. ÆN. vii. line 1 & 2.

Imitated.
* We come to the Ææan ifle, where dwells
Circe with braided hair.

Imitated.
† Æneian nurfe, Caieta, dear to fame,
Thou to our coafts from diftant Ilium came,
And dying left them an eternal name.

And

LETTER XXI.

And to shew you that every step we take is upon classic ground; a little further is the silent Liris † (Liristaciturnus Amnis) now Il Gariglano, on the banks of which some say the first battle between Pyrrhus and the Romans was fought, though others suppose, and with more probability, it was on those of the Siris, near Tarentum in Magna Græcia.. We crossed it in a ferry boat, and on the passage were told, that the servant of an English nobleman was assassinated there a few years ago by one of the postillions who drove his master's carriage, in consequence of some trivial dispute about the buona mano, or money he had given him. I was sorry to learn upon farther enquiry, that the villain had escaped. The Liris divided Latium from Campania, near its mouth were the marshes of Minturnæ, in which you may remember, that Marius in his seventieth year, when driven from Rome by Sylla, took refuge, and to avoid discovery, passed a night up to his chin in

† Liris—a silent brook.

mud

mud and water.—Happy were it for Rome had he died there.

We found the road moſt excellent, and ſoon arrived at modern Capua. The ruins of the ancient city (the principal of which is an amphitheatre almoſt entire) are a mile and a half higher up the country. I am perſuaded that the mere mention of this once luxurious place will remind you of Hannibal, and his fatal error after the victory of Cannæ. From Capua we ſoon came to Naples.

On the coaſt of the Campagna Felice, the paradiſe of Italy, and at the extremity of a deep and ſecure bay, not leſs than 80 miles in circuit, whoſe ſhores offer to the enraptured beholder every thing that is in nature ſublime and beautiful, is this celebrated city. Notwithſtanding every impediment to population, ſuch as religious celibacy, frequent aſſaſſination, and that extreme poverty which prevails among the lower orders of the people, in conſequence
of

of bad government, ill adminiftered; the inhabitants of Naples amount to 340,000 fouls, a number exceeded by no city in Europe; London, Paris, and Conftantinople excepted. It is upon the whole irregularly built, but contains many noble palaces. The Strada di Toledo is the principal ftreet, which is inferior to thofe of the fecond order in London. I remember being fhewn fome polifhed flabs of lava as a great curiofity a few months before I left England, but here I walk on nothing elfe, as all Naples is paved with it. Though hard as marble, I fhould fuppofe it too porous for the conftruction of houfes. We have been fo accuftomed to the magnificent edifices of Rome, that few buildings at Naples attract our attention; but there is one, the theatre of St. Carlo, which is fuperior to any thing of the kind we have ever feen; being at leaft equal to that of Milan in dimenfions, and far before it in decoration. On a gala night, when the houfe is illuminated, it prefents one of the moft brilliant fpectacles imaginable; as a profufion of mirrors, other glaſſes, and reverberators, aſſiſt and multiply the light, and conſequently diſplay to the greateſt advantage the carving, gilding, &c. The palace in which the king reſides is contiguous to St. Carlo, but contains nothing remarkable in ſculpture, painting, or other furniture, whilſt in that of the Capo di Monte, which, I believe, he never inhabits, are the choiceſt collections of pictures, medals, gems, &c. among the latter is a famous onyx, eight inches in diameter, repreſenting in cameo, on the one ſide, Meduſa's head: and on the other the apotheoſis of Hadrian. Though probably the largeſt gem in the world, it is leſs intereſting on that account, than for the beauty of its engraving, which is inimitable. Having ſaid ſo much of the city, I ſhall proceed to the environs and bay of Naples, the laſt of which the eye covers, as it were, at a glance from the windows of our apartments. The famous grotto of Pauſilipo is perhaps the moſt ſtupendous effort of labour in the world. Naples being excluded by the mountain of this name, which is immediately

mediately behind it, from a free communication with the country, Agrippa formed the defign of cutting a fubterraneous paffage through the folid rock (for fo it is) from the one to the other fide; and entrufted the execution of it to two freedmen, who had ftudied architecture. It is in length 2315 feet, from 16 to 20 in breadth, and from 40 to 60 in height. From the top of the mountain to the center of the grotto is an aperture cut for the purpofe of admitting into it air and light; but the laft is ftill fo fcanty, that fome perfon of authority, who knew how to convert the grofs fuperftition of the Neapolitans to their advantage, erected an image of the Virgin Mary in the moft obfcure part of the cavern, preaffured that they would never fuffer fo revered a figure to remain in the dark, but chearfully contribute their alms to fupply her fhrine with lamps. On the hill near the entrance of this grotto is a fmall fquare ruin called Virgil's Tomb; but to believe that it is fo, I require more fatisfactory evidence than the mere traditionary opinion of the Neapolitans.

politans. We always make our country excursions in calese, or light whiskeys, which stand for hire in Naples, as our hackney coaches in London, &c. because they are much pleasanter than a carriage, and being drawn by excellent ponies, infinitely more expeditious. In these we often pass the grotto of Pausilipo, and ever with all possible haste, the dust and confined air being so offensive. The road on the other side leads to the coast opposite the islands of Ischia and Procida, than which no maritime scenery can be more delightful; and perhaps you will give me full credit for this assertion, when I tell you, it is the country in which Virgil placed his Elysian fields, and Cicero, Lucullus, &c. &c. their villas. At Puzzuoli, the ancient Puteoli, we beheld magnificent ruins, particularly the entire ground-work of a temple sacred to the Egyptian deity Serapis, which has been lately discovered. About a mile from this place is the Zolfatàra, a small oval plain, the soil of which is one continued stratum of sulphur. It is surrounded by little hills,

having

LETTER XXI.

having been the crater of a volcano, from which the laſt eruption was in 1198. It ſtill has many mouths, which emit a hot ſulphureous ſteam, and is hollow below, as we perceived by the ſound of our feet in walking over it. I am ſatisfied its magazines of combuſtible matter are now augmenting for ſome terrible exploſion that may happen ſooner than expected. Not far from this place is the lake Agnano, a circular piece of water full of fiſh, particularly of tench, and I might ſay covered with moor-hens, which are preſerved for the king's diverſion, when he either fiſhes or ſhoots. Upon the borders are ſulphureous ſweating baths, which we had the curioſity to enter, but were ſoon compelled to leave, by the too powerful heat of the vapour. They are uſed by many who are afflicted with the gout, rheumatiſm, &c. and eſteemed a ſovereign remedy for ſuch diſorders. Near theſe is a ſmall cavern in a rock called La Grotta del Cane, from which mephitic effluvia exhale ſo powerfully, that within a foot of the ground they

prevent

prevent respiration. It was called del Cane, from the cruel custom of shewing people its effect upon dogs, kept for the purpose. In opposition to every thing we could say to the contrary, this was done when we were there. The poor animal (who from frequent experience was apparently conscious of his unfeeling master's intention) being put into the grotto became instantly convulsed; but on being thrown into the lake, he as quickly recovered, and swam to shore. To return to Puzzuoli, I must observe to you, that the pleasant coast of Baiæ is divided from this town by a bay two miles and a half across, over which Caligula, that monster of pride and cruelty, in vain attempted to build a bridge of stone. His intention by this work was to appear more powerful than Xerxes when he passed the Hellespont, but his vanity was not gratified; for when the artificers came to the middle of the channel, they found it too deep to proceed: he was therefore obliged to make use of boats chained together, as a substitute for his intended building. The ruins

ruins are still extant, and appear like an immense causeway in the sea. Near the extremity of this bay are the remains of Cumæ, the oldest city upon the western coast of Italy, founded, as some say, by a colony of Chalcians from Æubæa, or as others by adventurers from Cumæ of Æolis in Asia Minor. It was inhabited as late as the year 1207, when the Saracens utterly destroyed it. The castle gate-way however still remains entire. This charming coast is worthy of all that praise which the Roman poets have bestowed on it. The most elegant and descriptive prose is, in my opinion, insufficient to do it justice. Though now in the depth of winter the air is as soft as your summer breezes. The sea is calm, the sky clear, and all nature wears her kindest aspect.

> Hic ver assiduum, atque alienis mensibus æstas,
> Bis gravidæ pecudes, bis pomis utilis arbos*.
> VIRG. GEORG. lib. iii. l. 149 & 159.

Imitated.
* Here spring and summer every season share,
The cattle twice bring forth, and twice the fruit-trees bear.

Near the scite of Cumæ is Il Capo di Miseno, a bold promontory that bends over the sea, and was thus named after Misenus, the trumpeter of Hector, and the companion of Æneas. Virgil, who is always of our party in these excursions to this his favourite country, being the best and most agreeable guide, tells you that Misenus, for his presumption in supposing himself a better trumpeter than the gods, was thrown by Triton into the sea under this mountain, where he lost his life. The poet having described his funeral, and the grief of his companions, makes the following conclusion of the story.

> At pius Æneas ingenti mole sepulcrum
> Imposuit, suaque arma viro, remumq. tubamque
> Monte sub aerio, qui nunc Misenus ab illo
> Dicitur, æternumque tenet per sæcula nomen *.
> Virg. Æn. vi. l. 235.

Imitated.

> * High on a hill his tomb Æneas placed,
>   With his own arms, his oar and trumpet graced,
>   A hill from him Misenus call'd, that fame
>   To times, remotest age, might bear his honor'd name.

Within

Within a small circuit are the prisons and baths of Nero: the Elysian fields now over-run with vines: the ruins of several temples, &c: the river Acheron: mare morto; piscina mirabile, which seems to have been an immense reservoir of water: and the lake Avernus. The last of these, being the subject of one of the most finished pictures of so great a master of description as the Mantuan bard, is particularly interesting. You may suppose then that we viewed it with all the rapture that fine rural scenery, thus heightened to perfection by the fiction and enchanting language of poetry, can create in imaginations so alive to its impression as ours. We descended its steep banks, which, till cut down by Agrippa, were covered with venerable groves of ilex, to the ruined temple of Apollo.

" Arces quibus altus Apollo
" Præsidet *."   VIRG. ÆN. vi. l. 10.

Imitated.

* The tow'rs o'er which the god of day presides.

Part

Part of which stands in this clear and silent lake. In the surrounding hill is the grotto of the Cumæan Sibyl.

> Quæ rupe sub ima
> Fata canit, foliisque notas et nomina mandat.
> Quæcunque in foliis descripsit carmina virgo
> Digerit in numerum atque antro seclusa relinquit.
> Illa manent immota locis, neque ab ordine cedunt,
> Verum eadem verso tenuis cum cardine ventus
> Impulit, et teneras turbavit janua frondes,
> Nunquam deinde cavo volitantia prendere saxo,
> Nec revocare situs, aut jungere carmina curat,
> Inconsulti abeunt sedemque odere Sibyllæ *.
>
> VIRG. ÆN. iv. l. 452.

Each having taken a guide (Dundas being with us) we determined to explore this mansion of prophecy. In the middle of a long passage (which like that of Pausilipo

---

Imitated.

* Who in deep cave declares what fate conceals,
  And names and signs by written leaves reveals.
  On these she writes whate'er the god inspires,
  Lays them in form, and to her den retires.
  There they remain ranged in prophetic verse.
  Yet should a breath of wind these leaves disperse,
  She never cares to call them back again.
  But e'er consulted by the sons of men, ⎫
  Far, far they fly, and seem to hate her den. ⎭

is cut through the hill) we turned on the right, and by torch light defcended a narrow alley, until our progrefs was obftructed by water. Finding it not deep, we made our conductors take off their fhoes and ftockings, and got on their backs, each rider carrying his flambeaux. We foon entered a fquare apartment, in which we found two baths, and from this went into a fmaller room, both overflowed with water knee deep. Determined to proceed, we looked for the paffage that fhould lead us onward, but to our great mortification found that the earth had fallen in, and choked it. Our intention was to have walked directly through, there being (as reported) another entrance at Cumæ This cavern too is noticed by Ovid, who makes it his palace of fleep.

Eft prope Cimerios longo fpelunca receffu
Mons cavus, ignavi domus, et penetralia fomni, &c.*
OVID. MET. lib. ii. l. 592.

Imitated.
* There is a den near the Cimerian fhore,
Whofe deep recefs no mortal can explore.
The flumb'rous feat of floth—th' abode of fleep.

I fhould

I should suppose that the lake Avernus was, but at a time antecedent to the annals of history, the crater of a volcano, the circumference is not less than a mile and three quarters, the water deep, transparent, and well tasted. When its banks were covered with wood, the air being too confined, and charged with the vapour of the stagnate water, was so fatal to respiration, that Virgil tells you the birds, which attempted to fly over, fell lifeless into the lake, and that it was thence called Αορνος.

> Quem super hand ullæ poterant impune volantes
> Tendere iter pennis, talis sese halitus atris
> Faucibus effundens, supera ad convexa ferebant.
> Unde loca Graii dixerunt nomine Aornon *.
>
> ÆN. vi. l. 242.

You perceive that I have no room to say any more, therefore I shall beg leave to drop the subject until some future day,

Imitated.

* O'er which no birds on buoyant wing can sail,
Such fatal gusts from its dark throat exhale;
That from on high precipitate they fall,
And hence its gulf the Greeks Aornon call.

when

LETTER XXI.

when probably I shall have more matter, and more leisure, than I now have.

Naples.

UPON the bay of Naples, four miles south east of the city, are the towns of Resina and Portici. In the latter is a royal palace and a museum, richer in antique curiosities than all the cabinets of Europe, being filled with a variety of articles collected from Herculaneum and Pompeii, such as valuable statues, vases of silver, of bronze, and of glass: instruments of surgery, among which we were shewn some for extracting the stone, an operation which I had hitherto thought unknown to the ancients: weights: measures: hooks and fishing-nets: armour: weapons: musical instruments: loaded dice larger than those of the present day: metallic mirrors: earthen ware, and glass, of an inferior quality to that now made: toilet furniture, and even provisions, namely, figs, nuts, currants, eggs, meat, bread, corn, wine, and oil, dried to
a hard

a hard substance; in short, every thing that could administer not only to the necessities and convenience, but to the most refined luxuries of life. One of the rooms in this museum is the exact counterpart of a Roman kitchen, with all its furniture, hung as when discovered in the original. Many of the vessels are similar to those used at present, but of superior quality, being made of bronze, and highly finished. The most interesting and most valuable room, however, is the library, from the numerous manuscript rolls which it contains. What a field is here for conjecture! what room for hope! Among this inestimable collection how many great works are there, of which even the names are now unknown! how many unbroken volumes, whose very fragments preserved in the writings of the ancient scholiasts, convey to us moral improvement, information, and delight! perhaps all the dramatic pieces of Menander and Philemon, perhaps, nay certainly, the lost Decades of Livy; for it is impossible to suppose, that among so many rolls, the

most

moſt admired hiſtory of the people who poſſeſſed them is not to be found, what private library in Britain is without the beſt hiſtories of England? But how I tremble for their ſituation, as Portici is built on the lava that overwhelmed Herculaneum! How I tremble too for the indifference of the king of Naples towards this invaluable treaſure, in which all the moſt enlightened people of Europe are deeply intereſted! When I firſt ſaw them, I had no idea of what they were, as they reſemble wooden truncheons burnt almoſt to charcoal. They are ſo hard and brittle, that the greateſt caution muſt be uſed in removing them, leſt they crumble to duſt; neverthelefs, an ingenious friar of Genoa, named Raggio, undertook to unroll them, and by a moſt curious, though tedious procefs, ſo far ſucceeded, as to tranſcribe three Greek Treatiſes on Philoſophy and Muſick; but finding (as I hear) no other encouragement than his ſalary, which was but little more than you pay ſome of your ſervants, the work was unhappily diſcontinued. Were theſe manu-

ſcripts

scripts in England, they would not long remain a secret to the world. On leaving the palace we descended by stairs cut out of the lava, not less than fifty feet to the buried city of Herculaneum; but it was by no means as interesting as I expected. When at the bottom we thought ourselves in an immense quarry, and saw only the orchestra of a theatre, and part of the forum, which were so involved in obscurity, as to be scarce discernible. The difficulty and expence of working through the solid lava is so great, that few discoveries have been made, and it was found necessary to fill up many of the excavations, lest the foundations of Portici should be injured by them. But it is very different at Pompeii. This place is about nine miles from Herculaneum, being covered not by lava, but ashes, it has been cleared with little difficulty, so that an entire street, besides several detached houses, are laid open. In the suburbs are the soldiers barracks, a square building admirably planned. We perceived on the walls several names scratch-
ed

ed out with a knife, or some such instrument, particularly *Cn. Balbus, Lu. Jun. Rufus*, &c. &c. and were informed, that among the many skeletons found here (some of which we saw) four were discovered in the prison of these barracks with their legs confined in a stocks. These poor wretches were unable to liberate themselves, and forgotten in the general confusion. Having entered the town gate, we found the street narrow, and the pavement much damaged, and worn into deep ruts by cart-wheels. The houses, though low (none of them being above two stories high) consist of several small apartments stuccoed and painted, the colours of which are as fresh and vivid, as if recently laid on. Each has an inner court, some have two, and in one we perceived three, with marble basons or fountains in the middle. The cellars are built like cloisters, being four piazzas, at right angles one with another. We found in them several large wine jars of earthenware, ranged along the walls, and if I recollect well, marked and numbered. You may suppose that the houses of Pompeii are in high preservation, when I tell you, that we saw on the sill of a window stains of some such liquor as chocolate or coffee, made by the bottom of the cups.

Herculaneum and Pompeii were built at the foot of Vesuvius, each five miles distant from the crater. They were both destroyed A. D. 79, during the reign of Titus, but in a different manner. Pompeii, as the wind lay that way, was buried under a heavy and continued shower of hot ashes, and pumice stone, so thick as to darken that part of the country for three days successively, there being no light but from the flames of Vesuvius, and so immediate as to preclude escape. The fate of Herculaneum was still more sudden, as a deep torrent of lava rolled over it to the sea. I well remember that the younger Pliny, in one of his letters * relating the manner of his uncle's death, who was suffocated here in attempting to save his friend Pomponianus,

* See Epistle the 16th of the 6th Book.

and

and others of the wretched inhabitants, has left a moſt intereſting account of this tremendous eruption, the appearance of which, is (if I miſtake not) finely given by Martial in a ſingle line.

Cuncta jacent flammis et triſti merſa favillâ *.
MARTIAL, lib. xiv. Epigr. 42—44. l. 6.

In reflecting on this ſubject I have often been ſurprized that the Romans never attempted to lay open theſe cities, but what more ſurpriſes me is, that the Neapolitans ſhould build their palaces and villas on the very ſpot where Herculaneum was loſt. At every eruption they fly to Naples, but as what has happened may happen again, deſtruction no leſs ſudden than that of 79 may come upon them, and perhaps in future ages travellers will viſit the ſubterraneous towns of Reſina and Portici, as we now do that of Herculaneum. Being very deſirous of looking down the mouth of the volcano, we took guides and mules, and

Imitated.
* All is involved in flame, or mournful embers ſunk.

rode up its sides through the vineyards that produce the Lacryma Christi and Hermitage wines, which, like many other things, have, in my opinion, more fame than excellence. These vines grow in the dark blue ashes and cinders of the mountain. When arrived at a certain point, we alighted, and pursued the way on foot, as it was much too steep for even mules to climb. After two hours ascent, we got within five or six hundred yards of our destination. This point was once the summit of Vesuvius, but late eruptions have raised it considerably, and given it another top. Here we found it impossible to proceed without going round the mountain, which we did, but with great difficulty, as the foggy steams of sulphur almost prevented our breathing, and the heat of the ground had consumed our thick shoes to a cinder. Having at length gained the brink of the crater, which, like an immense cauldron, emitted a vapour that made it impossible to see the contents, until the wind should disperse it, we waited some time with great patience. But Pocock,

LETTER XXI.

cock, finding the smoke too oppressive, was obliged to retire. I however determined to remain as long as possible, and happily my perseverance was crowned with success, for a sudden gust entirely cleared the mouth, and gave me a full view of it. Instead of seeing, as I expected, a vast gulf with sides of shaggy and projecting rocks, I beheld a fine sloping bason formed as regularly as if it had been a work of art, the circumference of which is about 500 paces. In it were layers of sulphur of different colours beautifully clear, and at the bottom, about eighty yards deep, I perceived three mouths, but no fire or flame. It is a custom with the guides to shout whenever a breeze of wind clears the crater of its smoke. On this occasion I was surprised to hear, in addition to my man's voice, a loud English huzza; on looking about me I perceived a true John Bull, who, when he had almost cracked his windpipe with hollowing, swore that this was the most wonderful sight he had ever seen. He was the master of a merchant ship in the bay of Naples, and had come up to see the crater of Vesuvius; into which, insensible of the danger, he would have descended had I not prevented him, and by so doing, I flatter myself that I have preserved for my country one of its most valuable citizens—an able and intrepid seaman.

Some days after this expedition to Vesuvius we visited the palace of Caserta, which I had heard was the most magnificent in Europe; but conceive our disappointment when in an immense house, the external appearance of which is indeed full of promise, we could praise only the chapel, the theatre, and grand stair-case. These are very noble, and display a profusion of the richest and rarest marbles. The gardens, with their cascades and basons of water, though a la Françoise, are not undeserving of attention. From these we had a most grateful prospect of all the Campagna Felice, Mount Vesuvius, &c. &c. &c. Caserta is sixteen miles from Naples; we were persuaded to go about a league and a half further

further to see a modern aqueduct that supplied the palace with water. It was built by the late king of Naples over a deep valley, from one mountain to another. The architecture is very praise-worthy, as it is not only solid, but also light for an edifice of this kind. Near it are the celebrated Ferculæ Caudinæ, where the Roman army, being drawn into ambush by the Samnites, were compelled to pass under the yoke. Livy, whom I have been just reading on this subject, indicates the strong sense of shame that the vanquished felt on the occasion in this expressive sentence: " Quum ex saltu evasissent, etsi velut ab inferis extracti, tum primum lucem aspicere visi sunt, tamen ipsa lux ita deforme intuentibus agmen, omni morte tristior fuit.*" Book ix. Chap. 6.

We think ourselves particularly fortunate in having been introduced to society at

---

* When they had come out of the forest, like men raised from the shades below, they first beheld the light; but that light was to all more lamentable than death, as it shewed them their own army reduced to such ignominy.

Naples, as few Englishmen know more of it at their departure, than they do on their arrival. Indeed we expected this introduction to take place through the medium of Sir William Hamilton, the British minister, especially, as exclusive of the public and private letters we had for him, he was intimately acquainted with Sir George Pocock, but we were mistaken. He did us the honor of presenting us at court, and of inviting us to dinner twice at Naples, and once at his villa in Caserta, during a residence of two months. We were by another gentleman introduced to Monsieur de Taleyrande, the French ambassador, at whose house we met, and made acquaintance with the first company in Naples. His excellency keeps a superb table, from which he insisted that our *mauvaise honte Angloise* should not deter us, and indeed we are obliged to dine there seldom less than three times a week. We found the court very brilliant, and the king very gay; for as Sir William was reading over the *hard English* names of the gentlemen he presented, his majesty burst out a laughing a laughing in the middle, made his bow, and walked on. He is extremely partial to hunting, shooting, fishing, rowing, and a thousand other *things*, in which they say he is very clever. The queen removed out of the drawing room into another apartment, in which the officers of three or four Neapolitan regiments had the honor of kissing her hand, so that for an hour and a half there was nothing but kneeling and kissing. However, I should suppose this was not disagreeable to her, for she certainly held out to them *the finest hand and arm I ever saw*.

During the carnival, that grand Roman Catholic festival which precedes Lent, Naples is a scene of universal jubilee. Its operas, both serious and comic, are the best in Italy, the music being generally by Paesiello, who is thought to be, and I think with great reason, the finest composer that ever lived; though Naples can now boast of other great masters, such as Cimarosa, Guglielmi, &c. &c. Once every week during the latter part of the carnival, the

theatre

theatre of San Carlo is laid open for mafquerades, in which there is an infinite variety of character and humour unknown in England. At one of thefe I was introduced to the duchefs of San Clemente, the moſt elegant and accomplifhed woman of Naples, and in her parties I have fince generally paffed my evenings. She is nearly related to the duke of Leinſter, her mother the marchionefs Arezzo being a Fitzgerald. There is another amufement on certain days of this feſtival, which is peculiar to Naples. In the evening many of the nobility mafked, and in Dominos, parade up and down the Strada di Toledo in their coaches. Some go in open carriages, armed with fhields, and furnifhed with bags of fugar plumbs to throw at all they meet. When two of thefe carriages pafs each other, a warm engagement enfues. Our party on thefe occafions was generally made up at the French ambaffador's, and confifted of his two fons, the young Compte de Polignac, Pocock, and myfelf. On Thurfday laſt we had a very fevere action. I obferved that one

of

LETTER XXI.

of the enemy behaved uncommonly well; his exertions were at laſt ſo great, that his maſk dropped off, which he haſtily replaced, but not ſo ſoon as to prevent our ſeeing the face of his *Neapolitan Majeſty*. Beſides, of theſe diverſions there are (I believe every week in the year) two aſſemblies, or as here called Acadèmie; one, confined to the nobility is named L. Academia dei Nobili; and the other, confiſting of the firſt order of citizens, L. Academia degli Amici; their entertainment conſiſts of muſic, dancing, cards, billiards and converzationi; on our arrival we were politely ſent tickets of general admiſſion to each.

In ſo warm a country as Naples, the inhabitants during the ſummer ſleep the greater part of the day, and amuſe themſelves all night in the open air, either on the Chiaia, a beautiful walk near the ſea, or in their gardens on Mount Pauſilipo, &c. To their great partiality for muſic muſt be attributed that infamous cuſtom among

among the common people of making eunuchs of their children—a cuſtom in every other part of Italy forbidden under the ſevereſt penalties. Not one in fifty of theſe wretched martyrs to harmony and avarice ſucceed, but fortunately they are received as choiriſters by many of the religious fraternities, and are thus enabled to gain a bare ſubſiſtence. The Lazaroni are a body of near 4000 men peculiar to this city. Indeed in no other country, to which nature is ſo bountiful than this, could they exiſt, as they are without any ſettled employment, without money: without habitation, and almoſt without clothes. On our return to our lodgings every night we find the ſtair-caſe ſo covered with them aſleep, that it is with difficulty we paſs without treading on them. You may ſuppoſe that the appearance of ſo many ragged ill-looking fellows at firſt alarmed us; but we found they were extremely inoffenſive, and ready to run from one end of Naples to the other for the ſmalleſt gratuity.

In

In walking the streets I have often been robbed of my handkerchief, the Neapolitan pickpocket being a greater adept than Mr. Barrington. Some years since the boatswain of an English frigate had lost so many, that he determined to sew one to his pocket for the purpose of detecting the thief. Having done so he came on shore, and had not walked an hundred yards before he felt a pull; turning round on the instant, he struck the culprit with his fist in the stomach, and laid him breathless on the pavement. Many people immediately assembled, and turning the poor wretch about, were astonished not to perceive any marks of blood; for they supposed it impossible that one man could deprive another of his senses, without he had in their own common way stabbed him to the heart. I am afraid to tell you how many are killed and wounded annually in this kingdom by the coltellata, or cut of the knife; lest you should suppose I romanced, but I assure you I have it from the most respectable authority, that there are not less than 16,000.

The

The Neapolitan, you will obferve, never ftrikes with his fift, as an Englifhman would, but always with his long knife, and when he has done the deed, no man ever thinks of arrefting him. A few years fince an affaffin, grown grey in murder, was by fome unforefeen accident taken up. He not only acknowledged the crimes laid to his charge, but mentioned feveral others unknown. A monk who was prefent happened to fay, that probably too he had never confeffed himfelf, or obferved the difcipline of the church. This reflection was too fevere, he loft all patience, and addreffing himfelf to the prieft with extreme anger and indignation, Come padre, mi fofpettate dunque di non effer Chriftiano *?

The common people kill one another openly, but the better fort of citizens in a more refined manner. They have here, and I believe only here, the fecret of pre-

* How father (faid he) and can you fufpect me then to be no Chriftian?

paring

paring the acqua toffana, a poifon that all are by law forbidden either to make or keep. A gentleman of the faculty affured me, that its principal ingredients are cantharides and opium. It is as clear and as taftelefs as water, flow in operation, but fure in effect, without producing any internal inflammation, or leaving any marks that might lead even to fufpicion.

Adieu. I am really afhamed of this long letter.

LETTER XXII.

Pæstum, Feb. 16th, 1788.

IF I except my excursion into Spain, we had, previous to our leaving Naples, confined ourselves to the common rout of English travellers in France, Swisserland, and Italy; but the very favourable accounts of the Calabrias and Sicily determined us to strike out a new course, and to visit those countries, which not only from modern description, but from being so generally the subject of ancient history, we considered as a Land of Promise. Having procured every thing we thought necessary to alleviate the many difficulties of the journey, particularly letters of introduction from the duchess of San-Clemente, a good chart, and a few Greek authors as guides, we yesterday embarked in a Maltese Speronara, or open boat, managed by seven men, whose appearance was quite new to us, they being a mongrel race between the Italian and Moor, inheriting all the cunning of the one,

LETTER XXII.

one, and all the fiercenefs of the other;—dangerous company you will fay, but we took care to let them know two things effential to our future fafety; firft, that we had not money enough to pay for their boat, until we fhould arrive at Meffina; and again, that we were expected by fome knights of Malta, who would know of our departure with them. In failing down the bay of Naples, our view of the city, &c. was inexpreffibly fine, all its beauties being flufhed and heightened by the fetting fun. As the houfes, from the fituation of the ground on which they ftand, rife one above another, we were able at a confiderable diftance to diftinguifh thofe in which we had paffed the greater part of our time with people, whom it is impoffible to forget, or not to admire; and when night came on, the lamps, by reminding us that thofe people would foon affemble, led us into no favourable comparifon of their fituation with ours. They, happy in the fociety of a felect few, or charmed in their brilliant Académie with the mufic of their own incomparable Paeſiello: and we, expoſed to the night air, almoſt becalmed, and rocked to ſickneſs in the middle of the bay of Naples. At eleven P. M. we anchored in the Straits between the Iſle of Capræ*, and the Punto di Campanella on the main land, and having put up a covering of ſail cloth, lay down for the night. Our portmanteau made no bad ſubſtitute for a bolſter, and we luckily found a thick woollen rug, which ſerved as a comfortable counterpane; yet the ſwell of the ſea, and the roar of the waves againſt the rocks, made all our attempts to ſleep ineffectual, ſo that our only conſolation was the hope of a favourable breeze in the morning. But this proved deluſive; however, as the wind was not directly againſt us, we rowed acroſs the gulph of Salerno, and landed at the little village of Agropoli, where, having

* This charming iſland is ſituated in the entrance of the bay of Naples nineteen miles from the city. It was choſen by Sejanus for the retreat of the emperor Tiberius, in which he was guilty of every ſpecies of debauchery. Some remains of his palace, &c. &c. are ſtill extant.

hired

hired mules and a guide, we travelled a few miles back along the sea coast to visit the ruins of Pæstum.

In that part of Italy which the Elder Pliny calls the third region, and on the borders of one of those delightful plains, which extend in imperceptible descent from the Appenines to the Mediterranean, stood the city of Posidonia, or Pæstum, built, according to that general compiler Julius Solinus, by a colony of Dorians. We find in other authors, particularly in the fifth book of Strabo, a more satisfactory account of the origin of this celebrated city. After the destruction of Sybaris by the Crotoniats, a wandering troop of Thessalians endeavoured to settle near it, but were not permitted. Being too weak to oppose the conquerors, and their invincible champion Milo, they went back to Greece, and having allured many adventurers by the favourable description they gave of Italy, among whom was the historian Herodotus, returned with ten ships under the command of Lampon and Xenocratus, and founded Thurium. Among the new citizens were many Sybarites, who, having foon after their affociation with, incurred the difpleafure of the native Greeks, were driven from among them. Thefe exiles croffed the country, and fettled in this plain, where they built Pofidonia about 390 years before the Chriftian æra. As the Sybarites were the moft refined and voluptuous of the Grecian people that colonized in Italy, we might thence infer, even if its ruins were not a fufficient indication of it, that Pofidonia was a rich and magnificent city. It was firft conquered by the Lucanians, who changed its name to Pæftum. The citizens are mentioned by Livy as the allies of the Romans, to whom in the fecond Punic war they offered their golden cups and veffels, which however were not accepted—an undeniable proof of their wealth and luxury. In 920 it was burnt by the Saracens, yet happily thofe Barbarians did not fo entirely deftroy it, but that there ftill remain four noble monuments of its ancient grandeur,

which

which are, and probably will continue for many centuries, to be the admiration of the claffic traveller. The three firft are temples, which architects diftinguifh by appellations borrowed from the Greek, namely, the Hexaftyle Hypæthral: the Hexaftyle Peripteral: and the Pfeudodipteral or Bafilica. To explain this, I muft tell you that the firft ftands on a bafe of three fteps, and has two equal fronts of fix columns, and fourteen on each fide. Every fhaft confifts of four fluted ftones, they diminifh more in circumference from the bafe to the capital, than any I ever faw. Within the temple was another detached colonade, of which feven pillars ftill remain; and on thefe ftood a third row, fmaller and fluted. The fecond temple is not unlike the firft, nor very different from it in dimenfions; but the Pfeudodipteral is confiderably larger than either, having nine columns in each front, and 18 on each fide. As I well remember that you ufed to ridicule my partiality for Vitruvius and Palladio, I fhall fay nothing more upon the venerable remains of Pæstum, than that their order is a rude (and in my opinion) an unpleasing specimen of the Doric, which is a strong argument in favour of their antiquity. The fourth ruin is an oblong amphitheatre, 170 by 116 feet. Exclusive of these are a gateway: part of the city walls: and watch towers; but they (I should suppose) were built many years after the temples and amphitheatre. The view of this plain, and of these its ancient inhabitants, is grand and interesting. Seven miles from it are the woods of Silarus, and the river Silo. I almost wished to be stung by one of those flies which Virgil notices as peculiar to this country, and so formidable to cattle.

>Est lucos Silari circa ilicibusque virentem
>Plurimus Alburnum volitans, cui nomen Asylo
>Romanum est, Æstron Graii vertére vocantes,
>Asper, acerba sonans, &c *.
>
> Geor. 3. l. 146, &c.

Imitated.

>* In the deep groves of Silarus is seen
>A fly, or near Alburnum ever green,
>Which the Greeks *Æstron*, we *Asylo* call,
>That buzzes with hoarse hum, &c.

Most

Moſt of the Roman poets have celebrated the Roſe Tree of Pæſtum for bearing twice a year. I have this inſtant enquired of the people, in whoſe houſe I am now writing, whether it be ſtill ſo, and they tell me that their children gather them in May and in October. Adieu, we are going into our Speronara at nine, P. M.

Scaléa, Feb. 25th.

THE firſt night of our voyage, having been altogether reſtleſs, we fell into a deep ſleep almoſt as ſoon as we had extended ourſelves on our beds of oak, when we re-embarked at Agropoli, and did not awake the next morning, until we felt our Malteſe drawing up the boat on ſhore. This was in conſequence of a ſtrong ſoutherly wind, which had ſet in before they had rowed three leagues from the place we had left in the night. Our ſituation was now truly diſtreſsful, being caſt on the rude inhoſpitable coaſt of Salerno, where there was no food to refreſh, no houſe to receive us, us, nor any prospect at sea of favourable weather to proceed. The next day we walked up the country, and ascended a lofty mountain, on the peak of which is the village of Castel Abbate; but suspicious of the sallow and inhuman aspect of its inhabitants, we returned to the Speronara, in which we passed a dreadful night of wind and incessant rain. The day after, not judging a second walk altogether prudent, we amused ourselves with *sitting still* under the damp covering of our boat. At night I in vain attempted to sleep; in the morning however nature, overcome with fatigue, sunk into sound repose; but oh! how glad I was to be disturbed with tidings that the wind had fallen, and we were again going out to sea. The exertion of our sailors was very great, as if they were determined to make up the time they had lost, for before nine, P. M. we had gained 18 leagues by rowing, and never were poor fellows more chearful in their labour, though indeed we could not understand them, as their language is a corrupt Arabic. We doubled

the

LETTER XXII.

the capes Licofa and Palinuro; the laſt of theſe has retained its name near 3000 years, being called after Æneas's pilot, who, falling from the helm when aſleep, was driven to this promontory, where he was murdered by the natives, who were not however more inhuman than their preſent deſcendants. Near the brow is a ruin, which might be the remains of his monument. This ſtory is charmingly related in the fifth book of Virgil, and in the ſixth Æneas is repreſented as meeting him in the ſhades below, where the attendant Sybil comforts his wandering ghoſt with this aſſurance.

> Tua finitimi longé latéque per urbes
> Prodigiis acti cæleſtibus oſſa piabunt.
> Et ſtatuent tumulum, et tumulo ſolennia mittent,
> Æternumque locus Palinuri nomen habebit *.
>
> Æn. vi. line 381.

Imitated.

* The neighb'ring people ſhall repent thy doom,
  And warn'd by heav'n raiſe o'er thy grave a tomb.
  On which, as each revolving year goes round,
  All ſhall hang gifts, and conſecrate the ground.
  Call'd by thy name the mountain ſhall be ſhown,
  To future men in ages now unknown.

A few

A few miles to the south of this classical promontory we entered the gulf of Policastro, and carried our Speronara into a secure little port near the Capo di Infreschi, where we not only found a house, but fresh eggs and sweet oil, with which one of the servants, whom we had hired for the tour, being a good cook, though a most consummate rogue, made us an excellent omlette. We sat here over a wood fire more than three hours, except when driven by the smoke at intervals (there being no chimney) into the open air for the preservation of our eyes. About midnight the wind veer'd a little to the north, which occasioned our immediate re embarkation. Soon after our departure the breeze freshened, and we sailed in triumph across the gulf, when, to our inexpressible mortification, it not only fell, but rose again in the south; and blowing with great violence, dashed our boat upon the shores of Calabria, under the little town of Scaléa, which are still ruder than those of Salerno. Here we have been five heavy days and nights, and here

LETTER XXII.

we are likely to continue, as the moon, on which was all our hope, has changed, but produced no alteration in the weather. Our situation is now bad, but what would it have been, if on the melancholy day of our arrival we had not found a little convent of Francifcan friars, who have charitably received us: fpared us one of their own cells, with a bed, two chairs, and a table, and provided us with food. The honefty, the fimplicity, and the attention of thefe good men have greatly alleviated our diftrefs; indeed without the protection of their convent, we had probably been murdered, as *in a country of affaffination,* this fpot is the *moft* noted for it. About five years ago a knight of Malta, and the failors of fuch a Speronara as ours, were killed and plundered within two miles of Scaléa.

I have had an opportunity of obferving the foil and produce of this part of Calabria Citra. Though little cultivated, the earth is naturally rich and abundant, particularly in olives, figs, and grapes. The two former are

are remarkable for their delicious flavour, and the latter would be equal to any in the world, were the vines properly cultivated and dressed. The wild aromatic herbs of the mountains are so nutritious, that cattle cannot feed upon them without becoming too grofs in six weeks. All the coast is covered with a variety of myrtles, very different from the forced production of our northern hemisphere, as every gale is scented by their odour. The Calabrian peasant never knows what winter is: for even now the country wears the full appearance of summer, from the softness of the climate, and infinite variety of ever-greens. But the beneficence of nature is ill repaid in this charming country, for the inhabitants are worse than Barbarians, and the nobility, who possess immense tracts of land here, never see them, but reside altogether at Naples.

On the summit of one of the neighbouring hills that commands an extensive sweep of prospect over the Mediterranean, the Adriatic,

Adriatic, and the two Calabrias, ſtands an hermitage, whoſe lonely tenant (as our monks report) is an Engliſhman. He has reſided there nine years, and ſubſiſted on the alms of the country people, who are extremely partial to him from the happy ſuppoſition that he is a ſaint. Padre Vicenzo, the guardian of our little convent, tells me that he has often met him, and that once in a deep wood below the hermitage he found him weeping over a miniature, which, on being ſurprized, he put haſtily into his boſom, and retired. He ſuppoſes him to be about forty years of age, and ſays his appearance is very noble and intereſting. We have been, as you may imagine, very deſirous of *coping* with this melancholy man, but our continual expectation of a favourable wind has prevented it.

This is a fine ſporting country too, as it abounds in wild boars, ſtags, deer, wolves, foxes, hares, pheaſants, partridges, woodcocks, and a variety of water-fowl.

We

We shall never depart, but
———— ———— Superanda omnis fortuna ferendo est,
must now be our only motto *.

———————————

Messina, March 1st.

ON the seventh morning of our detention at Scaléa, I arose about two hours before day to observe the weather; and finding it the same as before, went to bed again, and slept. Some time after this, we were joyfully roused by one of the sailors, who could speak a little Italian, with the ever memorable words of Abbiamo il Tramontana Signori †. We hurried on our clothes, made our acknowledgements to our benevolent hosts, on whom with difficulty we forced a few pieces of gold, and in ten minutes got under way with our sails full of the rising gale. As we passed the coast of Calabria Ultra, our pleasure was extreme; because, the night before our departure, we had determined to run all hazards, and

* We must subdue our misfortunes by patience.
† We have a north wind, gentlemen.

LETTER XXII.

travel over it on horseback—a journey of four days at least. About sunset we had a most pleasing view of the volcanic little island of Stromboli, the ancient residence of Æolus, and at eleven P. M. entered a small inlet under Cape Vaticano, 34 leagues from Scaléa. This made ample amends for our long long week of confinement. The next morning we beheld Sicily before us; on our left was the southern extremity of Italy, and to the right the islands of Lipari. The sky was clear, the sun just risen, and the calm sea covered with boats employed in the anchovy fishery; so that upon the whole, I think I never saw a scene more chearful. We rowed and sailed 30 miles along the shore, beholding many buildings ruined by the terrible earthquake of 1783, and about ten A. M. disembarked at Giöja, a little town, in which we hired a guide and three mules *haltered and packsaddled*, and rode through one of the most charming, though neglected, countries of Europe, to the ruins of Oppido. What a scene of sorrow is there, what a glut of desolation!

I remem-

I remember to have shuddered at our newspaper recital of this destructive earthquake, but how faint a picture was that of the reality! I know not indeed how to describe it, as it resembles nothing in nature. Could you however bring your fancy to form an idea of the field of battle, on which Jupiter and the giants hurled rocks and mountains at each other, when they disputed the government of heaven, you may conceive the appearance of Oppido and its neighbourhood. The ground on which the town stood is a continued heap of stones, and on the northern side near its castle is a deep winding valley, where the earth has gaped most tremendously, at the bottom of which are two large lakes. This calamity happened very early on the 6th of February 1783. The crush was so sudden, and so general, that six thousand people were buried under the ruins. In addition to this we observed all the way from Gioja, villages and houses rebuilt, and large olive trees, &c. torn up by their roots, and thrown in confusion one across another. Having regained

LETTER XXII.

regained our Speronara we re-embarked, and foon reached the Faro of Meffina, where we entered the Straits that divide Sicily from the continent. The two countries were probably torn afunder at a period antecedent to all hiftory, by fuch another earthquake as that of 1783; and fo thought Virgil, who however only follows the opinion of Æfchylus and Diodorus Siculus.

> Hæc loca vi quondam et vaftâ convulfa ruinâ
> Diffiluiffe ferunt, cum protinus utraque tellus
> Una foret, venit medio vi pontus, et undis
> Hefperium Siculo latus abfcidit †.
>
> Æn. B. 3. l. 414.

The breadth of this channel is from four to twelve miles, and the length thirty. There is a continual ebb and flow in it, though no tides in the Mediterranean; the current running fix hours one way, and fix the other. As we failed under the little

Imitated.

† Thefe places they report as one, at firft,
  Which the convulfive earth afunder burft
  With monftrous ruin; when th' impetuous tide
  Rufh'd in between, and the Hefperian fide
  Did from Sicilia's new-made ifle divide.

town of Scylla, now Sciglo, we saw an immense rock, which in the late earthquake had been cleaved from the shore, and had fallen into the sea. You may remember that Æneas was advised by his prophetic countryman Helenus to beware of these Straits, where the currents and eddies are even in the present improved state of navigation most dangerous.

> Ast ubi digressum Siculæ te admoverit orâ
> Ventus, et angusti rarescent clauftra Pelori,
> Læva tibi tellus, et longo læva petantur.
> Æquora circuitu; dextrum fuge littus et undas ‡.
>
>   Æn. B. 3. l. 410.

As the Greeks personified mountains, rocks, trees, and rivers, we are not surprized to find that Scylla was the beautiful daughter of Phorcus and the nymph Cretis. Being beloved by the sea-god Glaucus, she incurred the jealousy and resentment of the enchantress Circe, who poisoned the fountain in which she used to bathe. The infected

    Imitated.
‡ When you obliquely to Sicilia steer,
 And the Pelorian Straits shall scarce appear,
 Far to the left th' intended way explore,
 Avoid the channel, and its dang'rous shore.

LETTER XXII.

water inftantly produced the change which the poet defcribes.

> Prima hominis facies, et pulchro pectore virgo
> Pube tenus, poftrema immani corpore priftis
> Delphinûm caudas utero commiffa luporum *.
>
>   ÆN. B. 3. l. 426.

And fhe (poor nymph) to conceal her deformity, threw herfelf into the fea, where her lover Glaucus changed her into a rock. Her oppofite neighbour Charybdis was a rapacious female, who ftole the cows of Hercules, and being ftruck for it by one of Jupiter's thunderbolts, underwent a fimilar metamorphofe.

I believe that tradition never dies, if there be any thing fupernatural in it. The feafaring people of Meffina will tell you, that they often hear the rocks of Scylla refound with the barking of her dogs.

>   " cæruleis canibus refonantia Saxa. †"
>
>   ÆN. iii. l. 432.

            Imitated.
* In face a man with breafts of woman kind,
  A monftrous form below of fifh and dog combined.

            Imitated.
† " Rocks yelping with their fea-green dogs."

END OF VOL. I.

www.ingramcontent.com/pod-product-compliance
Lightning Source LLC
Chambersburg PA
CBHW031956300426
44117CB00008B/782